ANITA DESAI AND HER FICTIONAL WORLD

ANITA DESAI AND HER FICTIONAL WORLD

Neeru Tandon

ATLANTIC
PUBLISHERS & DISTRIBUTORS (P) LTD

Published by

ATLANTIC

PUBLISHERS & DISTRIBUTORS (P) LTD

7/22, Ansari Road, Darya Ganj,
New Delhi-110002
Phones : +91-11-40775252, 23273880, 23275880, 23280451
Fax : +91-11-23285873
Web : www.atlanticbooks.com
E-mail : orders@atlanticbooks.com

Branch Office
5, Nallathambi Street, Wallajah Road,
Chennai-600002
Phones : +91-44-64611085, 32413319
E-mail : chennai@atlanticbooks.com

Printed in India at Nice Printing Press, A-33/3A, Site-IV, Industrial Area, Sahibabad, Ghaziabad, U.P.

Foreword

Indian English fiction, as a mode of expression, arrived quite late on the literary scene. From the sixties up to the end of the nineteenth century only a few novels, imitating the models of British fiction writers like Defoe, Fielding and Scott, could be written. With the turn of the century, however, substantial and powerful fiction writers like Mulk Raj Anand, R.K. Narayan and Raja Rao began to emerge and establish their distinct identity in the domain of fiction writing. The first half of the twentieth century was governed by the trend setting socio-political and ideological events caused by the Gandhian movement which had its deep impact on the fiction writing of the era.

In the Post-Independence era women novelists form a distinct identity of their own. Among the women fiction writers like Ruth Prawar Jhabvala, Kamala Markandaya, Nayantara Sahgal, Shanta Rama Rau, Raji Narasimhan, Bharati Mukherjee, Veena Nagpal, Arundhati Roy, Shashi Deshpande and Shobhaa De, Anita Desai occupies a unique place in the history of Indian English fiction. In the exploration of the inner consciousness or the psychological state of human mind Anita Desai has been appropriately compared to the powerful British fiction writer, Virginia Woolf.

In addition to a large number of essays, articles, reviews, short stories, Anita Desai has about a dozen popular novels to her credit. Besides being a Professor at various educational centres in different parts of the world, she is the recipient of Sahitya Akademi Award (1978), Guardian Award (1984), Booker McConnell Prize (1980), Padma Shri (1990) and Neil

Gunn Award (1994), etc. She is such an appealing and influential novelist that several critical books, research articles and Ph.D. dissertations have been written on the different aspects of her creative genius. In her novels she has successfully explored what Ortega Y Gasset calls 'the ferocious assaults of existence'.

The present critical anthology of Dr. Neeru Tandon on Anita Desai is an admirable effort on the presentation of a coherent and comprehensive assessment of Anita Desai as a powerful Indian fiction writer. In her collection she has included certain burning topics of the day such as 'male-female dichotomy', 'existentialist vision', 'religion and culture', 'concept of marriage' and 'narrative technique' in the fiction of Anita Desai. The uncomplicated language and the natural flow of words make for easy reading. I believe, the present book will be extremely useful and rewarding to the students and research scholars of Anita Desai.

R.N. Rai

Professor of English
Banaras Hindu University
Varanasi

Preface

> *"Knowledge emerges only through invention and reinvention, through the restless, impatient, continuing hopeful enquiry, men pursue in the world, within world and with each other."* — Paulo Freire

At the level of inner consciousness, words are not mere meanings recorded in a dictionary or in any other book. Words are symbols, which trigger feelings and meanings that each individual draws out of his/her subconscious storehouse. This is clear from the fictional writings of Anita Desai. She is moving forward with her strong and sure stride, matching the pace of the world. We see her bursting out on full bloom spreading her own individual fragrance. Today she is recognised for her originality, versatility and the indigenous flavour of her character-portrayal that she brings to her work. Her women characters are real flesh-and-blood protagonists who make you look at them with awe with their relationships to their surroundings, their society, their men, their children, their families, their mental and psychological make-ups and themselves. The present book purports to be a pioneering attempt to evaluate Desai's fiction and fictional art from various points of view and assess her contribution to the Indian English fiction. Her novels being nominated for the Booker Prize three times further consolidated her international acceptance and reputation showcasing Desai's immense dexterity in handling complex interrelationships and probing deep into the psyche of her characters. The painstakingly perfected chiseling is perhaps the secret of her four decades long success. What is unique about this book is the attempt to include

Desai's complete fictional oeuvre from her maiden attempt *Cry, the Peacock* (1963) till her latest published work *The Zigzag Way* (2004).

I cannot close these prefatory remarks without thanking the people who made this project possible. I put on record my sincere gratitude to Prof. R.N. Rai, Department of English, Banaras Hindu University, who kindly wrote the foreword to this book. My friends Satish and Sandeep deserve my sincere thanks to whom I am beholden for their perennial inspiration and encouragement behind this work. I also acknowledge my gratefulness to all the scholars and critics whose views and opinion have been cited and commented upon in this book. I must acknowledge my gratitude to my loving and caring husband Mr. Sanjay Tandon, without whose support and cooperation, this book would not have seen the light of the day. I especially thank Shubhangi and Shashwat for their patience and understanding of a mother who always had a book to write.

I discussed the framework and scope of this book with Dr. K.R. Gupta of Atlantic Publishers and Distributors (P) Ltd., New Delhi and gained from his advice. Dr. Gupta deserves my sincerest thanks and warm appreciation for his keen interest in the present venture and for bringing out the volume elegantly and expeditiously.

Neeru Tandon

CONTENTS

General Introduction: The Indian English Fiction

Fiction, being the most characteristic and powerful form of literary expression, has acquired a prestigious position in Indian English literature, popularly known as Indian writing in English. It is generally agreed that in India, the novel is the the most acceptable way of embodying experiences and ideas in the context of our time. Fiction, as form of art, mirrors the social fabric and reflects the thoughts of an age. Many good Indian English novels and many more short stories have demonstrated the feasibility of Indians, writing fiction.

Since the novel provides a sort of documentation for the study of social traditions and socio-cultural change, the achievement of the Indian writers in English has been more significant in the realm of the novel than in poetry or drama, both quantitatively and qualitatively.

Although the Indian fiction in English has been relatively delayed manifestation of the modern Indian imagination, it has always been instrumental in an artistic rendering of the contemporary social reality. It made its appearance during the nineteen twenties and thirties, when most of the vernacular literatures in India had already achieved tremendous maturity especially in the medium of fiction reflecting the universal consciousness of change.

The term Indian English neither refers to baboo English nor indiscriminate use of Indian words in English by an Indian writer who makes his English Indian. In fact the best definition is given by Prof. V.K. Gokak, "Indian English represents the evolution of a distinct standard whose body consists of correct English usage, but the soul is Indian in colour, thought and imagery". It shows that Indian social, cultural and linguistic set-up has affected the features of the English language as used by the Indian creative writers in English, especially the fiction writers and Indian writing in English is only a variety of English whose characteristics stem from the life and culture of the Indian people. A skilful novelist weaves the explanatory details into the pattern of the novel and converts them into a dense web.

The first ever Indian novel in English was written by Bankim Chandra Chatterjee, who established the novel as a major literary form in India. His *Raj Mohan's Wife* was the first and the only English novel he wrote. Thereafter he wrote fiction only in Bengali. Lal Behari Dey's *Govind Samanta* published in 1874 may be considered to be the first ever important Indian novel to appear in English. It represents the emergence of the novel in India with that formal realism which distinguishes it from romance. The last quarter of the nineteenth century, the period following the publication of *Govind Samanta*, may said to be a significant period in the history of Indian fiction in English. Though a very few good novels made their appearance between 1874 and 1900, the quarter century saw the emergence of a number of good writers of fiction in English.

EARLY PERIOD OF FICTION

The marvellous Toru Dutt, besides her many poems and her French novel, wrote in her teens an English novel named *Bianca or The Young Spanish Maiden*. Romesh Chander Dutt was a gifted novelist as well. Two of his Bengali novels were also published in English. *The Slave Girl of Agra* (1909) deals with Mughal times. Another novel *The Lake of Palms* (1902) is an intimate and reliable picture of social life in Bengal.

The various English translations of Bankim Chandra Chatterji's celebrated novels largely contributed to the literary renaissance in India during the last quarter of the nineteenth century. His novels gave at once a standing and status to the Indian novel. Among South Indian writers, B.R. Rajam wrote an English novel *Vasudeva Sastri*. We may mention T. Ramakrishna, the author of *Padmini* (1909), *The Dive for Death* (1911) and P.A. Madhvian, the author of *Thillai Govindan*.

Writers from Punjab who have attempted English fiction are Miss Sorabhi, Sir Joginder Singh and Bal Krishna. Miss Sorabhi's short stories are *Love and Life behind the Purdah*, *Sun Babies* and *Between the Twilights*. Sardar Joginder Singh's first two novels, *Nur Jahan* and *Nasrin* appeared as serials in the East and West. The *Love of Kusuma* (1911) by Bal Krishna is disappointing.

Middle Period: After the First World War

Among the Indians who came to prominence in the first decade after the war, one of the most outstanding was K.S. Venkataramani. His first published book *Paper Bats* gave a few vignettes of South Indian village life. Another book of prose-poem by him is *On the Sand Dunes*, the form had by then been popularized by the Tagore's *Gitanjali*. After that Shankar Ram's three English publications are: *The Children of the Kaveri* (1927), *Creatures All* (1938) and the *Love of Dust* (1938).

After 1930, there came a sudden flowering in the Indian literature in English. A society compelled into self-awareness like that provides a fertile soil for fiction and it is no accident that the three major Indian novelists in English, viz. Mulk Raj Anand, R.K. Narayan and Raja Rao began their career during the phase.

Dr. Mulk Raj Anand hails from the extreme north-west of India. His birth place is Peshawar. His important publications are: *Across the Black Waters*, *The Coolie*, *Two Leaves and a Bud*, *The Untouchable*, and *The Village and the Big Heart*. He is an ardent believer in the doctrine of social revolution and socialistic pattern of society. His object is not merely to shock his readers by a representation of reality but to stimulate their consciousnesses, and his concern as fiction writer has always been the redemption of the poor and the oppressed.

R.K. Narayan is little concerned with the maladies in the society and shows no desire for reforming it. All his novels are concerned in and around Malgudi, a small town in south India. His first novel is *Swami and Friends*. His *The Bachelor of Art* is a more mature work. His short stories are appearing in the columns of *The Hindu* and other journals. He is master at his own chosen grounds.

Raja Rao is deemed as the finest portrayer of Indian sensibilities. He tries to revive the ancient tradition of epics and *Puranas*. He thus stands apart from the main current of Indian creative writers in English. *Kanthapura* is his well known novel. The technique of novel is as old as those of, *The Ramayana*, and *The Mahabharata*. The whole story is related through an old woman of the village.

Among other novelists of the period is S. Nagarajan. His *Athawar House* gives an enduring picture of a Maratha brahmin family living in south India. Dewan Sharar wrote, *The Gong of Shiva*. It is well planned, well executed and wholly an Indian novel. A.S.P. Ayyar is also a voluminous writer. He has published two historical novels: *Baladitya* and *Three Men of Destiny*.

Later Period: Post-Independence Era

The fiction writers were deeply affected by the radical changes which were brought about by the partition of the country. Whereas poverty, hunger, death and disease form the keynotes of the symphony, movements like humanitarianism, socialism and liberalism spotlight the finer aspects of their dream for the future. They seem to stand between the two worlds — one dead, the other yet to be born.

Major writers of this era are Sudhin Ghosh, Bhabani Bhattacharya (*Music for Mohini, So Many Hungers*) and Ruskin Bond (*The Room on the Roof*). Besides these novelists, the others are Dillip Kumar Roy, Khushawant Singh, Venu Chitale, Rama Sharma, K.A. Abbas, etc.

WOMEN NOVELISTS OF THE POST-INDEPENDENCE PERIOD

The very emergence of women writers during this period was of great significance. Kamala Markandaya, Ruth Prawar Jhabvala, Anita Desai, Nayantara Sahgal, Veena Paintal and Nergis Dalal have added new dimensions and depth to Indian fiction in English. The emergence of these women writers marks the birth of an era which promises a new deal for the Indian fiction in English. The battle of emancipation was taken over by a few educated women themselves who, in their effort to communicate to the world their own bitter experiences as women as well as their ideals of social reform, turned writers. These women writers particularly shared experiences of Indian women in general and presented them into fictional form. Women's inner self, their agonies, their pleasures are better and more truly depicted by the women novelists. Literature which until recently was male dominated, has started reflecting the sparks that have emanated from this struggle of woman to be herself. The extent of change in her status, in life and society could be assessed by reference to her image reflected in literature in general and literature produced by her. The reason may be the flowering of the educated women who began to feel an increasing urge to voice their feelings.

The women novelists of the nineteenth century tried to give their characters justice by posting various problems but it was the early experimental period. Owing to lack of experience of writing, they soon turned to didacticism, sentimentalism and romanticism which weakend their novels. But it was not so with the later women novelists who emerged in the post-Independence era such as Kamala Markandaya, Ruth Prawar Jhabvala, Nayantara Sahgal, Anita Desai, Shashi Deshpande, Shobhaa De, etc. The fiction of Kamala markandaya is largely sociological in its focus. Her novels give a faithful account of contemporary Indian reality, she trusts that literature can play a constructive role and teach humanity through the work of writers who will lay bare the very anatomy of destruction. Markandaya shot into prominene with her very first novel *Nectar in a Sieve* (1954) which was followed by *Some Inner Fury* (1955) and continued till the *Golden Honeycomb* (1977).

As an outsider inside India, Ruth Prawar Jhabvala enjoys a double perspecive. She has sometimes been described as an inside-outsider and at other times as an outside-insider. The most significant thing about her is, her awareness of man, society, human and moral dilemmas and the religious and aesthetic design that she projects through her experience. She can view the game of human affairs in an Indian family from a point of view which is both objective and sentimental. Khushwant

Singh calls her the adopted daughter of India. From her first novel *To Whom She Will* (1955) followed by *The Nature of Passion* and then *The Householder* (1960), A *Backward Place* (1965), *Esmond in India* etc., till *Heat and Dust* (which won the famous Booker Prize in London in 1975), she received universal recognition in India as Indian novelist. Thus Mrs. Jhabvala, though limited in her sphere proves to be a torch-bearer for coming generations of Indian women writers in English. In this chain another prominent novelist is Mrs. Nayantara Sahgal.

Nayantara Sahgal is undoubtedly a major Indian novelist who is also an established political columnist. She takes every occasion to demonstrate her view of Indian womanhood in her fictional work. She does not view her women characters as wage earners or career women but mainly as married women, as wives, daughters and mothers and it is in these roles that they wish to experience freedom and to become aware of themselves as individuals and to be accepted as equals. From her first novel *A Time to be Happy,* till her latest novel *A Situation in New Delhi* she has exercised judicious care in picking and choosing such aspects of Indian life as suited her point of view.

Anita Desai is another luminary of this brilliant group of women novelists in the firmament of Indian fiction in English. Desai, born in 1937, of a German mother and Bengali father, is a north Indian novelist remarkable for her sensibility of inner world rather than the queer world of action. She shows a remarkable skill in her use of highly suggestive imagery and in handling the stream of consciousness technique. She is gifted with a sensibility which suits her aesthetic goals. Though not admittedly a feminist, Anita Desai is aware of the peculiar predicament of the Indian woman writers. She says, "Whereas a man is concerned with action, experience, and achievement, a woman writer is more concerned with thought, emotion and sensation".

Desai appeared on the Indian literary horizon in the year 1963, when her first novel *Cry, the Peacock* was published. Her second novel *Voices in the City* was serialized in *The Illustrated Weekly of India* during 1965. Since then she has published nine more novels and added a new dimension to the Indian English fiction.

There are some other notable fiction writers with an impressive corpus of fiction to their credit such as Shashi Deshpande, Attia Husain, Rama Mehta, Nergis Dalal, Bharati Mukherjee and Santha Rama Rau. Again there are some emerging women writers whose output is not large, but each of them is talented in their own way like Namita Gokhale, Nina Sibal, Shourie Daniels, Arundhati Roy, Anita Nair, Anuradha Marwah, Kiran Desai etc. Indian novel in English reached its zenith of glory when Arundhati Roy received the Booker Prize for her novel *The God of Small Things* followed by Kiran Desai (*The Inheritance of Loss*). Roy has achieved the status of a celebrity with the publication of this maiden novel. This book along with the fiction of R.K. Narayan, Mulk Raj Anand, Shashi Deshpande and Anita Desai, has caught the attention of the readers for one or the other reason and the need for critical evaluation has become more urgent than ever before. The personal background and intellectual training of this novelist seem to have endowed the speciality which her fiction bears. Her high educational and intellectual standards have given a sharp edge to her observation. Her natural feminine sensibility and introspection have imparted to her observation human touch and a psychological depth. She shed her inhibitions in a marvelous fashion and showed surprise, frankness, boldness and honesty in the fictional treatment of the working of the human psyche.

Anita Desai has been rightly considered as the forerunner of contemporary woman's fiction as she has produced novels which have evoked an enthusiastic response from critics inside and outside India. She is special because turning inward her fiction grapples with the intangible realities of life, plunges into the innermost depths of the human psyhe to fathom its mysteries, the inner turmoil, and the chaos inside the mind. Her imagination is horrified by the emptiness of modern life just like Saul Bellow's or Ioneso's. During the last few decades the Indian English novel has really enjoyed the golden period. The abundant growth of the novel may be attributed to the fact that there is much more intellectual life in India now than there was before Independence.

1 Bio-Bibliographical Background of Anita Desai

Anita Desai is indisputably one of the most powerful contemporary Indian novelists in English. She was born Anita Mazumdar in Mussoorie, a hill station near Dehradun in northern India to a Bengali father and a German mother on June 24, 1937. She grew up surrounded by Western literature and music. Her father D.N. Mazumdar was a Bengali businessman and her mother Toni Nime was of German origin. She began to write in English at the age of seven and published her first story at the age of nine. Desai was educated in Delhi at Queen Mary's Higher Secondary School and Miranda House, Delhi University, where she received in 1957 a B.A. in English literature. In the following year she married Ashvin Desai, a businessman; they had four children.

Anita Desai has two sisters and a brother. She spoke German as a child. She says in an interview with Jasbir Jain in 1979, "My parents spoke German with each other so probably it was my first language. I should think as a child."[1] She was determined to be a writer, and it was prose, mainly fiction. Her stories appeared as favourite pieces in the children magazine and when she was in college she used to occasionally contribute short stories to the magazine. Desai herself describes her upbringing as 'the greatest gift I could have been given as a writer!' She has lived in Calcutta, Chandigarh, Delhi and Pune and this accounts for the fact that all her novels are set in one or the other of these cities. She is, as Tilottama Tharoor puts it, immensely familiar with the contemporary Indian milieu, from which she derives the background and characters for her novels.

As a novelist Desai made her debut in 1963 with *Cry, the Peacock*. She had started to write short stories regularly before her marriage. This novel was published in Britain by Peter Owen, a publisher specializing in literature of the British Commonwealth and continental Europe. She never considered trying to first get it published in India because there was a belief that no publisher would be interested in fiction by an Indian writer and it was first in England that her work became noticed. U.S. readers were slower to discover her. This may be because of England's natural interest in India and the U.S.'s law of comprehension regarding the foreigness of her subject.

Desai writes in English only. This, she has repeatedly said, was a natural and unconscious choice for her: "I can state definitely that I did not choose English in a deliberate and conscious act and I'd say perhaps it was the language that chose me and I started writing stories in English at the age of seven and have been doing so for thirty years now without stopping to think why."[2]

She is considered the writer who introduced the psychological novel in the tradition of Virginia Woolf to India. Included in this, is her pioneer status of writing of feminist issues. While many people today would not classify her work as feminist, she believes this is due to changing times : "The feminist movement in India is very new and a younger generation of readers in India tends to be rather impatient of my books and to think of them as books about completely helpless women, hopeless women. They find it somewhat unreal that the women don't fight back, but they don't seem to realize how very new this movement is."[3] Also, she says, her writing is realistic: "Women think I am doing a disservice to the feminist movement by writing about women who have no control over their lives. But I was trying, as every writer tries to do, even in fiction, to get at the truth, write the truth."[4] It would have been really fanciful if I had made Bim and Tara modern-day feminists."[5]

Desai considers *Clear Light of Day*, her most autobiographical novel, because she was writing about her neighbourhood in Delhi, although the characters are not based on her brothers and sisters. What she was exploring in this novel, she has said was the importance of childhood and memories as the source of a life. She wanted to start the book at the end and move backwards, into the characters' childhood and further, into the childhood of their parents, etc., but in the end when she had gone as far back as their infancy, the book just ground to a halt; it lost its momentum. She had a sense of disappointment about the book as her intention had been different. The character of Raja is identified with her in the sense that he is immersed in all different types of literature and culture, and is so concerned with protecting the multicultural heritage of India. Her worries about the Muslim neighbour family is not just about them particularly, but rather worry about the loss of all that the Muslim culture and literature contributes to India.

Anita Desai is a guide star for many bright young writers. Starting right at home she influenced her own daughter, Kiran Desai whose novel *Hullabaloo in the Guava Orchard* was a celebrated debut in 1997, and her second novel, *Inheritance of Loss* became a classic as it received the famous Booker Prize. Kiran dedicated this novel to her mother 'Anita Desai'.

Kiran Desai was born in India is 1971, and educated in India, England and the United States. She is currently a student in Columbia University's Creative writing course. She went to high school in Massachusetts and then undergraduate in Vermont-at Bennington and then to a writing program called Hollins, in Virginia. Anita Desai influenced her. Kiran Desai says in an interview, "All my life I've grown up hearing her talk about writing and literature and books. It was wonderful to have her (Anita Desai) around when I was writing this book, to talk to her through this whole process. She was wonderful through the whole thing. It's a big risk to take, spending years of your life doing something that you're not sure how it's going to turn out, and she was very good through that whole time, not providing critical support as much as emotional support. A very motherly role, really."[6]

Anita Desai grew up during World War II and could see the anxiety her German mother was experiencing about the situation and her family in Germany. After the War when she realized that the Germany she had known was devastated, her mother never returned there, nor had any desire to return. Anita Desai herself did not visit until she was an adult. Desai herself describes her upbringing as the greatest gift she could have been given as a writer.

Desai likes to lead a quiet life. Her colleagues who knew her in the 1950, describe her as intense and solitary. Even her choice of books reveals this tendency. She likes to read books which explore human nature. Her favourite authors are Chekhov, Henry James, Lawrence and Dostoevsky.

Truly speaking not much is known about her personal life and views on literature. She is hesitant talking about her personal life and biases. In her opinion, the creative art is a secret one. As sufficient material is not available we can just frame a picture of Anita Desai as a writer on the basis of various literary sources and her writings. Most of Professor Desai's novels are set in India and completely immersed in Indian life. According to Professor Alan Lightman, head of WHS, her novels are distinguished by her focus on the inner life of her characters and her concern with people previously marginalized in Indian fiction, primarily women, children and the elderly.

Professor Desai won the Winifred Holtby Prize of the Royal Society of Literature for the novel; *Fire on the Mountain* (1978) and the Guardian Award for Children's Literature for *Village by the Sea* (1984). She also received the Padma Sri Award from the Government of India and the Taraknath Das Award for promotion of Indo-US relations. She is a fellow of the Royal Society of Literature of London and was recently elected a fellow of the American Academy of Arts and Letters. She also won the Sahitya Academy Award and National Academy of Letters Award. Her three novels *Clear Light of Day*, *In Custody* and *Fasting, Feasting* have been nominated for the Booker Prize. What is important is that her writing has not prevented her from looking after her family and her four children. She says, 'I write for three and a half hours in the morning while the children are away at school. Once they are back my entire time is taken with them.[7] Thus maintaining a proper balance between home and literary career'. She has presented an ideal image of modern 'New Woman'. She is a member of the Advisory Board for

English of the National Academy of Letters in Delhi and fellow of the Royal Society of Literature in London, The American Academy of Arts and Letters, Girton College, Cambridge and Clare Hall, Cambridge. Her major works are as follows:

Cry, the Peacock (CTP) — Peter Owen, 1963
Voices in the City (VITC) — Peter Owen, 1965
Where Shall We Go This Summer? (WSWGTS) — Vikas Publication, 1975
Fire on the Mountain (FOTM) — Heinemann, 1977
Games at Twilight and Other Stories (GATAOS) — Heinemann, 1978
The Peacock Garden (TPG) — Heinemann, 1979
Clear Light of Day (CLOD) — Heinemann, 1980
The Village by the Sea (TVBTS) — Heinemann, 1982
In Custody (IC) — Heinemann, 1984
Baumgartner's Bombay (BB) — Heinemann, 1987
Journey to Ithaca (JTI) — Heinemann, 1995
Fasting, Feasting (FF) — Chalto and Windus, 1999
Diamond Dust and Other Stories (DDAOS) — Chalto and Windus, 2000
The Zigzag Way (TZW) — Chalto and Windus, 2004
Hill of Silver, Hill of Lead (HOSHOL) — Chalto and Windus, 2005

She has been awarded the Neil Gunn International Fellowship for 1944. Her novels have drawn world wide attention and she stands in the fore front in the world of fiction, in the company of Iris Murdock, Doris Lessing, Margaret Atwood and Flora Nwapa.

The reader's first impression of reading Anita Desai is one of brave originality and uniqueness. Her novels are certainly reflective of social realities from a psychological perspective. She closely examines the emotional world of womankind. In dealing with the interior landscape and the psychic odyssey of her characters, Desai has extended and enlarged the thematic horizon of the Indian English novels. Dealing with the thoughts, emotions and sensations at various levels of consciousness, Anita Desai found the technique used by D.H. Lawrence,

Virginia Woolf and Henry James, i.e. stream of consciousness technique and flashbacks in her novels.

According to Desai most marriages prove to be unions of incompatibility. Her women long for love and communion of the spirit which they perceive as the panacea of the ills of the world. In her novels one comes across a symbolic link between different images, which form an interface, a common bond. Imagery is primarily used to capture and crystallize a wide range of experiences. It lends clarity and vividness to the situation she describes, events she documents and characters she delineates. Most of the images used by Desai in her novels are so sharply condensed and chiseled that they resemble a piece of painting. She is a symbolist as well as an imagist. Her wide canvass, her experiences in various countries and places also contribute to it. Undoubtedly she is a much travelled person.

Before coming to MIT, where she is professor at present, she was Purington Professor of English at Mount Holyoke College and divided her time between the United States, India and England. Philip S. Knoury, Dean of the School of Humanities and Social Science (MIT) said,

> "Anita Desai is a tremendous addition to the humanities and to creative writing at MIT. She is a novelist of international distinction who brings a wonderfully bicultural approach to her fiction and teaching."[8]

No doubt, she is one of the world's best known authors, and a writer who has influenced generations of writers.

While Desai has taught for year at Mount Holyoke and MIT, and spends most of the year outside India. She does not consider herself part of the Indian diaspora. Although she does not fit in the Indian box anymore as she said, she considers herself lucky for having not left India until late in her life, because she feels that she has been drifting away from it ever since: 'I can't really write of it with the same intensity and familiarity that I once had.'[9] Yet she cannot feel at home in any other place or society. Speaking about her initial years in India (she left India at 45), Desai confirms that her whole life was about family and neighbours. It was very difficult for a woman to experience anything else.

Anita Desai has attained an immense popularity as a novelist. Probably no other woman writer in the Indian English fiction has been admired by such different tastes and intellects, by whole classes of readers unlike each other. Anita Desai is solely conscious of her role as a woman writer and has tried her best to maintain the tradition for other women writers. As a person she has a belief and concern more with thought, emotion and sensation than with action and achievement.

References

1. web.net.edu/newsoffice/1993/novelist-0929-html.
2. *Ibid.*
3. *Ibid.*
4. *Ibid.*
5. www.nriinternet.com
6. www.writers.com
7. web.nit.edu/newsoffice/1993/novelist-0929-html.
8. www.nriinternet.com
9. www.writers.com

2

Anita Desai: A Novelist with a Difference

Anita Desai is one of the few distinguished Indian writers in English of international repute, whose works have been greatly admired both at home and abroad. Her contribution to fiction writing has been quite commendable and substantial. She comes face to face with the intangible realities of life, the innermost depths of the human psyche and the chaotic underworld of human mind through her novels. Her distinctive stature as novelist derives primarily from the fact that she has made extensive use of the stream of consciousness technique in her novels. Her achievement lies in the fact that she employs a relatively new technique in her fiction with a remarkable consummate skill. The fiction of Anita Desai has become self-analytical and introspective and the individual's quest for a personal meaning in life has become a theme of unavoidable interest for her. Her primary emphasis is thus on sights and sounds, on movements and patterns both physical and mental as they impinge on the consciousness of her protagonists.

Desai has got a distinguished place as her works are different from those of other Indian women writers, Kamala Markandaya, Ruth Prawar Jhabvala, Nayantara Sahgal, Shashi Deshpande, Shobhaa De and Kamala Das. Markandaya stresses more on the rural background. In Jhabvala's fiction the social background is more important than the characters who execute the various roles. Sahgal emphasizes on political and social awareness and Kamla Das moves between the man-woman relationship. Shobhaa De is more for physical desires and social framework while Shashi Deshpande follows of Desai to a certain extent only. But in Desai's novels it is the exploration of sensibility, the inner working of mind that assumes the most important place and is unparalled. She unravels beautifully the mystery of the inner life of her characters. As a novelist she seems to be highly dissatisfied with most contemporary novelist's way of writing a novel. She voices her feelings in an article on 'women writers' with all the richness of material at hand. She made it clear that she would not be satisfied merely with uncritical prosaic documentation of social reality. Her real concern is nothing less than exploration of human psyche.

As a novelist, Desai excels in writing psychological novels. She would however call them surely subjective. Her writings reveal inner realities. She confides, "That my temperament and circumstances have combined to give me the shelter, privacy and solitude required for the writing of such novels thereby avoiding problems, a more objective writer has to deal with since he/she depends on observation rather than a private vision."[1] Desai's central pre-occupation as a novelist is with the existentialist-outlook on human life. Her characters are distinguished by the qualities of introspection, introversion and a refusal to surrender their individual selves. Deeply infected by the existential problems of modern industrial age, Anita Desai has created unique characters that are largely eccentric and abnormal in their mental make up and hence totally unable to conform. Rao has commented thus:

> "Mrs. Desai brings something new to Indo-Anglian novel, instead of portraying character in terms of the environment of defining an individual in terms of his social or caste functions. Mrs. Desai creates character and the environment is important only in so far as it enables the reader to understand the character. Moreover the true artist that she is, Mrs. Desai presents each individual as an unsolved mystery."[2]

As a novelist Desai is unique as she has deviated from the path of realism and taken to the path of subtle psycho-analysis probing deeply into the inner working of a man's mind. She believes in the process of discovering the truth. She has herself stated:

> "Writing is my way of plunging to the depths and exploring this underlying truth. All my writing is an

effort to discover to underline and convey the true significance of things."[3]

Anita Desai has evoked mixed response from her readers. Critics have acclaimed her as a great artist, whose 'writings reveal inner realities and psychic reverberations of her characters.'[4] Her prose has won praise even from Westerners. Desai is not interested so much in registering surface realities as in the probings of inner truths lying under the surface level. The single most distinction of the novelist is in suggesting (in quite a few of her novels), at times overtly, at times covertly, the small but significant change wrought in the perceptions of the other characters in the wake of the strivings of the central characters. Anita Desai's novels have excited both lay readers and critics alike. The central concerns in both the cases have not been very much dissimilar: alienation, the 'inscape' of a guest for the elusive self, existentialist yearnings in claustrophobic environs, the interaction between the old and the new, the dilemma of choosing between the instinct to conform and the urge to rebel. In her novels, there is no plot in the conventional sense of the term as she is never interested in telling a story, hence there is little plot and development of events in her novels. In the interview with Atma Ram she has herself made it clear, "I prefer the word pattern to plot as it sounds more natural ... while plot sounds arbitrary, heavy handed and artificial all that I wish to avoid. One should have a pattern and then fit the characters, the setting and the scene into it — each piece in keeping with the others and so forming a balanced whole."[5]

It is really difficult to tell a tale without a well-structured plot for any writer. But Anita Desai does it and succeeds in it. Her forte as a novelist becomes, in the words of K.R.S. Iyengar, "The exploration of sensibility, the particular kind of Indian sensibility that is ill at ease among barbarous and the philistines, the anarchists and the moralists."[6]

Anita Desai is solely conscious of her role as a woman writer and has tried her best to maintain the tradition for other women writers. Her novels are documented with Indian settings, Indian culture and Indian background. Her younger character often try to imitate the Western culture but do not succeed in their lives. The elder generation in all respects are Indians and they adhere to Indian culture. It is unimaginable to think of Anita Desai without the portrayal of inner psyche of her characters. In her novels the inner workings, the inner sensibilities are more compelling than the outer weather or the visible action. Her strong point is an exploration of sensibilities. Desai's interest in the consciousness of the woman in her novels enables us to see the Indian woman adequately from the inside. She is occupied with interiorzing the consciousness of the woman and the economics of life do not bother her except when they are noticed as adding to the monotonous aspect of existence. In Desai's fictional world, living happily ever after in the old-fashioned sense, is the very fate her heroines struggle to escape. In fact Desai has fashioned a new concept of feminist fiction. The woman in her literary world is on a ceaseless quest, for a more meaningful life not only for herself but for humanity in general. Anita Desai has dealt with several types of severe psychological and social pressures. She has visualized society from the viewpoint of solitary individuals who look upon themselves as permanently uprooted beings. She has effectively used recurring images and symbols.

Anita Desai has found the artistic potential of the solitariness of the individual in an increasingly complex society. Desai's art as a novelist is praiseworthy because she is a meticulous artist. Most of her novels are about human relationships although it is rather their absence that is at the heart of the thematic impulse of her stories. Her characters, no matter to what age group they belong to seem to use one of Heideggar's phrases 'on the fringe of being' and then are debarred from evolving (to recall ierkegaard) a purely aesthetic person. In fact in her novels she has dwelt upon the existentialist issues of the absurdity of human existence and the individuals tapped by circumstances. The great achievement of Desai rests on her beautifully recording the emotional turmoil, chaos and agonies of her oppressed protagonists. Another quality to note in her fiction is that there is not only a rejection of the passive acceptance of the traditional female role but also the deeply felt and suffered rebellion against the entire system of social relationship.

Anita Desai is a novelist of urban milieu. An uncrowned queen of the inner emotional world, she is endowed with soundless imaginative resourcefulness and creative vitality. She writes remarkably well about only those aspects of life that she has minutely observed and deeply experienced. Therefore, her fictional world full of imperfection and unfulfillment, hankering and helplessness, agony and anger, struggle and surrender is no doubt limited but within this limited world she reveals amazing variety and profundity.

Desai occupies an unassailable place in the galaxy of Indian English women novelists. She is one of the strongest voices of women writing in India today. Desai possesses sure and unerring satiric instincts. The several illuminating flashes of satire that break upon the narrative surface of her novels are evidence of her satiric mode. But satire with Anita Desai is only incidental. Her sense of irony embraces the whole emotional range of her characters. Unlike the satirists who distance themselves from their creatures and describe them from outside only, Desai probes into the inner psyche, inner recesses of her characters. That is why her whole style is ironical. Her delicate irony is the very essence of her style. Irony of style has been created by Desai deliberately.

It is not only in the use of subject matter, characterization and in presenting the atmosphere of minds but also in the use of narrative technique, symbols, images, flashback, the method of objective correlative and stream of consciousness, etc., that Anita Desai has achieved high recognition. In regard to the use of the stream of consciousness and interior monologue in her novels, she does it with a view to capturing the prismatic quality of life in her fiction. Every novel of Desai is unique in itself. In *Cry, the Peacock* the emotional disparity between Maya and her husband Gautama is the basic cause of her sufferings. The lack of marital harmony in their lives leads to the contingent situation of Maya's life. Arjun's conflict with his father's bourgeois values of life creates a crisis of situation for him. In *Voices in the City* Nirode suspects his mother of adultery and his cherished image of his mother is shattered. Monisha experiences a sense of imprisonment in her in-law's house. This fact coupled with a lack of love and lack of natural trust in her marital life puts her in a predicament. Sarah, in *Bye-Bye Blackbird*, finds herself in a quandary as a result of her marriage with Adit, an Indian immigrant in London. His hopes of going to India remains unfulfilled as Adit stays in England till he himself grows aware of his counterfeit life in England. The cause of Sita's predicament in *Where Shall We Go This Summer?* is rooted in her illusion about the magic personality of her deceased father and in the lack of love and communication in her marital and domestic life. Nanda Kaul in *Fire on the Mountain* also suffers as a result of the lack of love in her life because her husband neglects her in pursuit of his love affair with Miss David. In the state of despair and loneliness, she grows aware of the absurdity of human relationships. Raka, though a child, is also aware of the hostile forces of the world because she has often seen her father maltreat her mother. In *Clear Light of Day*, the parents spend their time playing cards at the club or at home and do not think of the emotional needs of their growing up children, Bim, Tara and Raja. This emotional starvation gives these children an awareness of the meaninglessness of their existence. Devan Sharma, the protagonist of Anita Desai's latest novel *In Custody* suffers as a result of inconsistency between activity and success. His unsuccessful interview of the great Urdu poet, Nur puts him in a quandary. Ithaca is presented in the novel *Journey to Ithaca. Fasting-Feasting* tells the story of Arun, Anuna and Uma in a very interesting way. *Zipzap Way* is set in Mexico.

The comparative achievement of Anita Desai becomes clear when we notice that her fellow women writers like Kamala Markandaya, Ruth Jhabvala, Nayantara Sahgal, Shashi Deshpande, seldom try to portray the psychic elements involved in their themes on outwardly level. But most of these writers have overlooked the psychological reality. Anita Desai thus clearly stands ahead the group in as much as she introduces a shift of focus from the outer in the inner part of human existence. She insists on analyzing her characters and the story is important only in so far as it reflects the obsessions of her characters. Each work of her is a haunting exploration of the psychic self.

Another quality of her fiction is her characters who are generally neurotic females, highly sensitive and alienated from their surroundings. Coming to her themes, Anita Desai seems to be quietly sliding in her scenes settings and characters without much of an advance preparation. In fact main cause of popularity is that in her fiction, life is depicted as it really is. In her world action is subordinated to psychology. In this respect the novelist shows close affinity with Virginia Woolf who also entered the consciousness of the characters. These qualities of her contribute a lot to understand how she has attained remarkable success as a novelist.

References

1. Desai, Anita, 'Replies to the Questionnaire', *Kakatiya Journal in English Studies,* Vol. 3, No. 1, 1978.
2. Rao, B. Ramachandra, 'The Novels of Anita Desai : A Study', New Delhi: Kalyani Publishers, 1972, p. 87.
3. Desai, Anita, *Comments in Contemporary Novelists*, Ed. James Vinson, New York: St Martin's Press, 1972, p. 348.
4. Bande, Usha, *The Novels of Anita Desai,* New Delhi: Prestige Books, 1988, p. 7.
5. Desai, Anita, in an interview with Atma Ram, *WLWE*, Vol. 30, No. 1, Spring 1990.
6. Iyengar, K.R.S., *Indian Writing in English*, New Delhi: Sterling Publishers Pvt. Unit, 1985, p. 464.

Novels of Initial Phase: Shift from Collective to Personal — *CTP, VITC, BBB*

3

Anita Desai belongs to the group of women writes who have offered their experience to literature and therefore a certain representation of femininity is available in current literary discourse which in parts differentiates itself from the patriarchal mainstream literary tradition. Subsequent to the publication of Anita Desai's *Cry, the Peacock* in 1963, the mainstream critical scene conceded, as early as the beginning of the seventies, that there had been a shift in emphasis and that the psychological novel had emerged. K.R. Srinivasa Iyengar included a critical analysis of Anita Desai's fiction in the second edition of Indian writing in English, in which he stated that Anita Desai through her two novels *Cry, the Peacock* (1963) and *Voices in the City* (1965) was considered to have 'added a new dimension to the achievement of the Indian women writers in India.'[1]

In Desai's work of her initial phase we notice the shift from the collective to the personal and from the communal to the individual. As he further said:

> ".... in Anita Desai's two novels, the inner climate, the climate of sensibility that clears or rumbles like thunder or suddenly blazes forth like lightening, is more compelling than the outer weather, the physical geography or the visible action. Her forte, in other words, is the exploration of sensibility."[2]

The women protagonists in Desai's earlier novels live in a world of delusions like the cocoon of childhood. They do not possess 'homeostasis' or the capacity to adjust and adapt easily and naturally to a changed set of circumstances. Consequently many of them meet a very violent, unnatural end.

Anita Desai's first novel, *Cry, the Peacock* is an exploration into the psychic world of Maya, the main character, in the novel. The novel treats of the contingency of her situation: her despair, anxiety, dread, anguish and her choice in the given situation, which ultimately leads her to insanity. Part I of the novel depicts Maya as a hysteric character and forebodes the impending tragedy in her life. The death of her pet-dog, Toto, throws her into a frenzy of grief. She wishes to provide a decent burial to her dead dog, but the unsympathetic gardener fails to understand and fulfil her wish. Later on, when Gautama her husband, comes home in the evening, he telephones the Public Works Department to send the scavenging truck to take the corpse away. What shocks Maya is the unfeeling and matter of fact behaviour of her husband in disposing of the dead body of her dog.

Part II of the novel is Maya's long narration of her inner life and her relation with the world outside. Anita Desai employs the stream of consciousness technique to depict Maya's moods, emotions, her despair, her search for identity and her dread of death.

Maya is young, childless wife of Gautama, a lawyer. Gautama, much elder to Maya, is a friend of Maya's father. Gautama keeps on criticizing Maya's father as he knows that Maya suffers from father-fixation. He says to Maya:

> "If you knew your Freud it would all be very straightforward, and then appear as merely inevitable to you—taking your childhood and upbringing into consideration. You have a very obvious father-obsession which is also the reason why you married me, a man so much older than yourself. It is a complex that, unless you mature rapidly, you will not be able to deal with, to destroy..."[3]

Like his mother and his sister, Nila, he is a man of the world. He runs after fact and reason and has nothing to do with the world of feelings and emotions which forms the core of Maya's existence. It hurts Maya to discover that Gautama is incapable of appreciating the sensuous beauty of the world of nature. Lost in his world of intellect and reason, he fails to notice the difference between the smell of lemons and that of petunias. Gautama's myopic intelligence fails to establish communion with the emotional self of his wife. Maya suffers in her loneliness and tries to gratify her emotional starvation with her nostalgic reveries of childhood days. She was brought up tenderly by a doting father as 'a toy princess in a toy world'. She fails to grow out of childhood. No wonder that Maya's childhood world of fantasies and adult world of realities clash, producing more imbalances in life. Inner demands and outer realities also create a conflicting situation. In Gautama's family the atmosphere is heavily charged with intellectual, social and political discussions. Maya cannot participate in these discussions and they know it. With her, they discussed babies, shopping, meals and marriage for she was their toy, not to be taken seriously. Gautama, critical of her temperament, says:

> "Neurotic .... Neurotic, that is what you are. A spoilt baby, so spoilt she cannot bear one adverse word. Everyone must bring a present for little Maya that is what her father taught her."[4]

Gradually, when Gautama devotes more and more time to his work, Maya turns more and more inward. She clings to fantasy as she is unable to relate to reality. She wants to escape from reality whereas Gautama desires to live in it. She considers Gautama's theory of detachment as the negation of life and feels miserable.

The novelist highlights Maya's sexual demands with the help of two powerful symbols: The peacock's voluptuous dance and the mating calls of the pigeons. She compares herself to the peacocks who mate only after fighting. The cries of peacock, 'Pia, Pia, Mio, Mio' — assimilate in Maya's mind with her own anguish. Like the peacocks she loves intensely and her love is unreciprocated. Like Maya, peacocks are creatures of exotic world and will not rest till they had danced the dance of death. According to the albino astrologer one of them would die after four years of marriage. Maya is as much haunted by the prophecy as by the myth of peacocks. In all her moments of crisis she reverts to the moon which has lewd associations in her mind and symbolically becomes a demonic pursuance. Gautama was only a 'figure of granite' to her for 'there were countless nights when I had been tortured by a humiliating sense of neglect, of loneliness, of desperation.'[5] In a fit of frenzy, one evening she pushed down Gautama to death and later commits suicide by jumping out of the balcony. During their walk on the roof, Maya is charmed by the beauty of the moon. It appears to her a symbol of love and the life that emanates from love. Gautama, engrossed in his thoughts of a law-suit, walks in front of Maya. As his figure obstructs her view of adored moon, she falls into a fit of frenzy and hurls Gautama down the parapet:

> "And then Gautama made a mistake — his last, decisive one. In talking, gesturing, he moved in front of me, thus coming between me and the worshipped moon, his figure on ugly, crooked grey shadow 'that transgressed its sorrowing chastity. 'Gautama' I screamed in fury, and thrust out my arms towards him, out at him, into him and past him, saw him fall then, pass through an immensity of air, down to the very bottom."[6]

In Part III of the novel, the scene of action shifts from Delhi to Lucknow. Both Nila and her mother await the arrival of Maya's father from Switzerland. Suddenly, Maya's shrill and childish laughter turns into a desperate scream. Nila's mother runs upstairs to help the frightened Maya, who jumps down the balcony and carries her mother-in-law along with her. Desai narrates:

> "Then they heard the patter of a child's laughter cascading up and down the scales of some new delight a brilliant peacock's feather perhaps? Then it stopped, suddenly, and they heard a different voice calling, shrilly and desperately, from some unimaginable realm of horror calling out in great dread.
>
> The old lady was up on her feet .... They met for an instance, there was silence, and then both disappeared into the dark quiet. All around the dark was quiet then."[7]

Desai's second novel *Voices in the City* written after two years (1965) offers a moving picture of the life of another Maya named Monisha. Like Maya, Monisha also suffers emptiness within as well as without but unlike Maya, Monisha has stilled her emotions and has trained them to submit. Maya pushes Gautama off the roof so as to protect her world of sensuous abundance but Monisha sets herself afire to reach the case of intense feelings.

Monisha, Nirode's sister is married against her wishes in a middle-class stolid family. Her relationship with her husband is characterized only by 'loneliness and lack of communication'. She is always haunted by a sense of her life dedicated to nothing. She is also childless like Maya. She wishes to have peace and silence which she does not get. In her in-laws house, she does not mind the great amount of work she is made to do. But the fact that she is always under the scrutinizing eyes of others, causes her discomfort. It seems to threaten her individuality. The fact that she is childless and is incapable of bearing a baby snatches from her the privacy, even of her own room. In such circumstances when she realizes that her husband Jiban is unable to understand and fulfil her emotional needs, she begins to grow world-weary. The crowded city of Calcutta makes her feel tired in mind and she finds the atmosphere uncomfortable. At the zoo, where she goes to escape the suffocating environment of her home, the sight of a kangaroo lying in the sun makes her conscious of her being childless.

Nirode, Monisha's brother is the chief protagonist of the novel. He remains the most dominant character in all the four parts of the novel. He is observed with the desire to meet failure after failure in life:

> "Then I want to see if I have the spirit to start moving again, towards my next failure. I want to move from failure to failure to failure, step by step to rock bottom. I want to explore that depth. When you climb a ladder, all you find at the top is space all you can do is leap off fall to the bottom. I want to get there without that meaningful climbing. I want to descend, quickly."[8]

Nirode's belief in this negative attitude is sufficiently deep and he quotes Camus to prove the rightness of his belief:

> "I have been reading Camus, you know. He says, 'In default of inexhaustible happiness, eternal suffering at least would give us a destiny. But we do not have even that consolation, and our worst agonies come to an end one day.'"[9]

He is engaged in an unequal fight against the social and commercial values of life which the city of Calcutta symbolizes. He is conscious of the fact that the values of the contemporary society are hollow. He used to despise his father and worship his mother. But after the death of his father he always pities him and hates his mother because she has been unfaithful to his father by having intimate relation with Major Chadha who lives next door to their house at Kalimpong. In Calcutta, Nirode is dissatisfied with his life, although he calls himself a journalist to keep up his dignity. But his job offers him no opportunity to express his creativity. He is an artist at heart and can see beauty even in the turmoil and darkness of the city. The artist in Nirode makes him despise his present job of a clerk. Therefore, he plans to edit a magazine to bring the scattered intellectuals of the country together. He tells Jit Nair that: "The newspaper carries the writer further and further into the impersonal, it only follows you. The you is everything in news. There is never an I. It is the I that interests me now."[10]

However, when the first issue of the magazine *Voices* is released from the press, he goes to Dharma, a recluse painter to seek his opinion about the magazine because he is the only man whose advice and criticism he takes seriously. Dharma advises him to change the cover design and enlarge the size of the magazine and use a better quality of paper to make it more attractive and successful. Nirode regrets at having confided to Dharma of his involvement in the magazine. He is angry at the thought that the magazine has betrayed his need to communicate with others. The next issue of his magazine is a success because of the publication of three short poems by a famous English poet. It gives prestige to the magazine. He fears that his friends want to take away his freedom by thrusting the burden of success on his shoulder. Nirode recognizes a lack of individuality and commitment to some higher purpose in life in all those who come and flatter him on the success of his magazine. People like Jit, Sonny, and Bose are leading their lives on animal plane. They all are in pursuit of wealth and physical pleasures. Their narrowness of purpose in life arouses disgust in Nirode. He opens a bookshop near the university, but the place is difficult to reach, but it protects Nirode from meeting the people he dislikes. In the meanwhile, he writes a play, the theme of which reflects his own quest for identity. His broken faith in the idol of his mother prevents him from trusting other people and from being in their contact. But he falls sick and in a state of semi-unconsciousness, caused by high fever, he talks to Monisha about the mother of their childhood days. However, this is not the last stage of Nirode's evolution. He discovers a new meaning of life in Monisha's suicide. Her death does not leave him in a state of grief and distress. He goes to Amla and aunt Leila, and pressing them against his body he speaks to them in a consoling manner:

> "He pressed them to him with hunger and joy, as if he rejoiced in this sensation of touching other flesh, others' pains, longed to make them mingle with his own, which till now had been agonizingly neglected. There was so much he wanted to tell them — to reassure them that no outrage had been committed, that Monisha had died from an excess of caring in a fire of care and conscience, and that they too must accept, with a like intensity, the vigilance of heart and conscience, allowing no deed of indifference or incomprehension to drift by, but to seize each moment, each person, each fragment of the world, and reverence it with that acute care that had driven Monisha to her splendid death."[11]

Monisha's death has given Nirode a glimpse of the secret of life and death. But his ecstasy and relief soon vanish during the hours between Monisha's cremation and the arrival of his mother. He thinks that once again he will meet his mother and will be caught in a trap of communion, relationship, joy and responsibility. But when his mother arrives and pushes Nirode away, Nirode's passion for his mother dries up, and he reads a meaning of rejection in the mother's changed treatment of him. This rejection gives him his long sought liberty. He identifies his mother with Goddess Kali who is the cause of both the existence and dissolution of this world. Now like a true existentialist, he knows that it is a pure fact and another facet of life. His search for meaning in life is complete.

Nirode's another sister Amla comes to Calcutta in search of joy, independence and a new job. She faces Monisha's captivity and Nirode's poverty and starvation. She is young, and come fresh from some school of art in Bombay. The novelist describes the phenomenon of decay and waste through the symbol of decaying flowers used to describe Amla's awareness of the ephemeral nature of the joys of life. She has 'heaps of ideas' which she wants to use as a commercial artist, but she feels that a sense of hollowness has already entered her life. Her life appears meaningless to her. Her experiences at the party, which she attends at Mrs. Basu's house prove unpleasant, and her need for friendship and communication remains unfulfilled. She feels frustrated and wants to escape her fears and anxieties. She goes to Dharma with Nirode and Dharma requests Amla to sit for a portrait. Amla grows desperate to share her feelings with someone regarding her love for Dharma, but in vain. Later Amla is shocked to see the sketches because this dissection of her body in the paintings suggests to her the loss of the wholeness of her being. She discovers a symbol of disintegration in it. But later on Dharma changes and in Dharma's presence, she becomes another Amla, a flowering Amla. She grows aware of the fact that he took interest in her as a model only. But at the same time Amla's innocence revives Dharma's faith and interest in the human world.

Desai explains in detail about the city of Calcutta. Calcutta poses a threat to the integrity of the individual. It is a city of the false values of life. There is no chance of survival of human values in the dehumanized Calcutta. On the one hand, it represents the ethos of corrupt commercial life, on the other hand, its poverty, misery, death, and decay make it an embodiment of disintegration.

The third and the last novel of this phase by Anita Desai is *Bye-Bye Blackbird* (1971). Now Desai comes out of the theme dealt in first two novels. While dealing with Maya's neurosis, Desai goes deep into the sources of marital disharmony in a male dominated society. She communicates the sense of social fashion with the tender sensibility of a woman and gives it depth and meaning through a highly communicative symbolism. While in this novel, the father in the unconscious dominated the life of the protagonist, in *Voices in the City*, the mother governs the life and destiny of the major protagonists. Nirode's psychic imbalance is due, partly, to his unresolved oedipal fixations also. If Maya's tragedy emanated from the father, Nirode's tragedy lies in his love-hate relationship with the mother. The mother figure is not merely a person, it symbolizes in Nirode's psyche a complex cluster of dream and fantasy to which he returns psychically and emotionally after every encounter with reality. Here Desai consciously portrays the creative-destructive influence that Calcutta city exercises on her inhabitants. In *Bye-Bye Blackbird*, the interaction between the locale and the individual acquires a new dimension, for the tension here between the white locale and the immigrant blackbird involves issues of alienation and accommodation that the immigrant has to confront in an alien and yet familiar world. Anita Desai selects a microscopic minority of educated Indian immigrants to dwell on the interaction that takes place between the locale and the individual sensibility. The milieu that she selects is rather narrow but it is a milieu she is most familiar with. Desai focuses on the disturbing aspect of loss of identity that immigration necessarily involves. The pathos of a culturally alienated girl are most movingly rendered in Sarah's girl.

Caught between acceptance and rejection, between nationalism and cosmopolitanism, Dev is tortured emotionally and intellectually. Dev suffers because he keeps wavering between his choices. England is the golden world, the price of which is too high for him to pay. Dev, a new immigrant, comes to London to stay with the Sens in their Claphan house. The absurdity of Dev's existence in England and its drab superficiality is recorded beautifully by Desai in the novel. Dev is unhappy with the treatment accorded to immigrants in England. In his uncertainty, he develops a schizophrenic attitude to England. He changes place with Adit whom he called 'spineless imperialist lover'. Later on Adit longs to go back to India and Dev decides to stay on in England. However, the fact is that Adit's love for England is superficial. After his engagement to Sarah, he goes back to India in the hope of settling there. But lack of better financial prospects drives him back to England. In spite of his professed love of the English world, Adit is an Indian at heart. He plans to go to Calcutta and visit his parents when he would have saved one month's salary. He wishes to idle away his time listening to Sitar and Shahnai till midnight. Adit's complacency and his illusion about his belonging to England come to an end after a weekend visit to his parents-in-law at Hampshire. On the occasion of their wedding anniversary, Adit insists that Sarah should wear a sari and put on the golden necklace. But when he finds that Sarah is not willing, his hatred of the English life and manners reaches its climax in his accusation of his wife of the typical English prejudice and hatred against the un-English people and things. His hatred of the London life and his sense of alienation intensify his homesickness.

Anita Desai presents Sarah as a better realized character. She portrays her as a woman, and reveals her dilemma and split pensonality which are the result of her marriage with Adit. Sarah married Adit in the hope of filling the hollowness of her life with the exotic but romantic world of her husband. But she is deceived in her hopes, as Adit stays in England living the unreal life of an immigrant. Her sense of loneliness and her anguish are further aggravated by her awareness that her marriage with an Indian has created a secret antipathy among her colleagues at the school where she works as the Head's secretary. In her marriage with Adit, Sarah has lost her parents, her former friends and the English world, but she has not been able to identify herself with the Indian world which she hoped her marriage would bring to her. In her anguish, she feels that she is neither English nor Indian. The theme of conjugal disharmony and emotional incompatibility between husband and wife, which Desai successfully delineates in *Cry, the Peacock*, and *Voices in the City* finds a faint and subdued expression in this novel. The cause of the emotional disharmony between Sarah and Adit is not to be found in the difference of their cultures; it emanates from their different temperaments rooted in their individualities. In his indifference towards Sarah, Adit corresponds to his counterparts in the other novels of Anita Desai. But Sarah is not as imaginative and emotional as Maya and Monisha. Adit's indifference towards Sarah's emotional sufferings is reflected in his half-hearted attempt to know the cause of her anguish. Towards the end of the novel, the novelist-shows that he does not care to know Sarah's feelings when he decides to return to India and settle there. He tells her about his decision in fragments and creates a dreadful suspense in her. She dreads that he may alone return to India and ruin their marriage. As she is pregnant, her concern for her unborn baby intensifies the gravity of the situation for her. She comes out of her anguish, despair and dread, when he asks her to accompany him to India. Sarah's choice of going to her husband's country fills her with the hope of acquiring 'a new, a different personality'.

Though apparently Dev stands in contrast to Adit, he is similar to him in his strings to achieve an authenticity of his subjective view of England. Dev comes to London with the intention of studying at the London School of Economics, and hopes to impress his professors. As he perceives the hostility of the natives to Indian immigrants, his cherished image of England begins to shatter. He tells Adit that he cannot think of living in a country where he was insulted and unwanted. The novelist depicts Dev's dilemma, agony and sense of isolation through the latter's instructive responses to the London life. In this respect, Dev reminds of Nirode of *Voices in the City*, who also reacts in a similar manner to the claustrophobic atmosphere of Calcutta. In fact, his mood of uncertainty is an expression of his determination. Whether he should accept England as he finds her or reject her because she finds to conform to his image of England. Dev's dilemma makes him forget his original purpose of coming to England. The meager sum of five pounds changes the look of London for him. At night he dreams of Rose and realizes that he badly needs a job. His desperate search for employment shows his longing for the economic and social freedom with which he hopes to achieve the realization of his new identity:

> "I can't go to college, not now, I want freedom, not restriction. I want enterprise, not discipline. I want money I want life. But I don't want to take a secretarial course. I don't want to take a correspondence course in radio-engineering or social service or any bunkum. I just want a job, that's all a real, paid job. I can't sit around like this any longer, Sen."[12]

As Dev has not studied for any profession, he is left with the choice of accepting a less respectable job in a restaurant or in a shop. He feels frustrated and grows envious of Adit's job and position. Desai portrays the various aspects of Dev's distraught psychic state through the language of images and symbols. Dev's recognition of the England of his vision and his realization of the pattern of nature give him a new identity and a deeper understanding of life. His one week adventure in the countryside of Hampshire completes his season for his ideal, and he discovers his true identity in relation to this ideal. He realizes that life acquires meaning only when it is lived with a sense of relatedness and an all-encompassing love. Now he sees London as someone before whom vistas of love, success and joy had opened. He decides to stay in England, and does so on the strength of his inner conviction. Adit's departure from England provides him a job in the former's office, and he shifts to the flat vacated by Adit and Sarah.

In fact, inspite of all the lavishness of its local details, the novel does not make any clear impression on the mind of the reader. Desai's forte — her uncanny ability to probe into the minds and hearts of her characters, both major and minor — is missing in this book. B. Ramchandra Rao comments:

> "Rural England is presented in a more idyllic fashion. The failure of the novel is due to the fact that while Mrs. Desai is moderately successful in creating the

> English environment, her characters are wooden ...... In can be argued, in defence of Mrs. Desai's puppets, that the English and the Indian immigrants do not see each other, and that they only see what they want to see stereotypes of each-other, coloured by prejudice."[13]

In the same way R.S. Sharma concludes:

> "Beyond assimilation and rejection, the novel deals with the temptation that the colonial culture has for the colonized. The blackbird, thus, stands both for the temptation and the gloom that this temptation creates for the excolonial. If Adit is free of his temptation, Dev is free of his gloom. The novel, therefore, rightly bids the blackbird a 'bye-bye'. It employs as the preceding analysis reveals, the metaphor of voyage or quest to suggest a pattern of action where each soul, after initial shock, puzzlement and anguish, discovers its own 'natural condition'. The tri-section plan of the novel 'Arrival, discover and recognition and departure', also seems to suggest this. While we recognise the intricacy of this pattern, we are aware that Anita Desai takes recourse to a great deal of authorial intrusion to achieve this end and that some of her narrative intrusions into metaphysics and psychology finally remain vague and inadequately fictionalized."[14]

References

1. Iyengar, K.R. Srinivasa, *Indian Writing in English*, New Delhi, 1983, p. 464.
2. *Ibid.*, pp. 464-465.
3. Desai, Anita, *Cry, the Peacock*, p. 146.
4. *Ibid.*, p. 99.
5. *Ibid.*, p. 201.
6. *Ibid.*, p. 208.
7. *Ibid.*, pp. 217-218.
8. Desai, Anita, *Voices in the City* Delhi: Hind Pocket Books 1968, p. 40.
9. *Ibid.*
10. *Ibid.*, p. 32.

11. Desai, Anita, *Voices in the City*, p. 248.
12. Desai, Anita, *Bye-Bye Blackbird*, New Delhi: Orient Paperbacks, 1982, p. 116.
13. Rao, B. Ramchandra, *The Novels of Mrs. Anita Desai: A Study*, New Delhi: Kalyani Publishers, 1977, p. 49.
14. Sharma, R.S., *Anita Desai*, Arnold Publications (I) Pvt. Ltd., 1981, pp. 92-93.

Novels of Middle Phase: Progressive Phase of Feminine Self-Perception — *WSWGTS, FOTM, TVBTS, CLOD*

4

The interaction between the poetic texture and the narrative structure in the novels written in the first decade of her writing career raises the Indian fiction in English to a higher level of artistic success. But after ten years or so Desai enters into the middle phase of her writing career where her characters are from the well-to-do sections of Indian society. Their problems are psychological or spiritual, not social, or economical. They passionately discuss issues like conformity and rebellion, attachment and detachment. But the ordinary problems of everyday life are never really touched upon. Since Desai's characters belong to the affluent sections of Indian Society they never really have to face the problems of the struggle for existence. However, starvation, poverty, the mute misery of the millions of Indians are never touched upon by Desai. From Maya's fears and superstitions in the first novel we move to the city of Calcutta where young men sip their leisurely cups of coffee and discuss metaphysical, spiritual or literary problems. The third novel takes the reader to England to see the blackbirds in the white man's country.

In the novels of middle phase (1973-82) Desai has again produced three novels. *Where Shall We Go This Summer?*, *Fire on the Mountain* and *Clear Light of Day*. Here she takes us back to the upper-middle class milieu. She writes about characters of this class because she knows them very well and can understand them sympathetically. In *Where Shall We Go This Summer?*, Desai takes up for treatment the theme which had engaged her attention in her first two novels. The major protagonist of her first novel of the middle phase is a nervous, sensitive middle aged woman who finds herself alienated from her husband and children because of her emotional and explosive reactions to many things that happen to her. Sita is as introverted and subjective as Maya . Likewise *Fire on the Mountain* is the story of Nanda Kaul; who is withdrawn and totally detached. And in her new 'four dimensional piece', Desai seems to have moved closer to the aesthetic goal she had been striving at, in all her earlier novels. Here she recapitulates in a musical structure the themes and characters that she had explored earlier so that in relation to her entire work the novel reverberates with echoes that suggest points and counterpoints like the moves of a subtle musical composition, the unassertive Sarah, over-sensitive Sita, alienated Nanda. We come across practical Bim, who is an intelligent independent minded protagonist. Bim who is willing to enter the traditional male domain, fends for herself, chooses a career and earns her livelihood. We see a precursory Bim in Sita too, who is able to face the challenge of life when she decides to go back to Bombay with Raman and accept the responsibility of child-bearing and child-rearing. Bim tries to and succeeds in rising above the constricting influences of her family, breaking off the shackles of her past and brining order to her life. The positive note on which the novel ends is a personal victory for Bim. She faces the reality around her with courage.

Where Shall We Go This Summer? (1975) is a story of Sita, who is badly disturbed by the violence and cruelty around her. It deals with the problems of human existence, the conflict of life-denying and life-affirming impulses and the instinctual inability of an individual to conform or adopt to the social conventions. Sita's father was a freedom fighter, who after India's Independence wanted to quit political life, and hence retired to a lonely house on the island of Manori offered to him by one of his rich followers, a Parsi millionaire, named Dalwala. Sita's father had liked this place since he wanted to put his social theories into practice here, carrying out certain personal experiments, most probably religious ones. The house was named, 'Jeewan Ashram'. In a separate room upstairs sitting on the strew mat, he offered his prayers to him several times a day, where Sita's elder sister Rekha also used to sing in her sharp piercing tone.

Sita's father, a social worker, revolted angrily. When Mr. Dalwala proposed a tubewell there, saying.:

> "No, I will have no machines here. I can prove that machinery is not essential to civilization, even that it is inimical. For Indian civilization, I think it is fatal. Gandhi taught us that."[1]

He suggested to his disciples to dig a well, working for two hours every morning and two hours every evening after prayers. The well at the island proved a miraculous one for its water could cure a disease easily. The fisherwoman, Champa, claimed that her boils were cured by drinking its water. Such strange things always happened there. The childless Phoolmaya could have a son by the miracle of Babaji. When Kanti Amma's child was bitten with scorpion, Babaji took the poison away by herbal medicines that he had kept hidden in his kurta.

Sita's father suggested the way of better farming, of growing better crops to the villagers. Sometimes he used the medicine of the soil to increase production. People thought of him as a saint, as a charltan, as a wizard and a social worker. Once Sita had watched him crushing pearls and gold to mix in the medicines to give it a sparkling touch. He told his friend Deedar that it was only the faith of the people that cured them. Sita had never seen her mother. She was a mystery to Sita. Jivan told her that she ran away to Benaras, and that Rekha was her step-sister. Her father's personality grew more and more mysterious to her when Sita came to think of her mother's desertion of him:

> "Why had she left? She continued to wonder. Why had she left three children .... Rekha, who it was true, may not have been her own but another woman's child, the child of another ghost in her father's life. Jivan the quick, clever, unscrupulous and irresistible boy, and Sita? Why had she left her husband whom they called the second Gandhi? Why was she not at the island with them, participating in the experiment that

> all called unique, great and Gandhian? Did she not agree with them?"[2]

In fact both Sita and her father were not aware of each others mentality and inner life. While others accepted the sweetness of the water in the well, Sita found none. She suspected the relation of her father with Phoolmaya; but she always enjoyed the peace and beauty of the island. Shyam M. Asnani writes about the island as a symbol of purity and innocence:

> "The island is more a symbol than a place. It is an apt metaphor to concretize Sita's condition. She retreats into it as into a womb, with an obsessive desire to recapture once again her childhood innocence and purity. Her obsession for child like purity and innocence in the sense that she is herself carrying a child and has come on the pilgrimage to the island in search of this pristine world for the sake of her child."[3]

Sita's father suddenly fell ill and grew weak gradually. He refused to take any medicine saying he had his own remedies. But Sita could not see any. Jivan, her brother, left the island knowing that his father was going to die. Rekha too left on his death, and became the nightingale of All India Radio, while Jivan became a 'turbulent trade union leader'. Sita had planned nothing. Raman, the son of her father's friend Deedar had came to cremate her father:

> "Shut the house, fetch her away, send her to college, install her in a college hostel and finally out of pity, out of lust, out of a sudden will for adventure, and because it was inevitable ... married her."[4]

Sita was a sensitive woman, who hankered for love and affection in life, detested sharply the violence and cruelty anywhere, expected a close communion with her husband, Raman, but all in vain. The way ladies behaved in the house of Raman, the violence she witnessed there, made her utterly helpless, desperate and disappointed in life. In the meantime Sita is blessed with four children. Living with her rational and non-chalant husband, she finds her surroundings too unpleasant and cruel to cope with. When pregnant for the fifth time, Sita decides rather foolishly not to give birth to the fifth child in a world of violence and hatred—the world where there are crows attacking a helpless eagle, where there are ayahs fighting in the streets, where one's children may be assaulted at any time, where there is no love and sympathy but combat and attack only, where people lived for nothing but 'appetite and sex'. Sita's intention of keeping her baby unborn appears to be foolish, but through this foolishness of her behaviour, she has succeeded in maintaining her individuality. She took the benefit of Raman's querry Where Shall We Go This Summer? replying at once 'To Manori' a pilgrimage, to that place of wonder and miracles where she can keep her unborn baby safe and sound.

Accompanied by her two children Karan and Menaka, Sita reaches the island house where nobody, neither Moses, the caretaker nor the villagers who simply stared at her, has a liking for her but for the loving memory of her father. This trip to Manori becomes for her a trip of self discovery and a recognition of reality. All her hopes are belied when she discovers that the fields are 'only pits of mud and slush', and the tank is overflowing with dirty water. And ultimately she feels betrayed when she learns that Raman has come to Manori not to see her but to fetch Menaka, she feels that she is a woman unloved and rejected by everyone. She too realises that this island now lacks all miracles or magical charms.

Menaka writes to her father Raman about her ensuing admission to the college, and the father comes to the island to take her back to Bombay. She wants to become a doctor. For all of them except Sita, life is there in Bombay and not in Manori:

> "Menaka's admission to medical college gained, wife led to hospital, new child safely brought forth, the children reared, the factory seen to a salary earned, a salary spent."[5]

In order to bridge the gap, Raman speaks to her in a very calm, quest tone and informs her that he is prepared to do some farming here but it sounds him foolish. To Sita, suddenly he has become the nicest man in the world. She thinks that she was performing in a play on the island:

> "The storm ended, the play over, the stage had now to be cleared ... then the players could go home ... she had actually been playing the part here of an actress in a theatrical performance and was now to return to a life of retirement, off stage."[6]

But Sita cannot really determine which one was the real life ... the life on island or the life on mainland. Some critics have criticized the sudden harmony and reconciliation between the couple as unnatural and unconvincing. D.S. Maini observes:

> "But such a weak epiphany does not connect. Nor are we prepared for the sudden flow and the decision to return to Bombay and to sanity. Her final view which seems to uphold the exciting and teasing ambiguity of life again is not well-earned."[7]

Explicitly the compromise between illusion and reality, individual and society, has been the intention of the novelist. In an interview, when Prof. Desai was asked about the fate of Sita's fifth child, she replied:

> "It is born. It lives, it compromises. It accepts dullness, mediocrity .... In other words, it leads an ordinary life of the kind its mother tries so desperately to change only to find she could not."[8]

Thus through this novel Desai offers a positive solution to the temperamental maladjustment and alienation in the present day situations, although after a long period of acute suffering and desperation. Thus compromise with the circumstances marks a significant change in her second phase in Anita Desai's outlook as she herself says, "Had I written the book ten years ago I would have ended it with Sita's suicide."[9] She has adopted a new mature attitude towards the hopelessness of an individual in the society.

The novel *Fire on the Mountain (1977)* deals with a fascinating female character, Nanda Kaul and her female psyche. Like Sita, Nanda Kaul lives alone in her villa in the Simla hills. She is a vice-chancellor's wife, living presenting in utter solitude, free from the claims and demands of the family, servants and position. She also fights against the odds around her with a good deal of confidence and strength, but the fight eventually leads to destruction.

Having been rejected and discarded all her life by her husband and children, Nanda Kaul decides to live in the Simla hills of the distant Himalayas at Carignano, in Kasauli — a hilly restort, ignoring all the contact and relations. The arrival of Raka her great granddaughter, will be a danger to her self-imposed seclusion, yet she cannot deny the request of her daughter Asha to allow Raka to come after her long illness. She recalls her past and the moments when she had felt alone among children and various relations, including Miss David, whom the vice-chancellor deeply loved, though he could not marry her.

When Raka arrives, she embraces Nanda Kaul with deep love, watching her great grandmother curiously. Both are unable to communicate with each other. Raka is even worse. She herself avoids meeting with her great grandmother, having a gift of disappearing suddenly and silently into the forest and hills. Raka places before her no demand or need, and desires only one thing — 'to be left alone and pursue her own secret life'. Raka is all for freedom and does not wish anyone to meddle with her. Nanda takes her to Monkey Row as an exploser and discoverer. Mrs. Kaul finds in Raka a perfect model of what she once aspired to be herself. She says, "You are more like me than any of my children or grandchildren. You are exactly like me, Raka."[10] Raka is a complete and perfect solitary figure and solitude never disturbs her. Mrs. Kaul thinks that Carignano is an ideal place for Raka. She should leave it for her. Certainly it belonged to no one else, had no meaning for any one else. Raka alone understood Carignano, knew what Carignano stood for — she alone valued that, Nanda Kaul knew.[11]

Raka never enjoys the company of the grey old ladies like Nanda Kaul and her peculiar jolly friend Ila Das. Their talks bore her to the extent of depression and restlessness. Then Nanda Kaul diverts all her attention to possess Raka. But all the same Nanda has a desire not to drive the child into boredom and embarrassment, and strives to find some interesting subject for the child when she discovers that her fantastic stories of childhood have failed to bring the desired effect.

Ila Das is appointed as a Social Welfare Officer to work in the Himalayas. Earlier, she was appointed in Home Science department by the husband of Nanda Kaul, but later on she had to resign on being superseded for the post of Principal. Since then she has had hard days, but she is a very jolly and humourous person. She is curious to meet Nanda in order to revive the memory of her childhood, though Nanda wishes to avoid her. Ultimately Ila comes to visit Carignano — the villa of Nanda Kaul, her school friend. In the village over hills she had waged a war against the priests and traditional rotten beliefs. At the stance of the priest a woman Maya Devi does not take her child to hospital for anti-tetanus and the child expires. In another case, Ila persuades one Preet Singh and his family not to get their seven-years-old daughter married to an old man. On her way to the village, she is attacked by Preet Singh, raped and strangled. The Police Officer, Garphal Thana, informs Nanda of the sad news on telephone, which shocked Nanda so deeply that despite of all her sincere social work, Ila dies in such tragic circumstances. To quote Asnani again:

> "Ila's real involvement in people's welfare assumes tremendous symbolic significance when contrasted with the barren, unfulfilled and lonely existence of Nanda Kaul. Yet there is an irony in her tragic death, for if Nanda's self-imposed withdrawal and alienation was meaningless; Ila's involvement brings only tragic death to her so much so that on the way home to her rat infested shack, she is raped and murdered."[12]

Anita Desai has tried to suggest a middle path, but her characters fail in this because of their eccentricities, although Nanda Kaul has tried it. Desai has given more attention to the character portrayal than to writing a gripping story. Her characters are individual rather than types. They behave in an uncommon extraordinary way. The problems and the unhappiness in the life of Sita spring from her constitutional inability to accept the values and the attitudes of society. The society at large, as it is represented by the ayahs, the cook, the nameless and faceless multitudes, threatens the very life and existence of the heroine. Raman, the husband of Sita, represents the prose of life. Like Gautama in *Cry, the Peacock*, Raman is unable to understand the violence and the passion with which Sita reacts against every incident. *The Village by the Sea* is the only novel by Anita Desai which ends in total harmony. It is considered as 'children's fiction'. Hari, the central character, was heavily burdened with domestic responsibilities — useless and jobless father, sick and bed ridden mother, sisters to be married off and no dowries. Hari decided to go away, he left Thul, his village and reached Bombay. His modern and conventional ideas got a great shock with Mr. De Silva's absence in Bombay and his not getting a job there. He got nervous and lost his enthusiasm. But till he started working at Sri Krishna restaurant run by Jaggu. Gradually he got accustomed to his new environment where lights were never put out. Hari soon got tired of this modern life. His tired eyes longed for the deep darkness and the quite light of the seaside village. Hari had to go through a number of hardships in Bombay but the next-door watchmendor panwallah became friendly with Hari and made him his apprentice. He genuinely wished to make Hari a watchmendor. He began to brighten up and looked happy and alive as a result. Leila, Hari's elder sister worked equally hard in the village during his absence and gets poor Man's Plenty. She felt wonderful to earn money and having rice, tea, sugar, etc., in her kitchen. She used to take her father to hospital also. Leila and Hari change their traditional lifestyle of immobility and worklessness. Biju becomes Desai's mouthpiece when he says things have to change. Then they will improve. Yes improve/change. Even Hari could adapt himself to the changing condition of time. The experience made Hari wiser and mature. He was no longer the frightened, confused boy. He knew he could make choices and decisions on his own. He had known finally that he belonged to his village by the sea—Thul and that for happiness he would go back to his village. It was wonderful to be able to choose what you wanted to do in life.

There is no tragedy and the novel ends in a cheerful note. In the opening part of the novel, Hari is a helpless young man groping in the dark, but by the end, he is a caretaker of his father, mother and sisters. Hari's character grows and he learns to maintain a balance between tradition and modernity.

This story based entirely on fact, won the 1982 Guardian award for children's fiction. No other novel of Desai presents external reality with such clarity.

Clear Light of Day (1980) presents Bim, who is neither baffled by her past nor is she crazy for any aspect of life. Bim is an interesting study of 'self' in transition from childhood onwards, she cherishes and sustains the feelings and thoughts that lead her to a life of social obligations. She is free from any psychological trauma like Maya and Monisha. The only trauma she passes through is to understand the cyclic change of time. Tara is her sister and two brothers are Raja and Baba. They are growing up with their rather indifferent parents — a diabetic mother and a father who is nothing more for the children but a master of 'entrance and exit'. Bim being close in age to Raja, has a very close emotional relationship with him. Bim is Raja's admirer and his equal. She encourages him in every speculation, act and ambition. Both find a great mental temperamental affinity with each other. Both are bold and independent. The novel begins with the return of Tara to India with her husband Bakul, a foreign executive, in order to attend the marriage of Raja's daughter in Hyderabad. At first they visit their Old Delhi house where only Baba, the younger brother and Bimla the elder sister, are living presently. Tara is all happy to see the house of childhood after a long interval. She requests Bimla to accompany her to Hyderabad; but is shocked to learn the rudeness and indifference of Bimla towards Raja whom she had once deeply loved. Bimla makes it clear that she is in no mood to tolerate the pride and arrogance of her brother. She is an independent entity now.

Aunt Mira was a virgin when she was widowed, her young student husband, having left for England for his study immediately after their wedding, caught cold in the rain one winter night, and expired prematurely. It was her horoscope that had brought about her misfortune, they said — 'Her wedding fineries were given away to her sister-in-law.' The aunt was a charm to the children who were discarded by their own parents.

Hamid, the driver's son, used to take Raja for rides on his bicycle and taught him how to get on cycle. They participated in wrestling and other sports together. The girls were sickened with the dull and boring atmosphere of their house where they always waited for their parents, having no communication with them at all, a place of total inactivity and eventlessness. They had desired for a change, but that was denied to them. The school was a challenge to Bimla, while it was a terror to Tara. Tara lacked the needed stamina and vigour for games, study and other activities. The girls at school considered Tara as unbearably snobbish and conceited, never willing to join them in their songs and their gossips. She even hesitated in going to the hospital with other girls to nurse the patients in charity. On the other hand, Bim was a worshipper of Florence Nightingale, loving dedication and sacrifice. Bim had always supported the cause of the Principal who wanted to maintain discipline and order in the school. She stood first in her exams and won honours. This would create for her, she thought, a way out of that unworthy and unsatisfactory atmosphere of their home. Raja also won a poetry prize for his poem on the *Battle of Panipat*. He was then referred to as the young Lord Byron in their midst.

The neighbourly Misra family once took Bim and Tara for picnic at Lodi Gardens, Bim was badly bitten by the bees, while Tara received some stings on her body. Tara was always envious of Misra girls for their freedom. Her friendship with Jaya and Sarla Misra went on growing and they often took her to cinema shows and Roshnara club. According to Bimla, college was more important than their marriage. She told Tara that she would never marry in order to support Baba, Raja and Mira masi. She actually believed in earning for herself and leading an independent life.

Raja used to contrast the charm and grandeur of Hyder Ali's house to the shabbiness of his own and found that he had an emotional affinity with the house of Hyder. Raju loved Urdu and had a desire to join the Jamia Millia College and wanted to get perfection in Islamic studies. But he was scolded by his father when he had purchased an admission form from this Muslim institution. The father reminded him that there were riots all over the country, and a demand for Pakistan was being mooted. If he took admission in the Jamia Millia, he would be burnt alive by the Muslims because they would not trust him and the Hindus would call him a traitor. Their mother died and Raja continued his study in the Hindu college as a student of English literature. Then Raja fell ill and was advised complete rest. His classmates visited him frequently and informed him about the riots, partition, willings, looting and burning in the city. They also reminded him that the police was looking for the traitors like him and very soon Raja was suspected of an alliance with Muslims.

Once Tara brought Bakul to her house who requested Bimla to send Tara to a party the next day at his house along with the Misra sisters. She was allowed to attend the party. In the meantime, their father died suddenly in an accident. His children were indifferent to his death in the same way as they had been to the death of their mother. Novelist narrates:

> "Few of the people, mostly club members and bridge players, who came to condole, realised how little difference his death made to the household — they were so accustomed to his absence that it was a small transition from the temporary to the permanent."[13]

Bimla wanted Raja to look after his father's business, but Raja was not interested in it and told that either Baba or Mr. Sharma would do this trivial job. Bim was responsible for the maintenance of the house, total expenditure, their food and Tara's marriage. Dr. Biswas, who was treating Raja, was interested in Bimla as he was charmed by her beautiful manners and nice personality. Bim appears as an ideal of sacrifice and dedication amidst the frustrating situations which surrounded them. Bakul expressed his desire and seeks permission to marry Tara and Bim allows it. She has to nurse both Mira Masi and Raja simultaneously. Bim accompanies Dr. Biswas to mozard and concert, thereafter he requests her to meet his mother at home. Raja had improved gradually, but Mira Masi had not.

Bim visits Dr. Biswas's house to have tea with his mother. She was given a warm welcome at his house. That day only they heard about Gandhiji's murder. Later Raja decides to leave for Hyderabad to work for Hyder Ali. Bimla was too perplexed to decide her future course. The doctor rightly understood her pitiable condition, he said:

> "Now I understand why you do not wish to marry. You have dedicated your life to others — to your sick brother and your aged aunt and your little brother who will be dependent on you all his life. You have sacrificed your own life for them."[14]

Later it happened. Aunt Mira could not survive. Raja lit her pyre and left for Hyderabad, where he married Benajir, the only daughter of Hyder Ali. Tara, who had married long ago, has now two young daughters. Tara comes to India along with her husband Bakul to attend the marriage of Raja's daughter in Hyderabad, who had become the owner of all the estate and property of Hyder Ali. Bim shows her displeasure with Raja who has become arrogant since his marriage with Benajir. Bim shows Raja's letter to Tara:

> "Perhaps you are also a bit worried about the future. But you must remember that when I left you, I promised I would always look after you ... about the house. ... I want to assure you that now that he is dead and left all his property to us you may continue to have it at the same rent, I shall never think of raising it or of selling the house as long as you and Baba need it. If you have any worries, Bim, you have only to tell."[15]

This letter is sufficient to generate a grudge in Bim against Raja. Tara becomes sad because she knew that Bimla had loved them all deeply. Tara thinks that Bim has developed some misunderstanding about Raja. They have a long discussion about their childhood, Misra family and life in school. Once they all were dependent on her; now only Baba is there, who is as indifferent as an inanimate object in that shabby house. Now who is there to deal with, Mr. Sharma with reference to the business of their father? Bim knows nothing about insurance.

She wants to sell out her share to Mr. Sharma, but she cannot decide. Tara is surprised at the revelation of Bim's anxieties and fears. She wants to consult everyone to solve the family problem, which has disturbed Bimla. Bakul also thinks over the issue and suggests Tara to arrange for a meeting of Bim and Raja. Bim knows that Raja is not concerned with them at all, she decides to sell her parents' share in the firm to Mr. Sharma and proposes to Baba that he should go to Hyderabad and live there with Raja because of financial constraints at home. Baba keeps silent. It is the climax of Bim's anger and despair. Through a dismal and shadowy atmosphere Bim can see in the *Clear Light of Day* now that she bears only love and yearning for all of them, and if she is hurt at present it is only because of her imperfect love, that does not extend to all equally. She should extend her net of love so that it could encompass everyone. She should forgive Raja for that unsavory letter. Then she tears up all the papers collected by Raja in her room and even the letter which is never answered and all the journals, old cheque books, pamphlets and catalogues kept by her father. Then she thinks, she is released from the conflict of resentment and acceptance, love and hostility, which is accelerated by Tara's arrival at Old Delhi. By their departure all this commotion would end.

Unlike other female protagonists of Anita Desai, Bimla, who is free from the danger of a shattered childhood or an incompatible marriage, is symbolic of forces that have sustained the foundation of all family life. She has gone beyond the existential problems that torment her other fictional countcrparts Maya and Sita. Bim's life acquires a heroic dimension in her character. Unlike many other Indian girls Bimla opts for her own way of life. She is admired and adored by Dr. Biswas and Bakul (Tara's husband) and despite a sure offer of marriage, she refused to play the conventional role of a sex object and a submissive wife and becomes a truly liberated woman.

But at the same time the clear and bright light of a day, in which she can see everything has also made her miserable because she realised her imperfect love for them all. She wants to live in shade, quiet and darkness. Thus Bimla's despair and loudness is given a spiritual dimension in the novel. In her denial and acceptance, she is like a mother who can sacrifice herself for others. The writer has shifted from the depths of human psyche to the depths of time as a 'destroyer' and as a 'preserver' and 'what the bondage of time does to people'. We find Bim as self-reliant and a sturdy support of the others: Tara sensitive and impressionable; Raja imaginative and self-centred; Baba strange and distant figure, the retarted product of the parent's middle age. The perspective of childhood dominates the novel for the adult life of the children is seen as an extension of their childhood. In this second phase Desai has attracted most critical attention due to the complexity of form and theme of her novels, conforming of the broad parameters of psychological novel. She focuses her attention on the status of women in India in the male-oriented and male-defined social and moral codes. She portrays their quest of self-assertion and self-actualization in the face of rigid norms of behaviour in a conformist and status-quo society. "Though Mrs. Desai traverses a broad territory of themes, yet she mainly focuses on the trials and tribulation, fears and apprehensions, joys and hopes, dilemmas and predicaments, perplexities and paradoxes, in the physical and psychological lives of her characters in general and the protagonists in particular, to mirror the multi-dimentional reality in all its contours."[16] She is interested is characters who are not average, as Sita, Nanda or Bim, and are driven into despair and as a result turned against the general environment and trend. The basic problem for her characters is how to exist in society and yet maintain their individuality. In the fictional world of Anita Desai, the creed is to discover value of the individual and individualization. In the novels of this phase the maturity of Desai's art, the nature of identity crisis becomes more complex. She stresses on the existential problems of womankind. Although she does not belong to any feminist movement yet there is a touch of persuasive feminism in her writings. She successfully depicts the inner world of sensibility and the chaos inside the mind of characters with a special stress on female psyche. Her protagonists possess a defiant individuality and fight against the commonplace conformity and stick to their own vision of life. For the novels of this period, Desai herself comments, "My novels are no reflections of an Indian society, politics or characters. They are part of my private efforts to seize upon the raw material of life — its shapelessness, its meaninglessness despair and to mould it.[17] Yes, her women characters like Bim, Nanda, Raka or Sita desire to be respected and recognised as individuals in their own right and not taken for granted. They all represent progressive phase of feminine self-perception. First it shows a journey from Maya's self-destructive sensuous involvement to the meaningless detachment of Monisha from the world of people around, which does not save her from a fate similar to that of Maya. Then Sita's dilemma between rejection and acceptance is presented by Desai to show her longing to escape the brutal realities of life. Then Desai shows Nanda Kaul's predicament of pulling on a life of pretence, braving deceptions and unfaithfulness. The courage, poise and balance with which she carried on a life uninvolved and unloved is an improvement on the preceding harness. It is only at the fag end of life after having discharged all her duties and obligations that Nanda Kaul retreats from active life. Since her courage, poise and balance are only acquired and assumed qualities, they fail her at the crucial movement of the arrival of the news of Ila Das's death. The journey from negation to affirmation is completed in Bim's perception of the truth of life that in order to keep oneself whole, one has to relate oneself with others and that fulfillment lies in connectedness — a truth achieved through love and forgiveness.

References

1. Desai, Anita, *Where Shall We Go This Summer?* Delhi: Vikas Publishing House, 1975, p. 49.
2. *Ibid.*, p. 62.
3. Asnani, Shyam M., 'Anita Desai's Fiction: A New Dimension', *Indian Literature*, Vol. XXIV, No. 2, March-April, 1981, p. 49.
4. Desai, Anita, *Where Shall We Go This Summer?* p. 71.
5. *Ibid.*, p. 101.
6. Desai, Anita, *Where Shall We Go This Summer?* pp. 110-111.

7. Maina, D.S., 'The Achievements of Anita Desai', *Indo-English Literature,* Ed. K.K. Sharma, Ghaziabad: Vimal Prakashan, 1977, p. 229.

8. Desai, Anita, in an interview with Alma Ravi, *World Literature Written in English*, Vol. XVI, No. 1, April, 1977, pp. 97-98.

9. Desai, Anita, in an interview with Atma Ram, Loc. cit., p. 97.

10. Desai, Anita, *Fire on the Mountain,* New Delhi: Allied Publications, 1977, p. 64.

11. *Ibid.*, p. 80.

12. Asnaw, Shyam M., 'The Theme of Withdrawal and Loudness in Anita Desai's *Fire on the Mountain*', *The Journal of Indian Writing in English*, Vol. IX, No. I, January 1981, pp. 89-90.

13. Desai, Anita, *Clear Light of Day,* New Delhi: Allied Publishers, 1980, p. 64.

14. *Ibid.*, p. 97.

15. *Ibid.*, p. 27.

16. Bale, Suman and Pabby, D.K., *The Fiction of Anita Desai*, p. 2.

17. Vinson, James, *Contemporary Novels,* London: St. James Press, 1976, p. 356.

Novels of Third Phase: Analysing Male Consciousness — *IC, BB*

5

Third phase of Desai's career as a novelist deals with male phychology. She switches from a woman-centered to a male-centred narrative. In this phase she has written two novels *In Custody* and *Baumgartner's Bombay*. Theoretically, these two novels present some deviation from Anita Desai's earlier novels. Whereas her earlier novels are mostly female oriented, where one or the other angle of the female psyche is explored deeply, in these novels, the main focus is shifted towards the male psychology. The major protagonists Deven and Hugo represent male psyche. *In Custody* (1984) is an example of the idea of mutuality, of the relationship of the individual to society, of interdependence between the creator and receptor of poetry. The novel brings out the unfortunate experiences of Deven, the protagonist who is deceived and trapped by a friend. Her *Baumgartner's Bombay* (1988) is a portrait of loneliness, of alienation and immigrants' existential problems. It is a moving account of the travails of Hugo, a simple and submissive Jew. The barriers and betrayals and his disillusionments with human company are beautifully depicted. Hugo and Deven both are victims of strained relationship with society and with family. Desai herself says about her characters delineated in this third phase:

> "They are those who can handle situations and those who cannot and my stories ... are generally about those who cannot. They find themselves trapped in situations over which they have no control."[1]

The theme of outlandishness of *Bye-Bye Blackbird* is repeated in this phase also by Desai in *Baumgartner's Bombay*, too with the difference that Adit and Sarah get their redemption while Baumgartner does not. He ultimately meets the tragic end of his life. The novel presents that Hugo has been victimized, time and again, by different people in Germany and India. Baumgartner prepared foreground for her next novel in next phase *Journey to Ithaca* in revealing a super-sensitive mental vision. Desai stresses Hugo's homelessness through the image of cats. The locale of the novel is Germany and India. The first chapter of the novel uses flashback technique from the present to past. His childhood recalled through many of German songs. Anita Desai has done justice to portray the mind of Baumgartner, his confusion, his maladjustment both in his own country and his adopted country. The pre-war Calcutta and the contemporary Bombay of the novel come to life admirably. Desai captures the feel of life in the back alleys of Bombay, with the cheap restaurants and the hippies haunting them. *Baumgartner's Bombay* is a serious study of a lone human being at the mercy of impersonal forces too large for him to comprehend. Yet the picture is not completely somber, it is lit by flashes of humanity.

In Custody marks a departure from her earlier novels in the sense that the protagonist in this novel is not a female but a male. He is Deven and not his wife Sarla. Deven is married to Sarla who is not his choice. Sarla is usual, ordinary, compromising and a lady of normal temperament. That's why she is not like Maya, or Sita or Amla or Monisha, the typical heroines of Desai. The theme of the novel is probed through nature, the city, the house, the circus and the comet and stars. In fact we can easily identify that Anita Desai has systematically fused three thematic threads in the novel, *In Custody*: craze for freedom, problem of love and marriage and imprisonment and death in life through various apparent objects. The novelist tries to discover the true significance of things in life. In reality Desai here explores the psyche of male protagonist outside the circumscriptions of familial ties and obligations. She successfully makes a departure from her earlier obsessive per-occupation with the interior landscape of hypersensitive and neurotic women.

In Custody is a novel about an unassertive lecturer of Hindi in a mofussil Degree College in Mirpore near Delhi. His name is Deven Sharma. He is an Urdu enthusiast and wants to interview which is beset with many obstacles and mishaps and when at long last it materializes, the tape recorder is not operated well and what is recorded is a string of nonsense utterance of a senile poet about biryani, pigeon flight, wrestling and memories of his young days. The interview is to be deposited in the college. But the irony is that there is nothing worth depositing in the tape. Deven is in a dilemma and he seems to be in custody of the poet.

In Custody marks the continuation of some of Desai's earlier themes and narrative tendencies. The novel deals with issues like poetry, language and even monetary problems. In reality, Desai here explores the psyche of male protagonist outside the circumscriptions of familial ties and obligations. Deven is endowed with different kinds of sensibility. He is not an alienated self, in the sense the female protagonists of Desai's earlier novels are. The main theme revolves round Deven and focuses on his awareness of the meaninglessness of his existence, his yearning to discover meaning in the world of Urdu poetry. Deven Sharma, is frantically busy in pursuit of his ideal, but the fact is that he also stands in the moment and passes through the agonizing states of anxiety, dread and concern. His dread of being ruined gives him an insight unto his authentic existence, and he gains the courage of his convictions. Deven and Sarla therefore, are constantly confronted with the stupendous task of defining their relation to themselves and to their immediate human context. Acceptable behavioural pattern is alien to them. The root is not far to find. He craves for freedom. Deven by and large has strange childhood from when he develops a negative self-image and aversion. The immediate result is, his fragmented psyche to view world as a hostile place. For him the domestic life is not his world, rather it is a trap where his individuality is endangered and thus complete lack of interest and dissonance in his relationship bring solitary confinement and show his reluctance to face reality. He knows how he has been trapped and how he can begin to live afresh. He cries, he tries and he flies too but all in vain. There are many obstacles too. Soon he is caught by fantasy. The next thing is marital disharmony. It is one of the main issues dealt in the novel. Desai refuses male as super power. Even Deven plays negative role in his relation with Sarla. They have an unhappy married life. Both of them are frustrated in their own way, but they're unable to do anything for each-other. Deven feels as if they were in a trap. Marriage, his family responsibilities and his job have placed him in a sort of cage and there was no way out of it. Desai's main concern is to depict the psychic and social status of Deven at this crucial juncture of his life. Deven is cheated and bullied with a project that ends in his disaster and ruin. The whole narrative oscillates between Deven's dreams and realities, his aspiration for poetry and its illusory nature and finally into ultimate disaster. Defeated aims, frustrated ends, and thwarted wishes fill Deven's heart with gloomy darkness. The financial and social factors are mostly responsible for the drooping spirit of Deven-self-pity resulting from his self-defeat weakens him further. Deven is further humiliated, cheated, bullied and thrown away. The idea of death occurs in his mind. In the process of visualizing Nur's death, Deven becomes conscious of the eternal nature of his relationship with Nur. He learns that even his death cannot end this relationship. At the same time during his morning walk beside canal, he wishes that it would have been good if his students were to emerge to stab him. There is an insistent longing for death as a possible exit out of this ordeal, but very soon this longing for death is sought by an all pervasive awareness and consciousness. Towards the end of the novel he is a changed person altogether. As the novel ends with a positive note. Deven is able to perceive a ray of hope even in his boundless suffering and humiliation. He is convinced that 'perhaps when everyone had cut him off and he was absolutely alone, he would begin to find himself and his own strength'. Deven's sufferings gave him a philosophical outlook. In fact each new misfortune and calamity fills him with the iron of resistance. The great Indian English Poet Keki N. Daruwalla finds fault with the novel's ending regarding the character of Deven as the reader does not know what exactly happens to

Deven at the close of the novel. He comments that at the ending whether one takes it that Deven commits suicide or refrains from committing it frankly left him surprised and untouched.

Desai uses zoological imagery and the animal imagery is predominantly drawn from circus animals. The fight between Nur's wives is presented 'as between jeolous tigresses'. Nur's young wife has reptilian hand and for Deven she is a jackal. There is the figure of a dog to describe Deven's dejected and futile life. He identifies his fate with the dog which had come under the bus. As for characterization, this novel, *In Custody*, as also most of Desai's novels, is very successful. All the important characters are well developed. Even Mr. Trivedi, a minor character is characterized sufficiently well. Of all the characters Murad is unforgettable. He is very interesting. Thus *In Custody* is by and large, a flawless creation of Desai's craft singularized by a happy fusion of structure, content and language. It reveals the remarkable measure of Desai's succors in having dealt with a theme and male character. He cannot but admire its novelistic excellences which even the western critics, have come to recognize and accept.

Baumgartner's Bombay (1988) presents the multifarious vision of racial distinction, human predicament, historical awareness, seeming poverty and total violence and social obligation. Spending his childhood with his parents in Germany, Hugo arrives in Calcutta for his business. He meets Habibullah here and on his advice he comes to Bombay and becomes a partner of Chimanlal in the business of timber and finally he is stabbed to death by a German neurotic boy, Kurt. Thus the entire life of Hugo from Berlin to Bombay unfolds the multifarious vision of human relationships. Hugo's entire life seems to be a mysterious one. The vision of this lovelorn man is clearly discernible in him. As a man, a 'firangi' he craves for human love.

> "Accepting but not accepted, that was the story of his life, the one thread that ran through it all. In Germany, he had been dark — his darkness had marked him the Jew-derjude. In India he was fair and that marked him the 'firangi'. In both lands, the unacceptable."[2]

With this novel Desai has again made a place for herself in immigrant writing too. She uses autobiographical material as base for her multi-dimensional novel *Baumgartner's Bombay*. When asked why she chose to write a novel about a German in Bombay, in an interview, she replied:

> "And it was when I saw this Austrian Jew in Bombay — I actually saw the man pottering around the streets picking up scraps for his cats that I began to imagine his past. And that gave me the key to open that German world. And I was able to use my mother's memories of pre-war Germany and our own perception of the war far away from India simply as a set of rumours and news that came to us."[3]

Thus, Hugo was an alien in a strange land, came from a foreign country, was of a different colour, spoke a different language, had a different religion, is established early in the novel. In Germany, his dark complexion marked him for a Jew, in India, after fifty years the land was familiar to him, but the eyes of the people who passed by glanced at him who was still strange and unfamiliar to them, and all said: 'Firangni, Foreigner' (19). And for Indians he was fair, therefore, ostracized in both countries. By interiorishing the feelings of a marginalized person in Hugo, Anita Desai portrays him not just as Gramsci's simplified 'Subaltern' but as a complex victim of multiple marginality. Even after the war, Hugo cannot entertain hopes of returning to his homeland because of his race. His bitter experiences in Berlin and later with fellow Germans in the internment camp had even killed his desire for the language and gradually he found 'the language slipping away from him replaced by English and Hindustan.' With frayed, troubled roots Hugo's life's journey literally turns out to running in circles, like the circular tracks of the race course, never arriving, because in India he is unaccepted and betrayed to the state of a permanent refugee. The immigrant resident syndrome takes over. From a consciousness of race, Hugo is made painfully aware of the difference in colour and language throwing him out of the normal existence.

There are other voices from the periphery as well that cannot be overworked. Hugo's mother, Frau Baumgartner embodies a fragile beauty that is readily consumed by the fiery Nazi extermination campaigns. Here is a world overflowing with poetry, violets and books. Sadly deficient in her capacity to comprehend the precarious conditions surrounding her and lacking the courage to take the 'leap of faith' and move to a safer corner of the world with her son, and fate correspondingly fades with her sentimental song. Gisele and Lotto were twin dancers at Prince's in Calcutta. When Hugo first meets them, Lotto succumbs to her lot submissively accepting the existing order of things in society. Gisela, on the other hand, is the 'empowered' female dominating the male, thereby subverting the social order.

Isolated and deceived, Baumgartner feels seclusion and for the fear of loneliness, he leans upon Lotto with brotherly affection to share his isolation with her. She is also in constant search for identity in Indian society. She marries Kanti Sethia in order to have Indian citizenship, but he leaves her in Bombay like a widow and lives in Calcutta himself, (201). After the death of her husband Kanti, Lotto learns upon Baumgartner for companionship. As Hugo is pure in his heart and mind, he develops a telepathic insight.

Anita Desai employs a distinct narrative strategy that not only enforces rhythm and pattern to her story but also marks the regular alternating from past to present in a zig-zag movement that inscribes time not as linear or circular but as the swing of the pendulum. Metaphorically it is emblematic of the passage from childhood to adulthood, from colonization to decolonisation, from trauma to creativity. This is further reinforced by her use of German necessary rhymes and English songs.

Thus, Anita Desai has dedicated this decade of her creative writing to male characters. Speaking about her initial years in India, Desai says that she left India at 45. Before that her whole life was about family and neighbours, it was very difficult for a woman like her to experience anything else. She said:

> "I was bored, and I needed to find more range, which is why I started to write about men in books like *Baumgartner's Bombay* (in which a German Jew flees the War in India) and *In Custody* (in which a college lecturer goes in search of a famous poet). Men led lives of adventure, chance and risk. It just wasn't possible to write that from an Indian female perspective."[4]

References

1. Rao, Madhusudan Sinha, 'Silent Spaces of Inner Vastness', *Times of India*, Delhi, 18th June 1992.
2. Desai, Anita, *Baumgartner's Bombay*, Harmondsworth: Penguin Books 1988, p. 48.
3. Libert, Florence, 'An Interview with Anita Desai', *WLWE*, Vol. 30, No. 1, Spring 1990, p. 54.
4. www.amazon.com

Novels of Mature Phase: A Tinge of Variety — *JTI, FF, TZW*

6

Recent Phase/Mature Phase

Recently Anita Desai has produced three novels in this mature phase of writing novels when her daughter Kiran Desai has also started writing novels. These novels she had written after she moved to New York, first novel is about Egyptian culture. It is a positive story and it is called superior religious and spiritual novel to the novels of Raja Roy. It is called a miracle work by the critics. It is Journey to Ithaca.

Recent Phase 1993-2004

Anita Desai has won well-deserved praise as a woman writer for her elegant, evocative prose and for the keen intelligence with which she explores culture and character. In all the three novels *Journey to Ithaca*, *Fasting, Feasting* and *The Zigzag Way*, this Indian novelist and short story writer especially noted for her sensitive portrayal of the inner life of her female characters appears a bit different. Several of Desai's novels explore tensions between family members and the alienation of middle-class and upper-class women. In her later novels Desai has dealt with such themes as German anti-semitism, the demise of traditions, and Western stereotypical views of India. Professor Lightman of MIT said about her:

> "She is a novelist of the human psyche, and she approaches her subjects quietly and delicately. She is one of the world's most distinguished novelists in English."[1]

While *Journey to Ithaca* deals with a European couple Matteo and Sophie, *Fasting, Feasting* describes American Melony alongwith Arun and Uma in full detail. In her latest book, the half-Bengali, half-German, Desai, who has often focused on India and on Indians living elsewhere, turns to another land : Mexico. In *The Zigzag Way*, she illuminates, that country's vistas and history, and the interwined lives of three very different foreigners who venture there, with characteristic grace, skill and insight. She says, "Modern-day India is slipping away from me" and has set her new novel, *The Zigzag Way* in Mexico'. She continues, "To my friends and family in India. I am becoming a ghost."[2] She currently shuttles between Boston, Mexico, Cambridge and Delhi, but her visits to India have become less frequent. At an age when most writers are descending deeper into their own fictional worlds, into meditations on age, identity and the bankruptcy of the modern world; Desai is exploring lives increasingly remote from her own. Desai is said to have developed a passion for Mexico. She first went there six years ago, and immediately felt its affinity with India. Desai tells about Mexico, "Its such an ancient country, you feel every stone has a history to tell. Mexico and India share a history of colonialism — 300 years of Spanish and British rule along with this, much longer past that goes back into myth. Physically, we 're alike, too : I am constantly taken for a Mexican."[3]

Journey to Ithaca begins with Cavafy's poem 'Ithaca'. Translated by Rac Dolven. In the novel, India appears as a kind of Ithaca. Paranjape maintains that Desai no doubt, intended India to be a type of Ithaca. The main characters are Matteo and Sophie, an European couple who came to India together to share an adventure as hippies in the early 1970's. The story begins with Matteo lying sick in a hospital in India. Sophie who had deserted him, fed up with his foolish craving after gurus, hurries to him to fetch him back home to live with her and her two children Giacomo and Istabel. Of the three major characters in the novel Sophie is at the centre of the narrative. The novel beautifully documents the journey of two characters Matteo and Leila searching for enlightenment. The novel also portrays the pathetic conditions of Indian artists who have been selling Indian spirituality abroad. To a secular rational reader *Journey to Ithaca* remains a significant work because the central issue of the novel is 'search for truth, ultimate reality, beauty, joy, ecstasy or whatever form truth has.'[4] Sophie, a German journalist follows her husband Matteo to India and wanders with him from one ashram to another. She has a Western oriented approach towards life and does not have a blind faith in ashrams and gurus in Bihar. As a young wife she has desires to fulfil herself but this is not possible in the stuffy and unruly environment of the ashrams. She is upset and baffled to see 'the unequal living of different devotees there. She feels neglected and outcast among the pilgrims. She smokes with a mixed feeling of guilt and gratefulness. Matteo is at peace and feels fully adjusted to the filthy environment because his sole purpose in life seems to reach the truth. This difference of opinion and attitude create a gap between the couple.

'Yet when Matteo comes to her in the night she fights him off fiercely. 'I can't - I can't here, in this zoo, I want to go away. I want to be ourselves. 'By ourselves', Matteo withdrew in distress. 'By ourselves we'll never come to know India'. 'Why not? I want to go to Goa and eat shrimp. I want to go to Kashmir and live on a house boat. And lie in the sun and shampoo my hair and eat omelettes ....' Matteo was disgusted. 'That isn't India.' 'What is?' What is? We must search for what it is.'[5]

Sophie is treated as a second rate seeker of truth in the ashram. She looses her freedom here. Her smoking is symbolic of two things : first she breaks the code of ashram and secondly she relieves herself momentarily from her tense nervous systems. Her feeling 'guilty and grateful' at the same time brings forth the ambivalence of her mind. She feels guilty because she smokes as an ashramite and is grateful because she does not like to make an association and reconciliation with the inferior pilgrims in the ashram. The sense of belongingness to her own country so much overpowers her that she asks Matteo, "Couldn't we stay in our own country? To die there?"[6]

In that ashram in Bihar where Matteo and Sophie were staying, meals were served to foreigners not in the dining hall with the disciples but on the verandas outside and they were served on the disposable leaf plates, so there was no chance of a Hindu disciple being polluted. When Sophie understood the arrangement she refused to eat in the veranda and would only eat peanuts sitting on the steps behind the kitchen with a pack of stray dogs. Matteo hissed at Sophie after receiving complaints:

> "Sophie, please do not mind! If you don't live it here, please remember I have to stay in order to study. Can't you behave?"[7]

Sophie did not want to argue with Matteo as she was drained of all her strength due to summer and unhealthy environment. Her strength had dwindled away. They had come to India to share an adventure. Sophie wished to go through this adventure to recover their unique and essential love but her strength had run out. Matteo always stressed that he had come to the ashram to stay and study and Sophie's restlessness in the ashram disturbed him. Matteo tried to avoid her and would keep the company of his teachers. He would come to the room late at night:

> "Occasionally at this hour he would make love to her and this he did with a new contempt, and a violence that was so unlike him, it shocked her .... Sometimes, if she felt strong enough, she struck at him and fought him, this made him more violent."[8]

Sophie missed Matteo's presence and showed signs of nervousness and insecurity. She suffered from her husband's disgust. She was sick and after a thorough checkup by the ashram doctor, was found pregnant. The word 'ashram' baffled her severely. She longed to go back to her country. Matteo had joined the life of an ashramite for unveiling the secrets of life while Sophie followed her husband only to share his life and nothing more attracted her as an ashramite. The news of Sophie's pregnancy made everyone there discard her even more jealously. One of the woman disciples was heard saying, 'What do they think, that they can come here and live like animals in our ashram?'[9] This attitude was explicit not only to Sophie but also to Matteo through his Sanskrit teacher. Sophie was admitted to a hospital with poor medical aids and the unruly mob of so many ladies inside it and insanitation, which made Sophie very sad. To Sophie's utter displeasure Matteo shifts her to another hospital in the hills.

The insecurity and restlessness in Sophie's mind can be detected from Sophie's dreams where she gives birth to her baby in a stream of blood and she touches the baby and tries to unwrap it, it becomes a cold and limp snake and therefore she drew her hand back in horror. Confining Sophie to her bizarre world, Matteo joins another ashram, run by a woman known as Mother. Matteo is intoxicated with his quest for truth. He seeks in Mother some indefinable features and becomes her disciple. Sophie is put in the maternity ward of the hospital. The purpose of Matteo's life was just 'to experience bliss' and for Sophie:

> Tearing himself away from the ashram, he made his way to the hospital, in town as if it were a penance, and sat by her bed with a face of suffering which she lay — calmly, willingly, even contentedly — at the centre of the hospital world of beds, babies, food, bodies and other smell. To see her so was to have a vision of what the world was for the ordinary, the unblessed, a nightmare world of physicality.[10]

The differences between Matteo and Sophie assumes alarming dimensions as Sophie's pregnancy advances and Matteo continues advancing on the path of spirituality. Both of them grew indifferent to each other with one seeking for soul and the other for body. Matteo's attachment with Mother develops and he says:

> Any time spent away from the Mother, without her, was wasted time, empty time, dead time ....[11]

Sophie's rational mind and her logical outlook on life demanded scientific answers from the Mother. She questions:

> And what is she, this Mother — a hypnotist, a magician? "Are you afraid my question will expose her? Your questions do not expose her, they expose you — your pathetic ... 'he stammered' stupidity? 'Oh, call it what you like — it is your refusal to see and experience ...' what? 'what I see and experience.'[12]

Sophie as a normal woman becomes jealous of Matteo's affinity to the Mother. Her irritation becomes obvious with the question. "Would you work like this for your father if he asked you to join his business? No, you wouldn't, you'd refuse outright. So why do you do this for her?"[13]

When Sophie finds that there is no remedy and at least she cannot deviate Matteo from his path, she tries to isolate herself from Matteo's world by listening to her old tapes and stay busy with her separate world of pregnancy. Giacomo, a baby boy is her first child and after some years, staying in the ashram, she gives birth to baby girl, Isabel. Now she is worried about her kid's future as a mother and as a lady her tension builds up with the growing infatuation of her husband for the Mother. Her womanly weakness is quite apparent when she rebukes her husband in this matter:

> 'Oh, the Mother, once again, the Mother. Not a stone, not the shrine, Matteo it is a woman who keeps you here, call her what you like — the cosmic, the absolute — but it is woman. Don't you see?' Sophie's breath was coming short and hard. She turns and went back to the darkened room. There was nothing left to say.[14]

The suspicion in the mind of a wife regarding the presence and role of another woman in a man's life is authentically depicted. Though Desai has touched this problem very lightly but it is a different sort of relationship. Fundamentally their approach towards life is different. According to O.P. Budholia, "Matteo represents all that comes from the heart, while Sophie represents all that comes from the mind."[15] The bitterest quarrel is approached in regard to their son's education. Matteo wants him to be educated at the ashram school and Sophie wants him to go to a school in Europe. Now both of them are locked into what both of them feel is a fight to the end. Both are now desperate to protect what they believed to be right. Matteo stressed on 'sacred love' and for Sophie physical love and sacred love are the same. But ultimately "the arguments were turning into silences, and the silences were stretching and deepening. He was disappearing into them. She let him be, bitterly."[16]

Sophie, returns to Italy where she tries to fill the void created by Matteo's absence by Paolo's friendship but in vain. Sophie overcomes the onslaught of lower impulses and realizes that Mother was a great saint. This reveals the purity of Sophie's mind. Sophie seems to have left India behind her completely but when a telegram arrives about Matteo's sickness and hospitalization, she receives it with such surfeitness and eagerness that "it was clear her mind had been with Matteo all this time, her senses alert to receive any message from him."[17] Now nothing was more important for her, than to be with her husband instantly. She rushes to India, the third time, and learns about the death of the Mother and Matteo's departure from the ashram in quest of his 'self'. Now Desai presents materialistic Sophie filled with the fire of spiritual height. She perceives the higher vision of love in her husband and the Mother. Sophie is now determined to follow the ideal of Mother as a seeker, forgetting her children and parents and country. She collects that will-power to follow the path of higher vision. Some inner enlightenment makes her submit to the higher motives of life. She begins to complete the journey:

> 'Sophie is lying as still as a stone, with an arm across her eyes, thinking in the dark of that first pilgrimage she went to India that had ended in the death of a child. Now she knows why the Mother went on that pilgrimage, why anyone goes on a pilgrimage, and why she must go too. She says in a flat voice, 'I'll have to "and adds, what else"?[18]

She decides that she is to undertake a journey for mystic experience. 'Anita Desai achieves a grand success in presenting higher values of love, humanism, realism mysticism and a unified vision of universal brotherhood.'[19]

Unlike her earlier novels, *Journey to Ithaca* looks at India through an outsider's eyes, and sees only melodramatic horrors. Almost all the descriptions of day-to-day life in India strike false note. One suspects that it is currently fashionable to write about alternative sexual behaviour. It has a gratuitous description of childhood sexuality, with incest also included. When Sophie's little daughter Isabel, not old enough to go to school, and her brother Giacomo, three years older than her, fondle each other. Thus the novel is about making choices in life and not about framing judgments on the outcome of such choices.

After the huge success of *Journey to Ithaca* in the Western countries, Desai again felt the need to talk about Indian women, their psyche, their problems and attitude. Her next novel *Fasting, Feasting* deals with Indian women but in a different context. Her more mature approach is exhibited throughout the novel; be it story, technique or the psychological probing into the characters. Variety speaks in this phase as this novel again gives a good taste to her Indian readers.

Fasting, Feasting (1999) takes up a stock theme of post-colonial fiction : The encounter with the West. The book is in two parts. The first deals with the travails of Uma, a daughter with neither looks nor intellectual brilliance, who is treated as a domestic drudge by her parents, satirically presented as a single entity, 'Mama Papa'. She has to leave school to look after her baby brother Arun. The second part deals with Arun, who comes to study in America. Desai convincingly presents the Indian obsession with a son, but other details about life in India are all wrong : To mention just one instance, no explanation is given for Uma's father (a lawyer) not taking legal action against his bigamous son-in-law. The depiction of the discrimination against daughters loses much of its force because the parents are shown as absolute monsters.

Uma is a plain, simple, uneducated, spinster daughter from a close-unit orthodox Indian family. She is trapped at home, smothered by the overbearing parents and their traditions. The traditions 'Mama Papa' of Uma tried to bring up their daughers as just to get them married at the right age and their son for a career. Uma has to stay away from the school after the birth of her brother. 'We are not sending you back to school Uma. You are staying at home to help with Arun.'[20] Uma, as a student, has been producing depressing results at school so "you will be happier at home. You won't need to do any lessons. You are a big girl now. We are trying to arrange a marriage for you ... till then you can help me look after Arun. And learn to run the house."[21] Her mother has sigh of relief at the withdrawl of Uma from school because now the boy could be left to the care of his elder sister for bridge parties, "you know we can't leave the boy to the servant. He needs proper attention."[22] Mother was sharply vigilant on the performance of Uma or ayah when they bathed and dressed the boy.

Here, Anita Desai never bothered to give the parents a name. They are mentioned as parents by the authoress and addressed as 'Mama Papa' by Uma. The reason may be that they represent all the mothers-fathers of the typical middle-class Indian society. Uma's parents never think of giving her a career. Her depressing performance at school should have been no hindrance for attaining her some vocational qualification. Instead of sending her to dance, painting, tailoring classes she is kept back at home just to do the job of an attendant. Lot many restrictions are put on Uma. When Ramu, her cousin takes her to dinner, they received the typical reaction of an orthodox Indian family.

Papa comes thundering towards them with a face as black as the night and Mama's face glints like a knife in the dark, growing narrower, fiercer as it comes closer. 'Quiet you hurry! not another word from you, you idiot child! you, you disgrace to the family — nothing but disgrace, ever.'[23]

The less valued child, Uma proves to be as unlucky in the matters of wedding. The first proposal could not be materialized because the match liked the younger sister, Aruna. The second match was son of a wealthy cloth merchant of the city and so, eagerly responded by Mama Papa in an advertisement in the Sunday Newspaper. This family had recently begun to prosper and was building a new house. A negotiated sum was offered as dowry and the engagement ceremony was arranged simultaneously. But later on, the 'Son had decided to go to Roorkie for higher education and felt he should not be hampered by an early marriage at this stage and asked for the engagement to be indefinitely postponed.'[24] They had spent the dowry on the house hence it could not be returned. Uma's family now stands cheated by the Goel family. 'Everyone knows that they have played that trick before: Uma's ears were filled to saturation with mama's laments. Aruna's 'yelps of laughter' made fun of Uma. Nobody ever noticed that Uma's face was losing its childish openness of expression and taking on a look of continual care. The family stopped caring for this defeated girl. 'She missed his (Arun's) teasing, and she missed Aruna's sympathy and solidarity too.

Mama tried hard to 'dispose off' Uma and her photograph was sent to everyone who advertised in the matrimonial columns. Uma was never consulted regarding all this. A marriage was fixed without even arranging a meeting with the man. The ceremony was performed in a state of 'unenthusiasm'. The man seemed to be as old as 'Uma's own father. Mother-in-law informed Uma that Harish had gone to Meerut, who had never bothered to tell Uma and had left before the marriage was consummated. For several weeks Uma kept waiting and in these weeks, 'She learnt how to cut vegetables in pieces exactly the same size, how to grind spices into a wet paste and how to differentiate one dal from another. All speech directed at her was in the form of instruction, there was no other'. We see the plight of this innocent girl in the Indian context. She is in a trap - situation and is not capable or was not made capable of pulling herself out of it. It is direct attack by the authoress on the institution of arranged marriage. This is a story of the most middle class girls.

Uma's husband does not turn up and somehow the marriage is cancelled, annulled and Uma is never considered being told of the legal proceedings involved. Rather, Uma is never quiet certain if she has ever actually married. Having cost her parents two dowries, without a marriage to show in return. Uma is considered to be ill-fated by all without any fault of her own and no more attempts are made to find out a match for her. By all this Uma grows depressed and never could attord to arrest herself in the family. Another reason for Uma's depression is that the younger sister, Aruna is married off and started a 'fantastic' life in Bombay and won laurels of praise from parents and in-laws. Her family was scared of her. Her success in marriage had made her dominate everybody including her husband:

> The only thing that made them tolerate her behaviour was the avoidance that she directed it not only towards them but even at her husband Arvind .... Aruna had a vision of a perfect world.[25]

Aruna's assertiveness highlights Uma's depressed nature. Uma could never be like Aruna and felt disturbed to notice the discontent between her sister's eyebrow. Uma is reduced to the status of a maid servant in the family. Parents actually never cared for her and never wanted to spend on the treatment of Uma's eyes. No need, no need. Why waste money on a trip to Bombay? Our optician is good enough: Uma is not allowed to make any phone call because it:

> "Costs money! costs money! never earned anything in her life, made me spend and spend, on her dowry and her wedding. Oh, yes, spend till I am ruined, till I am a pauper ....."[26]

> Uma is kept confined to the house sans friends, enjoyment or entertainment. This is evident from the reactions of the parents to Mrs. O'Henry's invitation for Uma to a coffee party. Father never liked Uma and turned away his head as if it was of no use talking to someone as naïve and as backward as his old daughter. Father's retirement is to be spent finding ways to keep Uma occupied — She has to write a letter to Arun, to drive off urchins from ripe Mulberries, see that the cook had brought the green mangoes for pickle and all necessary spices, Papa's woolens must be spread out in the sun and sprinkled with dry neem leaves. Uma has no idea of escape from this trap-situation. When Uma tries to show a passive resistance her mother pretends to be sick just to hinder the way for Uma's job. But Uma is now ready to assert herself at least by ringing Dr. Dutt up, "Dr. Dutt Mama is not ill. She's not!" Dr. Dutt Mama is not ill. She's not!" Uma is taking up cudgels to release herself from a thankless occupation

at home. The readers would certainly appreciate this passive resistance while comparing Uma to the recources taken by Maya, Monish or Sarah.

There is another pathetic story of Anamika that runs parellel to it. Although the episode is just an appendage to the main story but it leaves an indelible mark on the psyche of the reader, especially women readers. Anamika was 'simply lovely as a flower is lovely, soft, petal skinned, bumble bee-eyed, pink lipped, always on the verge of bubbling dove like laughter, loving smiles ... whereever she was, there was peace, contentment, well being.'[27]

Daughter of a lawyer with thriving practice, Anamika won a scholarship to Oxford, to Oxford where only the most favoured sons could ever hope to go. She could not be sent abroad just because, she was of an age to marry. The letter of acceptance from Oxford was locked in a steel cupboard taken out to be shown around with pride.

Anamika's marriage to a man, so much older than herself, with higher degree, suffering from Oedipal complex, marred her life. The man married her because it was a custom and it will raise his status among other men in society. Joint family system becomes a curse for Anamika. She had been beaten regularly by her mother-in-law while her husband stood by and approved — or at least did not object. Anamika spent her entire time in the kitchen, cooking for everyone and she ate the remains in the pots before scouring them.

The story is a direct attack on the joint family system in Indian society, cruelty of the in-laws, apathy of the parents towards a married daughter. "How can she be happy if she is sent home? What will people say? What will they think? (p. 71) Anamika's own parents would not protect her and no one of the relatives even wanted to see Anamika.

Anamika died under mysterious circumstances. It was a death by fire. Nobody was sure whether it was a murder or suicide. She was tortured for twenty-five years in the name of marriage. Marriage is seen as the only course for women. The novel throws light on the misery that can follow a marriage too hastily arranged and the lot of women in a typical joint family where the new bride is a prisoner and a slave to the mother-in-law. Anamika has a miscarriage after being beaten and is treated like 'damaged goods' to be sent back to her family. The novel also throws light on many ugly practices in Indian society with regard to oppression of women.

Thus feasting by Aruna never gives a good taste and fasting by Uma cannot give her satisfaction. Another character Melony, daughter of an American family suffers from psychosis. She eats too much and vomits. She is carried to psychotic centre and then cured over there. Finally, at deeper level *Fasting, Feasting* believes in the diction of *Bhagwat Gita* as the theme is no pleasure from pleasure and no pain from pain. In it essence of equality and harmony and cheerfulness is everywhere to be found.

Then Desai has shifted to foreign land as the background of her latest novel *The Zigzag Way*. Desai again centres her attention on a male character Eric whose psyche is displayed. Unlike *Fasting, Feasting* where major characters were women like Uma, Aruna, Anamika or Melony; this novel presents Em, the girlfriend of Eric as a support to run the narrative. It reminds of Desai's another novel *In Custody* where Deven's psyche is probed and his wife Sarla merely stands as a minor character. After describing the locale of Mirpore in *In Custody* Desai narrates Mexico, its culture, vision, practices in detail in her latest novel *The Zigzag Way*. Desai continues the thematic experimentation with foreign characters in this novel too with the subject matter of foreign and their displacement.

In her long, distinguished career as a fiction writer, Anita Desai has focused her vision on questions of culture and identity. *The Zigzag Way* (2004), a magical novel of elegiac beauty, presents Mexico and in this Mexican landscape 'a young American stumbles upon an unlikely path to self-discovery.'[28]

Eric, a New England born student in history at Harvard, is a newly minted historian just out of graduate school, unsure of his past choices and future options. With no clear direction, he follows his lover, Em, when she travels to the Yucatan for her scientific research. But, unfortunately once she sets of with her colleagues to conduct fixed operations, Eric ends up alone and overwhelmed in this foreign place. Then he pursues his own private quest, tracing his family's history to a Mexican ghost town, where, a hundred years earlier, young Cornish Miners toiled to the death. With vivid sympathy, Desai conjures the struggles of Eric's grandparents and their community.

Now, in place of the Cornish workers, the native Huichol Indians suffer the cruelty of the mines. When he inquires into their lives, Eric provokes the ire of their self-appointed saviour, Dona Vera. She is known as the Queen of the Sierra. She is an eccentric, powerful European woman and has become a champion of indeginous culture but whose own past is mysterious. She is the widow of a mining baron, who has dedicated her fortune to preserving the Huichol culture. But her formidable presence belies a dubious past. The zigzag paths of these characters converge on the Day of the Dead, bringing together past and present in a moment of powerful epiphany.

Eric was disenchanted with his graduate studies and thesis dissertation at Harvard. He, then, decides to give it all a rest for a while and accompany his girl friend, Em, on her field studies to Mexico. He has just informed his family in Maine that he would shortly be visiting Mexico. His father informs him that many years ago Eric's father was born there, then he was taken to England as an infant and brought up there. Mexico remains just a fairy tale to Eric's father.

The seemingly casual piece of information soon becomes the focal point of the novel. On a casual rest stop in central Mexico, Eric takes a lecture about Huichol Indians and their belief in the powers of the 'peyote cactus' given by a lady with a 'Teutonic name', Dona Vera. While her lecture was in Spanish, a language foreign to Eric, she tosses around a few names that stir memories in him. He remembers his grandfather in far-away England mentioning these same names many years ago — "Words like Sierra Madre Oriental, Sierra de los Catorce, Real del Monte, La Purisima, La Asuncion, Los Lorenzos, La Luz Valenciana" ... and he heard them before, each had an image, a memory linked to it that he struggled to resurrect. It was as if they were the words of a song he used to know, or had sung.

The stories of Eric, his grandparents and Dona Vera are interwoven into a short contemplative narrative. Eric is a passive narrator clambering his way through the beautiful but beguiling scenery, which is described in florid, dense prose.

As Eric further moves on with his explorations in Mexico, he comes to find out more about the legend of Dona Vera and her escape to Mexico from Nazi Austria with a foreigner. Eric also learns details about his own past — his grandmother, Betty Jennings and grandfather, David Rowse, who travelled all the way from Cornwall, England, down to mines in Mexico after hard times in England had closed their own mines down. The miners set up their communities in the mining towns in central Mexico only to have it all abruptly disbanded at the outbreak of the Mexican revolution.

As the novel progresses, Desai neatly ties the loose ends of many stories and the reader is held fascinated by the mystery not only behind ancient family histories but just as much by the lure of Mexico painted incredibly beautifully by Desai.

Perhaps the most intriguing aspect of *The Zigzag Way* is the history of the Cornish people in Mexico — a pattern of migration enchanting not just for its simple occurrence and the economic forces that made it happen, but also for its similarities with more recent ones. The close-knit Cornish community in Mexico reads similar to many immigrant communities across the world. Betty writes in a letter back to Europe; 'Did you ever think that here on a mountain in Mexico, we would be celebrating the Durk of Comwall's birhday?'

It is a very slim novel of 176 pages. But somewhere it feels too rushed, and the complete recounting of Eric's past leaves Desai breathless in a few places. The novel's title comes from the zigzag way miners take on their way up out of mine shafts to prevent exhaustion. At one point Eric wonders of his own path across. Mexico follows a similar zigzag pattern illuminating traces of information on a journey back and forth across time and place. Learning that porters carried heavy bags up thousands of stairs in a zigzag direction to take advantage of air currents that helped them breathe; Eric ruminates on his own zigzag journey, his effort to enter the past. The book's magical, haunting final section follows. Eric on the '*Day of the Dead*' as he seeks Betty's grave and encounters both past and present.

Desai here paints a subtle, miniaturist history of twentieth century Mexico, seen from unexpected perspectives, that evokes the exploitation of the Mexican Indians. With vivid sympathy and brilliantly telling detail, Desai conjures up Eric's grandmother, and her poignant story, that of a young Cornish girl whose grave is in a cemetery on a Mexican hillside.

Desai shows that Eric has just completed his dissertation on immigration patterns in the early twentieth century Boston. Eric stays back to discover his ancestry by visiting the town where his grandparents lived. He comes to know of his past family specially of his grandmother Betty Jennings who died while giving birth to his father. Though the novel is presented through the eyes of Eric, Desai has also concentrated upon sketching the life story and character of Betty Jennings. Descriptions about her past and her youth add momentum to the novel. The novelist records the saga of Betty's adjustment to her new life in a strange land. Betty evolves from innocence, wonder, discovery and eventually a life of sorrow. However, Desai has not elaborated upon the story of Betty for the novel is more about the protagonist Eric and his adventures in Mexico. This is the first novel where the locale is not India but a foreign land Mexico which for long had fascinated the novelist and she wished to write about it. Desai invokes her renowned lush and occasionally dense prose to portray Eric's sensory stimulations. She obviously speaks with intimate knowledge of the land, and this combined with the wealth of historical detail, prompt several critics to sing her praises. More importantly, as *The New York Times* notes *The Zigzag Way* is 'not just a condensed' course in 20th century Mexican history but a meditation on the futility of our efforts to outrun the past : In other words, Desai does her job. Eric is a bit too passive as a narrator, and this slim novel does skip character development, but whatever difference is here is really very good.

Taking into consideration the novels of Desai it may well be concluded that her canvas is wide. She mainly deals with female psyche but her probing into the male consciousness also cannot be overlooked. The message in her writings is clear that women can extricate themselves out of the trauma of mental psychosis by realizing that they have the power of sustaining others. This realization gives them a lot of inner strength. At the same time she has successfully experimented with different fictional modes of subversion of male power. Recent novels depict the male consciousness and through them a healthy synthesis of the social and personal is achieved. Like many coloured glass, Desai's fiction reflects the various lights and shades of experience. The movement from the early (dealing with feminine sensibility) to the recent phase (giving a tinge of variety) marks increasingly self-assurance and mastery both in vision and technique. The human (both female and male) condition is accepted as something natural, without any trial or bitterness or resentment. These three novels of this decade *Journey to Ithaca*, *Fasting, Feasting* and *The Zigzag Way* are more than mere mediocre variation on the theme of cultural encounters; it has deeper overtones and a fascinating rhythm with different themes. This shift sanctions universality and human significance to her art. As Andrew Robson has rightly presented a complete picture:

> "Alienation, after *In Custody* and *Baumgartner's Bombay* gains a new artistic dimension. It grows into an estrangement of the adolescent in the rapidly changing spatio-temporal psychic continuum. The obsessions and fantasies of childhood no longer haunt the protagonists. They come as a fleeting impression of the past but not as a torturing obsession as in *Cry, the Peacock*. The sequestered world of the earlier novels now gives way to the socio-psychic entrapment of the self. The poetic outpourings of the long self are now replaced by a penetrating observation of the milieu."[29]

Thus Anita Desai, in her latest work, leads up always from extreme domesticity to a new realm and horizon where socio-spiritual awareness results in lasting ecstasy.

References

1. http://web.mit.edu/newsoffice/1993/novelist/0929.html.
2. *The Guardian*, Sept. 03, 04, London (Edinburgh book festival).
3. *Ibid.*
4. Tripathi, J.P., *The Mind and Art of 'Anita Desai'*, Bareilly: Prakash Book Depot, 1987, p. 60.
5. Desai, Anita, *Journey to Ithaca*, London: Vintage, 1998, pp. 47-48.
6. *Ibid.*, p. 57.
7. *Ibid.*, p. 77.
8. *Ibid.*, p. 80.
9. *Ibid.*, p. 81.
10. *Ibid.*, pp. 106-07.
11. *Ibid.*, p. 108.
12. *Ibid.*, p. 108
13. *Ibid.*, p. 92.
14. *Ibid.*, p. 143.
15. Budholia, O.P., *Anita Desai: Vision and Technique in Her Novels*, p. 187.
16. Desai, Anita, *Journey to Ithaca*, p. 143.
17. *Ibid.*, p. 156.
18. *Ibid.*, p. 305.
19. Budholia, O.P., *Anita Desai: Vision and Technique in Her Novels*, p. 187.
20. Desai, Anita, *Fasting, Feasting*, London: Chatto and Windus, 1989, p. 18.
21. *Ibid.*, p. 22.
22. *Ibid.*, p. 30.
23. Desai, *Fasting, Feasting*, pp. 52, 53.
24. *Ibid.*, p. 82.
25. *Ibid.*, p. 109.
26. *Ibid.*, p. 146
27. *Ibid.*, p. 67.
28. Desai, Anita, *The Zigzag Way*, Houghton Mifflin Books, 2004.
29. Robson, Andrew, 'Failed Householders : Renouncement and Distributive Strategies', *The Atlantic Literary Review*, Vol. 2, No. 1, New Delhi: Atlantic Publishers and Distributors (P) Ltd., Jan-March, 2001, p. 68.

Short Stories of Desai

7

Indian short story also known as short fiction or a by-product of Indian English fiction, began its history towards the close of the nineteenth century with the publication of Kamla Satthianandan's *Stories from Indian Christian Life* in 1898. Writers like R.N. Tagore, Mulk Raj Anand, R.K. Narayan, Raja Rao and Manjeri S. Isvaran supplemented the cause. One of the best stories ever written by Anand is 'The Lost Child' in *The Barbers' Trade Union. In Between Tears and Laughter* (1973) Anand's another collection, consisting of seventeen pieces, gives way to understanding and compassion. R.K. Narayan occupies a prominent place among those writers of short stories who prefer the lighter vein in presentation. Raja Rao writes mostly on social and political scenes around him with natural ease and philosophical speculation. With ten volumes of short stores, Manjeri S. Isvaran occupies a conspicuous place among the pioneers of short story writers. He manages to write skillfully, from different angles, on a wide variety of subjects.

After Independence Khushwant Singh made his debut as a short story writer. His stories are sweet, sow and peppery, but they are always pleasing. Ruth Prawar Jhabvala has published four volumes of short stories. Of all her short stories 'How I Became a Holy Mother' is perhaps the best. K.A. Abbas has also created a place for himself as a short story writer. His two volumes deal mainly with the problems people had to face in the wake of partition.

Though Anita Desai has not written much in this genre in comparison with her fiction; but in her first collection one can easily see the play of a delicate sensibility.

Anita Desai's first collection of short stories *Games at Twilight* was published in 1978. She has shown her craftsmanship even in the shorter fiction like short story. Her short stories which are witty, evocative, tender and perceptive reveal her skill and dexterity in handling this genre. She uses sincerely all her creative techniques and talents in her short stories too. The reason is clear as she works with the same material as in the novels but on a small scale. In her short stories she has taken up themes like the tension between convention and exploration, family solidarity and individualism, social requirements and the impersonal factors like death and art. In these stories, one finds the colours, smells and sounds of India. Her delicate strength of observation, her unique style of telling a tale emphatically, quietly precise characterization and gentle irony with a tinge of humour add a new dimension to her art of writing short stories. She has also dealt with the temperamental differences between husband and wife, pragmatic relationships, psychological complexes, and poor social conditions. Speaking of her novels, Anita Desai once observed:

> "My novels are no reflection on Indian society, politics or character. They are part of my private effort to seize upon the raw-material of life, and do mould it and impose on it a design...."[1]

Though Desai finds the short story form 'much less satisfying' than the novel, she began to write short stories as early as her college days. And the interest in psychological study of characters which distinguishes her novels, also characterizes her short stories, though they do not offer scope for full-length psychographs as the novels do. Her novels and short stories are also interrelated through the presence of similar ideas or scenes in both of them. For example, the scene of very tender and intense, almost divine love between an extremely beautiful tubercular, 'borkha' clad, Muslim woman and a very old man that Suno, the protagonist in the story *Studies in the Park* (pp. 30-31) sees, also occurs in the novel *Where Shall We Go This Summer?*' is seen by its heroine, Sita, who is similarly in dire need of such love.

Her short stories were published in such magazines as *Quest*, *Harper's Bazaar*, *Thought*, and *Fesmina*.

"All the characteristics of symbolic style musicality, pictorialness and synaesthetic experience are found in her short stories."[2] She has published a collection of short stories in 1978; entitled *Games at Twilight*. By this time her novels like *Cry, the Peacock*, *Voices in the City*, *Bye-Bye Blackbird* were published and she got fame as a novelist. Even then she gave proper attention towards the creation of short stories. The title story *Games at Twilight* is an indepth study of psychology of children at play. When the children decide to play, 'hide-n-seek', Ravi, in an attempt to come victorious in the game hides in a dark lumber room for hours together suppressing his fear. As he anticipates his victory over others, his fear dissipates. When he comes out to declare himself victorious, nobody recognises his victory as the children have left the old game and now playing a new game 'funeral game'. In this story Desai has successfully developed and depicted the struggle between Ravi's 'self-assertion and desire for recognition'. Desai chooses the subjective mode and adopts the strategy of sustained use of imagery.

In the story, *Studies in the Park*, we find a kind of withdrawal, withdrawal from material pursuits, from participation in the rat race, Suno, in a bid to get first in his examination, finds a suitable place in a park and sticks to his books. But books are 'like parasites and like parasites they suck him dry'. Under the overwhelming pressure of study, he gradually loses his ability to function suitably, both physically and psychologically. All other famous stories like 'Private Tution by Mr. Bose', 'Surface Textures', 'Sale', 'A Devoted Son' and 'Pigeons at Daybreak' depict beautifully and faithfully the life of Indian middle class families. 'Private Tution by Mr. Bose' portrays in a humourous vein, the domestic life of a middle-class Indian, Mr. Bose, who earns his living by giving private tuition. It depicts the love and consideration of Mr. and Mrs. Bose for each other. At the same time it also presents a scene of domestic anarchy once created by Mrs. Bose's jealousy. But, it is soon relaced by a scene of domestic happiness. The reconciliation is brought about by Mrs. Bose's frying hot purees for Mr. Bose and coaxing him to eat more, one more as though the extra puree were a peace-offering following her rebellion of half-an-hour ago. In 'Studies in the Park' the attitude of the protagonist's father to the education of his son is that of a typical middle class Indian who educates his son with a view to enable him to get a good job. In *Surface Textures*, the protagonist's wife reveals a typical Indian wife's characteristic. Her use of kumkum that daily 'cuts' a gash of red colour is also something uniquely Indian. In *Sale* we find poor artist's wife kneading dough in a brass bowl, with her head bowed and her long hair brooding down to her shoulders, and her child sitting beside her playing with a spoon, is a slice of middle class life in India. *A Devoted Son* presents Rakesh, who after getting success in the examination, touches his father's feet according to Indian customs, *Pigeons at Daybreak* depicts the devotion of a true Indian wife to her valetudinarian husband.

In the story *Studies in the Park*, we find withdrawal from material pursuits. Suno sticks to his books in order to come first in the exams and finds a suitable place in the park and studies there. But books are like parasites and like parasites they suck him dry. He gradually loses his ability to function suitably, both physically and psychologically. Then at one point Suno sees a young beautiful woman on a bench in the park, her head lying on the lap of a man, who is caressing her face.

In the story *The Accompanist*, Desai delineates the emotional state of a Tanpura player. The company of Ustad Rahim Khan makes a street urchin an accompanist. The alchemic touch of the master turned the crude and base boy into a noble and gentle accompanist.

Desai's second volume of short stories *Diamond Dust* (2000) is not as successful as her fist collection, *Games at Twilight and Other Stories* (1978). The earlier stories were set entirely in India, but three of the nine stories here are about life in the USA, while one is set in Mexico. The first story *Royalty* deals with Raja, Sarla and Ravi. Story starts with Sarla's declaration that Raja has come. He is in the south. He wants to visit us next week (2). Very beautifully Desai portrays the reaction of Ravi:

> "A great shiver ran through the house like a wind blowing that was not a wind so much as a stream of shining light, shimmering and undulating through the still, shadowy house, a radiant serpent, not without menace, some threat of danger. Whether it liked it or not, the house became the one chosen by Raja for a visitation, a house in waiting."[3]

Then finally Raja comes. Sarla suggests that he accompany them to the mountains, but refuses as he had come to Delhi, all the way to Delhi in the heat of June, to see them, to relive the remembered joys of their beautiful home. And he feels that there is so much for him to see, to do, to catch upon. Raja had been Ravi and Sarla's friend at Oxford, thirty years back. At his arrival Ravi and Sarla have to cancel their summer programmes of going to the hills and prepare for Raja's visit. Sarla's excitement reveals a strange attachment she had for Raja and a 'Shiver runs through the house'. He arrives and Sarla's sister Maya comes visiting. Both vie for Raja's attention and try to outdo the other. The rivalry between the two is evident. Raja stays with Sarla and Ravi but is enamoured of Maya and flatters her. He also asks them to arrange a dinner for his old friends and calls Ila Dutta Ray, who 'sang like a nightingale' (14) and Sarla forgets to invite her sister Maya. Maya retaliates by throwing a big party and not calling her sister. Sarla, requests Raja to accompany them to the hills to Winhaven but he keeps postponing it and ultimately announces that he is going to Kashmir with the Dutta Ray. Raja, as per his name, is the royal one — all the other characters run to do his bidding. The women are jealous of each other. Food is an important factor in 'Royalty'.

Raja enjoys Sarla's impatience. He says:

> "But darling Sarla," Raja beamed at her, showing both the pleasure he took in her suggestion and his determination not to be swept away by it. "Maya tells me there is to be a lecture at India International Centre next week on the Himalayas as an inspiration for Indian poets through the centuries. I would hate to

> miss it. It's to be given by Professor Dandavate, that old box-d you remember his?" (20)

The second story *Winterscape* also abounds in food imagery. *Winterscape* is a touching story about the deep love between two sisters, offering a strong, contrast to the antagonism between the sisters in 'Royalty'. Rakesh and Beth based in the States are expecting their first child. Rakesh's mothers — Ma and Masi as he calls them, come to assist in the delivery. Rakesh recounts to his wife Beth how the two women had nurtured him and, how he had always called his mother Masi and his aunt Ma — both the women had devoted their life to him. Asha and Anu were very close as sisters even when they were young. Asha, the first born was brought up as an ornament. Desai narrates:

> "There were three years between them and those seemed to have made all the difference. Asha was the first child in the family. So delighted was her father that it never crossed his mind she should have been a son. He tossed her up and caught her in his arms and put his face into her neck to make growling sounds that sent her into squeals of laughter. That she was fair skinned, plump and had curly hair and bright black eyes all pleased him." (27)

Asha's husband goes out to shoot partridges for the festive dinner, meets with an accident and dies. Asha is inconsolable and Anu decides to leave her son with her. Rakesh ultimately is brought up by Asha, his aunt whom he recognises as Ma. Anu comes to visit occasionally and becomes Masi. Anu loses her husband, shifts to Asha's house where they both shower their love on Rakesh. Both Rakesh's wife and his mother-in-law Doris cannot accept the idea of a mother giving up her child to her sister. Beth declares she can never do it.

Diamond Dust, a Tragedy is the story of Mr. Das' fatal love for his dog Diamond. Diamond troubles the family members, the neighbours, the school children and everyone who comes in the street. Mr. Das is unperturbed, even though his friends mock at him for Diamond. Diamond develops the habit of disappearing in the mating season. Twice, Mr. Das manages to bring him back. He goes sad, forlom and frantic when Diamond disappears. Ultimately, chasing and jumping onto the dog catchers van that was carrying street dogs and his beloved Diamond, Mr. Das falls off and hits his head on the road and dies. Desai narrates:

> "Diamond, who had been badly bitten and probably thrashed or stoned in the course of his latest affair, seemed to have quietened down a bit; at least there was a fairly long spell of obedience lethargy, comparative meekness. Mr. Das felt somewhat concerned about his health, but seeing him slip vitamin pills down the dog's throat, Mrs. Das grimaced, now what? He is too quiet for you? You need to give him strength to go back to his badmashi?" (61-62)

Next story 'Underground' is an intensively emotional love story between a husband and wife — Bod Mc Taggart and Helen. Bob, an engineer had done lots of traveling and a scene from one of his trips was deeply embedded in his heart. He had seen a close family scene — the mother nursing a babe at her breast, the father clapping and the daughter dancing. He feels that this is how he'd love to love his life. So, when Helen falls ill with a strange disease, he seeks out a faraway seaside spot and makes it into a hotel. Now he would always be with her, not traveling out on official tours. Helen is looked after by her husband; she deteriorates and finally dies. The couple's evening hours passed sitting out on the verandah, throwing out scraps for the badgers to come out and eat. Desai further narrates:

> "Bob and Helen were not deceived; they knew they were being watched as keenly as they themselves watched, and sometimes one of them gave a shiver at the closeness of these dark, furtive creatures, the close sharing of the silent evening with the badgers." (77-78)

The next story 'The Man Who Saw Himself Drown' is a story of a businessman on tour, who finds his look-alike drowned and dead. He hides and pretends to be dead and tries to escape from his own life. But this plan does not help him. The story is philosophical in theme, exploring the illusive nature of man's quest for freedom. When freedom is achieved, man realises that he feels disillusioned. The story is deeply symbolic. The man realises that by dying his double had not gifted him life instead 'by arriving at death, life had been closed to me'. His feelings are so very natural:

> "When his business associate telephoned to invite him out to dinner, he made an excuse, he was very tired, he wanted to go to bed early in order to be rested and ready for the meeting tomorrow. Actually, he could not stand the thought of spending the evening in the company of the man who had been annoying him and irritating him all day. Although it might have helped to discuss their business privately over a meal before going to the meeting tomorrow, he could summon no interest in it at all it seemed, no more important to him than anything he had been doing for the last twenty-five years. He would go through the motions tomorrow but he could not pretend that he thought it important enough for him to give up an evening like this. He sipped his beer, ate the sandwiches and potato chips they had brought him. When he decided not to go out to dinner, and contentedly watched the lights bob and sway in the pool of darkness below the veranda. What he found he could not do was go to bed and fall asleep early, after an evening so relaxing and calm. He was not sleepy at all, in spite of the long, frustrating day at work. He was, instead, totally relaxed but wide awake. So he decided to go for a stroll, although the evening was warm and humid, telling himself a little fresh air would help to make him sleepy. Besides, he might as well take a look at some other part of the city before returning home tomorrow night." (84-85)

Then the person escapes from the hotel without paying off the bill as in that case the hotel person would have informed others about him. He was feeling delighted to end the dull, wretched, routine ridden, unfulfilling life lead by him and to begin on another life filled with all those things that are derived by heart. But at the sametime there were so many questions, no answers, doubts and no certainties. He also wanted to know what would happen after his 'death'. He wished to go to attend his funeral but at the thought of the presence of his family and their grief, he abandoned the idea. Desai narrates his dilemma beautifully:

> "I did not trust myself to have the nerves or the self-control required for such a bizarre experience, and so I stayed away, but all the time in a kind of anguish that made me clench and unclench my fists and often wipe the tears that streamed down my face. I could not even tell the exact cause of my anguish was it for myself, the old self that had died, or was it for those I had been parted from and could not go to comfort." (93)

He visited his place and found that his family had left the native place and his father-in-law had taken them before his eyes. He could do nothing. The car passed by him. He crouched in the hedge, and none of those seated in the vehicle turned their heads to glance at him. He says, "And when I saw that, when I saw that they had a future, one that they looked forward to, or at least moved towards with resolution. I admit that also felt, mixed with the bitterness of disappointment, a certain relief. It was as though I had at last shed them. My wife, my children, my house, they were all gone from me, and curiously. I did not feel bereft so much as lightened of my load." (96)

After a long time of sitting in a state of sorrow and exhaustion he left his house and he went by small back streets, normally used by servants and peddles, came to the river that ran around the outskirts of the city. Then he walked down and across the sand and came to the water. Now he was free. But he was unable to enjoy his freedom, freedom from family, from job, from friends, colleagues and even freedom from his own self, own identity. Desai delves deeper into his self and narrates:

> "But that self, my other self, the self that had had a job and a wife and children and a home, that self was already gone. I wondered what it meant, that death of my mysterious double. It seemed to me that I had died with it, I was so convinced of this that I was not able to resume my life. But was that the only possible

> interpretation? Once again I felt my mind splinter into fragments that whirled wildly in some great vacuum, and one fragment that I seized upon as another possibility was this, could that death have meant that my double had died on my behalf, that his life was finished, freeing me, my new self, my second self, to go on with another life, a new life?" (98)

Then he was filled with such despair that he came out his knees in the mud and he was found dead by the child next morning.

Next story 'The Artists' Life' is about the unartistic life of an art teacher Polly, a young school girl was enamoured by Miss Abigail, an art teacher at a camp who asked her in her whispering bubbly disquieting voice to paint the dreams. Infatuated Polly imitates Miss Abigail and turns to live like an artist sitting in the attic for hours and coming up with weird paintings. To her utter disillusionment and terror, she discovered that their dirty looking tenant, Miss Dodd, who wallowed in dirt, was an artist and taught art. Polly is brought back to the reality. Desai very realistically narrates the reaction of Polly at this:

> "Polly's mouth opened to form a protest. Her lips formed the letter 'O' or else 'No'. She wanted to protest, She was not sure against what, but against something that had been presented to her, interposed between her and what she wanted and believed in — something objectionable, inadmissible, an imperfection. How was she to protest, to deny? Her lips stretched to form the word 'How'? but then she broke down and what burst from her was a surprising, 'Oh, Ma-ma'. Her mother looked at her, questioningly. What was she protesting? Polly had no idea. All she knew was disillusion. It made her stretch out and grasp a sandwich, then bury her teeth into it, despairingly." (114)

'Five Hours to Shimla or Faisla' is an interesting account of a highway incident. 'A goatherds' stone strikes and breaks the glass of a truck. The truck driver parks his truck across the road and says he will not move unless compensation is given to him. The goatherd is not to be found. After holding up the traffic for hours, he moves the truck quickly when the police arrive. A family that is travelling is held up in irritation, and hunger. What is interesting is that out of nowhere vendors arrive with a variety of goods. Hunger and anger are fought with food and as always food provides solace.

The children set up a clamour and are rudely shut down by the mother on the threat of 'germs'. The mother herself is seen succumbing to tea, without worry of cholera or typhoid. The picture of another adult, the truck driver chewing sugarcane presents his attitude. It is shown clearly how he has treated the public, drawing a sadistic mean pleasure out of it, disturbing everyone and showing his disregard for all. Finally traffic moves and the story ends with, 'The police, looking baffled, swing around, flourishing their canes. 'Get on! Chalo!' they bellowed. 'Chalo, Chalo, get on, all of you' and they did'. (129)

'Tepozatlan Tomorrow' is a picture of a small town suffering the pangs of change. No place can escape change. There is the unavoidable mingling of families, cultures and commercialising of the area. Louis has been away for higher studies and comes back to his town to meet and be with his mother's sister Dona Celia who hates and resists change. There is a conflict between the modern trends and traditional forces. Louis is welcome back. Nadyn has not changed and is not likely to. Louis is filled with disgust and ultimately decides to go out and smoke. After a short visit to old friends, Louis decides that he does not fit any more and is ready to leave. Through his change in food taste Desai shows how our deepest concerns and instincts also change with a change in our living style and life's objectives.

'Roof Top Dwellers' deals with the modern women's desire for independence. Moyna comes from a small town and lives first in a hostel and then in a barsati with the Bhallas. She works for the literary magazine *Book*. She faces many problems of stay, food and water crisis, landlords problems, thrift, ill-health and job crisis, yet she is content to live alone and exults in her independence and self-sufficiency. Ultimately with her mother's letter of a marriage proposal and joy in her heart the story comes to an end.

Moyna makes friends with a cat giving it 'bread and fried eggs'. Nostalgia is expressed through food imagery. Moyna takes great pains to buy fish and milk for her cat Mao. She wants to keep Mao happy, her only close companion. This imagery again heightens the loneliness and hunger for closeness in today's modern materialistic life. When Moyna's mother comes to her, she is shocked to see Moyna starving and she could not stop her mother and 'she is shocked to see her mother shopping and cooking and storing food in a storm of energy and activity.' (202)

Her maternal instincts are afire, this is what one witnesses in the imaging here. Mrs. Bhalla sends pickles, etc., to Moyna. Moyna's mother is impressed by the kindness of Mrs. Bhalla. Moyna knows the truth of these antics but does not speak of the theft and other problems. She quietly accepts the spinach curry and lentils served by her mother and sits back quietly. Gustatory imagery here reflects love, nostalgia and hunger for companionship and communication. The story ends with the letter from Moyna's mother and the reaction of Moyna and Mao too. Desai writes:

> "It was when she was in such a state that a letter arrived from her mother. She opened it listlessly; knowing in advance what it would contain advice on how to run her household, how to cook a specially strengthening stew, an offer of monetary help, pleas to return home, her father's message that she should consider studying for a higher degree before embarking on a career and she glanced at it cursorily, her mother did not understand even now the attraction of living alone, in Delhi, and could think of it only as a poor substitute for living at home." (205)

But at the bottom of this letter, her mother had added, craftily:

> "Our neighbours have invited us to a welcome party next week; their son Arun is returning from the United

> States. He has taken a degree in Geology and is expected to find a suitable job in the field. I am sure he would be pleased to meet you again. If you are planning a visit soon, we shall ask him over for a meal. I know his family is very keen ... Mao gave a leap off the bed as Moyna fling herself backwards, at the same time throwing the letter into the air with a shout of laughter. She rolled her head about on the pillow, spluttering, 'Oh, Mama - re-a-ll-y, Mama!' Mao had not seen such behaviour in a long time." (206-207)

Thus we see old relationships stir up buried resentments, a beloved dog causes havoc, a businessman away from house sees his own death, and freedom springs in surprising ways. This is a 'brilliant collection of funny, sad, compassionate and charming stories'. She creates unforgettable moments in the stories both visual and emotional.

Desai uses Indian words in her stories to evoke local colour. She uses them more sparingly than any other contemporary write. Moreover, Desai neither uses Indian phrases nor literally translates Indian expressions into English. Her use of Indian words is restricted mostly to nouns — names of Indian dishes, dresses, musical instruments, games, and certain other things which cannot be expressed with precision by using their English equivalents. She relies more on the technique of paying attention to details to achieve realism and to create the necessary atmosphere in her stories. Her short stories reflect to her Indian sensibility in themes, characterization, settings and language. As the usual narrative mode is inadequate for her purpose, she chooses the subjective mode and adopts the strategy of sustained use of imagery. She feels that this mode gives her ample scope for introspection, analysis, reflection and reverie. Truly, *The Times* has commented upon Desai's short stories and labelled them as 'Exquisite' ... "These are stories whose beauty is in the detail, and their knowledge of the human psyche. They sparkle, not with the brash glitter of rhinestones, but with the intenser, more complex fire of real diamonds." (www goole.com)

References

1. Cowasjee and Kumar, *Modern Indian Short Stories*, Delhi: OUP, 1983, p. 101.
2. Indira, S. *Anita Desai as an Artist*, New Delhi: Creative Publications, p. 101.
3. Anita Desai, *Diamond Dust*, New Delhi: Vintage, 2000.

   (All the references are from this book only, the pg. nos. are given in brackets.)

Narrative Technique of Anita Desai

8

Anita Desai has emerged as a very serious, skilled and promising novelist in India today. Of all the contemporary Indian English novelist, Anita Desai is undisputably the most powerful novelist. She really deserves, compels and invites plenty of critical attention. She seriously sets herself to voice the mute miseries and helplessness of millions of men and women tormented by existentialist problems. An uncrowned queen by the inner-emotional world, she dexterously transcribes the subconscious, the phantasmagoria of her highly sensitive protagonists. Endowed with boundless imaginative resourcefulness and creative vitality she reveals amazing variety and profundity in her fictional world. She has given a new dimension to the Indian novel in English by turning from outer to inner reality. G. Rai, has called her, 'a writer with an original voice'. Desai is well known for her use of technique.

The word TECHNIQUE is derived from the Greek word. 'Technique, means an art'. The method adopted by a writer to present life in the process of living may be described as the narrative technique. Though the novel gets its main sustenance from the story it intends to tell, its success depends on how it is narrated. The quality of readability, the most important of all the desirable qualities of a novel, may be achieved when there is compatibility between the narration and the narrative technique. Wayne Booth said, 'Narration is an art not a science, but this does not mean that we are necessarily doomed to fail when we attempt to formulate principle about it. There are systematic elements in every art and criticism of fiction can never avoid the responsibility of trying to explain technical successes and failures, by reference to general principles.'[1]

Desai's experiments with non-traditional materials and technique give her a distinct position among the Indian English novelists. Her fondness for quotes from various writers serves a definite purpose. Desai's style or technique of delivering the thematic thrust is the vital agent. Language is the main element of her narrative style. Her use of language and dialogues is one of the features of her artistically conceived novels. She has tried to present her themes organically with appropriate adjustment and adaptations in spheres of style and point of view. Desai is no doubt a great artist with a remarkable and astounding technical efficacy. Her techniques enrich the novel by lifting it above the mere narration of a story or depiction of a character and provides it the very life, blood and the soul. Technique is a matter of predominant concern for Anita Desai. She expresses her views on the skill of writing that:

> "Writing has become such a deeply ingrained habit. For her it is like chain smoking. She admits that she chain-smokes with words, with books."

Form and Structure, in the novels of Anita Desai 'take the shape of an exquisitely designed tapestry'.[2] The novels of Desai reveal her unique world view, but at the same time confirm to the existing tendencies in modern fiction. Her novels are technical innovations which 'combine features of both novel and lyrical poetry' and shift the reader's attention from men and events to a formal design. She herself prefers the word pattern to plot, she says:

> "I prefer the word 'pattern' to 'plot' as it sounds — more natural and even better, if I dare use it, is Hopkins, word 'inscape' while 'plot' sounds arbitrary heavy handed and artificial, all that I wish to avoid."[3]

Anita Desai has adopted a controlled method of stream of consciousness, 'Internal narration', a point of view within a character's consciousness, manifesting his or her feelings about and evaluations of the events and characters of the story. It is used extensively in *Cry, the Peacock* and to a limited extent in *Voices in the City*. Major part of these writings include 'free-indirect-discourse' an internal perspective, in which the subjective feelings of protagonists are transformed into third person narration and are interwoven with, and framed by the author's account of the character's inner state. For her writing is not an act of deliberation, reason and choice. Infact it is a matter of instinct, silence and waiting.

Desai uses the language of the interior to delineate the inner tensions and crisis in the lives of her characters. That's why her novels are called forte of poetic sensibility. Desai's exploration of sensibility and distinctive technique made her novels celebrities. Anita Desai uses the technique of contrast between various settings, situations, characters and even between different stages of the same characters. Her achievement consists in beautifully recording the emotional turbulence and chaos of her oppressed protagonists with a remarkable fidelity and seriousness. Her fiction is not at all transparent and predictable, unlike the fiction of R.K. Narayan and Kamala Markandaya. Nor does she use the traditional plot structure with linear movement in terms of exposition, conflict and resolution. She does not philosophize or indulge in self-conscious story telling in the manner of Raja Rao or Salman Rushdie. She often uses simple plot elements to propel plot development and depends on what may be called deconstructive devices for creations of meaning and atmosphere in her novels. She uses quotes from other writers and juxtaposes contradictory experiences for the reader by using techniques such as value reversal and surrealistic effects. Within the existential framework, she creates people with dreams and wills who in turn create the story, action and drama of the novels. Her characters come alive as they find situation where choices and commitments are involved despite the meaninglessness and shapelessness of the human condition. In her novels the attraction of the unusual attracts and the fantasy lies in the narrative technique which combines the realistic and the romantic modes. In her novels incident or situation is more important than character.

In order to present the submerged psychic truth she employs various linguistic devices. Carefully chosen clusters of images, symbols and myths, figure most prominently amongst the devices deployed by her. Apart from them, quite often she makes use of fresh collocation, deviations and parallelisms to render the uniqueness of the psyche of her characters. She exploits even phonological patterns like alliteration, assonance, consonance, rhyme, etc. Sometimes different levels of semantic interpretation also become significant for the presentation of her character. Her novels qualify her for stylistic distinction. We agree with Meenakshi Mukherjee's statement about Anita Desai's style when she says,

"Her language is marked by three characteristics: Sensuous richness, a high strung sensitiveness and a love for the sound of words."[4] Even Darshan Singh Maini is also of the same view as he finds that in Desai's fiction words appear to have sensuous appeal for her and she has a love for the sound of words.

Anita Desai uses native words for festivals, dress, food items, cultural practices, address, etc., in order to evoke the typically Indian atmosphere. Most of her novels present a unique aspect of life, handled in the peculiar manner the theme demanded. Her novels are mostly psychological studies, and the narration is aimed at delineating character through the objective world. She confirms to the tradition of the 'lyrical noel'. *Cry, the Peacock*, her first novel is a portrayal of personality types. The writer does not reveal the names of the protagonists, but highlights the qualities possessed by them. The words of Maya (woman) and Gautama (Man) are sharply contrasted in that both represent the extremities of feminine and masculine principle. Desai's second novel *Voices in the City* is based on contrasts, a gap between appearances and reality. The contrasts have been skillfully wrought in the scene from a railway platform. Arun has been the father's favourite and has accepted routine, while Nirode hates routine. I quote:

> "Nirode is aware of his love-hate relationship with Arun, of the envy which corrodes his very being, and is also aware that this is a final parting, yet the pretence is maintained that it is not so."[5]

In Desai's hands imagery becomes a very powerful mode to represent the perception of a character. Symbols also have a vital role to play in displaying different states. Generally the symbols used by Desai are a part of the circumstantial details of the narrative. They acquire significance because of the appropriate correlation between the object and its symbolic meaning. The houses in *Fire on the Maintain*, *Where Shall We To This Summer?* and in *In Custody* are an essential part of the created world. Their symbolical meanings are only semantic extra positions. Yet they are capable of objectifying the inner psychic layers of characters in a powerful way. At times, very minor objects seem to attain symbolical overtones and effectively outlay a particular shade of mind or a psychic tension. If symbols, generally through their extra semantic impositions help Desai to objectify the nuances of a character's subjective world, at times, also by only half revealing the truth they enable the novelist to delineate the psychological depth of the characters. For instance, in *Cry, the Peacock,* Desai suggests the subconscious decision of Maya to murder Gautam through the dust symbol. Through this 'dust storm', the novelist suggests the preceding psychic turmoil and the following peace. Some of the traditional symbols have been reinterpreted by Desai for the sake of rendering highly individualized psyches. In *Cry, the Peacock*, the repeated references to a peacock as a 'brain fever bird', 'a reminder of death' and 'ill-fated lover' are contrary to the traditionally popular image of the peacock. By presenting the peacock in her arbitrary symbolical colours, Desai is making an attempt to depict Maya's mental predicament — a deep love for life with a sure knowledge of death to follow.

Myths have also been deployed by Desai, which with all their religious and traditional associations lay out the psychological depths of characters. They serve as powerful instruments to suggest what cannot be expressed denotatively. Often Desai resorts to a skilful development of phonological sounds to render the inner world of her characters. Among the phonological devices used by her, alliteration, assonance, rhyme and use of harsh sounds figure most prominently. Thus, Desai's wizardry with words, especially in her recent novels is once again established. Each novel presents a unique aspect of life, handled in the peculiar manner as the theme demanded. Mostly psychological studies, the narration is aimed at delineating character through the objective world. She confirms to the tradition of the 'lyrical novel'. *Cry, the Peacock*, is a portrayal of personality types. *Voices in the City* is based on contrasts, a gap between appearance and reality. In *Bye-Bye Blackbird*, the first five hundred words express that the novelist deftly weaves the fine thread of an exotic design into the already tough and coloured cloth of Dev's Indian consciousness. The next novel, *Where Shall We Go This Summer*? is another discovery in the ingenious craftsmanship of Anita Desai. A commonplace character and locale are the materials which evoke the sardonic grin of the author. But all these novels with many more do reveal some common features of her narrative style. She prefers simple words to polysyllabic words. A discreet mixture of Saxon and Latin words give her English a native touch. While writing about human psyche she uses more concrete nouns than abstract. For vividness and visibility she includes adjectives, referring to physical and psychological states. A large number of adverbs of time, place, direction and degree give her writing a palpable quality and the adverbs of manner throw light on the personalities of the characters, so as to render their total image for immediate apprehension. A balanced use of transitive and intransitive verbs adds speed to the progression of images, which are created in order to dramatize an inner conflict and symbolize it objectively through a situation or object. The transitive verbs give the reader an impression of movement and activity and thus add liveliness to the description. Desai prefers complex sentences to simple ones. She favours non-finite clauses as it is a mark of careful writing. These clauses result in compactness and hence aid fluent reading. An interesting feature of her style is the use of articles.

Anita Desai like Jane Austen paints on a limited canvas. Parataxis, ellipsis and parenthesis are other devices employed freely. They save the narration from excessive formality, retaining naturalness of expression. For cohesion, Anita Desai takes recourse to lexical repetition, the use of pronouns and definite article. Besides these, the underlying idea is a strong unifying link between paragraphs. A careful arrangement of paragraphs is another distinctive feature which is very evident from the organisation of material. Despite being a part of a bulk, the beginnings are all self-contained units. Her novels are technical innovations which 'combine features of both novel and lyrical poetry and shift the readers attention from men and events to a formal design'.[6] It is so because for her it is not the theme, but the inner and outer rhythms of human psyche which are all important.

To prove my discussion I will exemplify this through my favourite novel *In Custody* by Desai.

In Custody is mainly the story of Deven Sharma. The implied author and this character come very close to each other and sometimes merge into each other. The other voices are that of Murad's (Deven's counterpart), and Nur Shajahanabadi, the Urdu poet, and minor characters, Sarla, Trevedi, Nur's wives, etc. Murad and Deven represent two different lifestyles, and although Deven Sharma is the less successful of two, it is he who gains the reader's sympathy because of his honesty and uprightness. Even Nur, with all his poetry and fame fails to impress us because of his disordered personal life. Deven, though not prosperous, displays a reverence for all that is good and noble in life, and the reader is won over by the sheer power of goodness which may not give us any material reward but is its own reward.

In this novel, to achieve stylistic effects, Anita Desai adopts varieties of speech and thought presentations. One can notice different versions of them in a single passage, for e.g. in the following passage the writer has included free indirect thought, free direct thought, direct speech and free direct speech, along with narrative report.

> "Deven was shocked (free IT). He looked furtively to the left and the right. They were walking up the stairs to the main hall (narrative report). Anyone could have heard, even someone of the staff (FDT — free direct thought). His eyebrows crept together in a furry

> scowl (narrative report) 'Please, Murad, leave me now,' he muttered anxiously, (direct speech), hunching his shoulders and clutching his books to his chest (narrative report). I must go to my class" (free direct speech).[7]

Desai's experiments with non-traditional materials and technique give her a distinct position among the Indian English novelists. Her fondness for quotes from various writers serves a definite purpose. Nur quotes lines from romantics like Byron, Shelley and Keats and poems like 'Ode to the West Wind', 'Ode to Nightingale' and 'La Balle Dame Sans Merci' are oft quoted poems in the novel. The plot of the novel is intricately connected with the characters of Deven and Nur. The central incident of novel is the interview and all other actions are either related to it or subordinate to it. The action of the whole novel is a long series of episodes related to the interview. The tone of the novel is ironical in the sense that in spite of the best efforts of Deven his circumstances go against him and everything leads him to further trouble. At the same time if we compare *In Custody* with Desai's more mature novels like *Bye-Bye Blackbird*, *Journey to Ithaca* etc. from the point of view of technique, it is not a very significant novel. But still it very well portrays the mind of an anti-hero Deven who is different, unsure of him, never able to fight successfully and always a victim of people and circumstances. In this novel, Desai at occasion achieves a fine blending of satire, irony and humours. She also makes use of certain Hindi words in her dialogues but their use is justified. Justification for using foreign words is that either the words are untranslatable or the words that come spontaneously when the characters are emotionally charged.

Thus it is clearly visible that Desai's style of technique of delivering the thematic thrust is the vital agent. Language is the main element of her style. Her use of language and dialogues is one of the features of her artistically conceived novels. She has tried to present her themes organically with appropriate adjustment and adaptations in spheres of style and point of view.

No doubt, Desai has a subtle and inimitable style. Her fiction is symbolic, sensitive, and psychological. Her work reflects her concerns with psyche of her characters. She is a painter of sensitive poetic pictures — the pictures are varied in hue and open to manifold interpretation. Mooving deep into the works of Anita Desai one notices her unique use of imagery along with symbolism. She appears, in her narrative strategy, subtle and sensitive. Her style is one of 'suggestive symbolism'. Brati Biswas says:

> "She unconsciously and intuitively chose not to write 'the kind of social document that demands the creation of realistic and typical characters and the use of realistic and typical dialogue.' By writing novels and stories that are psychological and purely subjective, she was free to employ, simply the language of the interior. She further states, even when two characters meet, they use this particular type of language — the language of their thoughts."[8]

Desai is no doubt a great artist with a remarkable and astounding technical efficacy. Her technique does not only suit the theme dwelt upon in the novel but also go a long way in her externalizing the inner turmoil of her protagonists. This technique is deftly used by Desai in capturing authentically a psychological realism, an intensified impressionism a multiplied consciousness. The result is her comparative superiority over other Indian women novelists writing in English. Her achievements are aptly summed up by Meenakshi Mukherjee. She, taking a note of Desai's language and style, relates the novelists manner of narration to the elements of her protagonist's personality. She believes that Desai's style shows a strong individuality. About her language she observes that it is marked by three characteristics, sensuous richness, a high strong sensitiveness and a love for the sounds of words. R.S. Sharma said, "Anita Desai's gifts as a prose stylist are now acknowledged. What is perhaps overlooked in the process is the fact that most of her problems as a fiction writer begin with her insistence on too much style on too small a canvas."[9]

References

1. Wayne, C. Booth, *The Rhetoric of Fiction,* Chicago: Chicago University Press, 1961, p. 164.
2. Ralph, Freedman, *The Lyrical Novel,* Princeton University Press, 1973, p. 9.
3. Ram, Atma, An Interview with Anita Desai, *World Literature Written in English*, Vol. 16, No. 1, April, 1977, p. 10.
4. Mukherjee, Meenakshi, *The Twice-Born Fiction,* New Delhi: Amold-Heimeman, 1974, p. 189.
5. Desai, Anita, *Voices in the City*, New Delhi: Hind Pocket Books, 1968, p. 112.
6. Ralph, Freedman, *The Lyrical Novel,* Princeton: University Press, 1973, p. 1.
7. Desai, *In Custody*, London: Heinmann, 1984, p. 10.
8. Shrivastava, K., "Indian Writers Problem", *Perspectives on Anita Desai*, Ghaziabad, Uimal, 1984.
9. Sharma, R.S. *Anita Desai*, Arnold Publications (I) Pvt. Ltd., 1981, pp. 92-93.

9 Feminism and Desai

> "In the 1990s it was Elaine Showalter, who claimed that feminist criticism has finished with her 'gyno-criticism' and needed to focus on gender and sexual difference in texts by men as much as by women. 'Speaking of Gender' (1989) focused on significations of the feminine in the works of Irigaray, Jardine and others. Thus from 1970s onward the growing interest in feminist criticism has taken speedy strides. Like political feminism which began with the Women's Liberation Movement in '70s, critical feminism today is shaped by a much richer understanding of difference .... With such conceptions feminism comes a long way from power politics to an understanding of cultural diversification."[1]
>
> — *Jayita Sengupta*

Women's writing which springs from the new concept of Indian womanhood is voluminous and it depicts in their phases of new liberation movement, the changing concept of the woman's subjectivity. The analysis of Desai's novels would unfold not a totalitarian ideology of their unified goal or a metaphysical absolute; rather it will reveal a prospect of achieving a feminine consensus where each novel voices her story.

With the rise of feminism in India in the seventies, the feminist literary critics came to believe that women had to create a literature of their own, in which the feminine sensibility could consider and confront the peculiarly feminine issues and experiences. It was essential to do so, because a large part of the feminine experience is out of the reach of the male psyche and, therefore, an authentic and sensitive portrayal of the conflicts and traumas, in all their nuances, ambiguities and contradictions, could be achieved only by women writers. We have, through women writers' writings, the pictures of women in flesh and blood, with a distinct mind of their own. She is no more a wooden creature, subject to suppression and male domination only. The transformative power of Anita Desai's novels lies in her taking up the task of revealing the process of self-awareness at work in feminine psyches. Her novels are an engrossing study in the progression of women from feminine to female as stipulated by Elaine Showalter. Her women characters are sensitively portrayed and therefore, are best appreciated in their psychological depths. Desai's feminism is not the same as hating man or abandoning families and relationships or indulging in lesbianism, etc. As a feminist she wants women to be accepted as responsible human beings.

Feminism in literature is essentially concerned with the representation of women in society. Feminism has always meant independence of mind, spirit and body. The demand of feminists is women's control over their own lives. With the advent of feminism, each and every female oriented subject has become an issue of contemporary literary debate. Feminists consider that male authored texts have obtained double standards in their treatment of male and female characters. Today female writer feels that she is helping to create a viable tradition which is at last definitively emerging. Thus, to become a feminist means to be prepared for a profound personal transformation.

The novels of Anita Desai are basically female oriented. She probes into their problems, be it of a daughter, sister, mother, grandmother or a wife. Her female figure appears as a victim in a patriarchal, patrilineal and father dominated Indian family. Anita Desai depicts the Indian woman as a fighter, a victim, a heroine and in later novels ultimately a winner because of her indomitable spirit and attitude of compromise. She has portrayed both kinds of women — those who are symbols of growth and change, those who are powerful means of withdrawl, regression, decay, death and destruction. She designs the exploration of the disturbed psyche of the Indian woman lying emphasis on the factors of loneliness and alienation. However, Desai's women do not give up the strife so easily. Desai focuses on the gender roles of women seen through the lense of female activities experiences, goals, values, institutions, relationships and modes of communication. Desai's contribution in the field of feminism does not merely involve revalidating the French theories or the western model. She presents in her writing, the pictures of women in flesh and blood, with a distinct mind of their own. Her characters are no more wooden creatures, subject to suppression and male domination only. The transformative power of Anita Desai's novels lies in her taking up the task of revealing the process of self-awareness at work in feminine psyche.

Anita Desai, along with Shobha De, Shashi Deshpande, Bharati Mukherjee and others, writes primarily women's novels — novels that are addressed to and deal with women. Desai is satisfied to dive deep into the inner working of the protagonists and brings out the hidden depths of human psyche. Her fictional world is just like an iceberg mostly hidden and partly visible, it is overcast by mist and fog, half revealed and half-concealed. Her inner voyage of the characters in her novels is greatly influenced by *Virginia Woolf*. She has been hailed as a pioneer of Indian feminism. She brilliantly exposes the grinding suppression of women in India:

> "Even if in reality she is nothing but a common drudge, first in her father's house and then her husband's — a beast of burden bearing an endless string of children, putting up with any brutality or disloyalty or failing of her husband — she has no alternative : She must live as Sita did, as Draupadi did, she is Durga incarnate. The myth keeps her bemused, bound hand and foot. To rebel against it — either in speech or action would mean that she is questioning the myth, attacking the legend, and that cannot be permitted; it is the cornerstone on which the Indian family and therefore Indian society are built."[2]

In her world, it is always the 'Sitas' who interrogate their patriarchies. The portrayals of men are indistinct and their psychological complexities are not taken into account. Men in her novels mostly exist only as projections of women's point of view. She explores the issue of gender from one Indian socio-historical perspective. But where comes the question of labeling as a feminist, like other women authors, Desai too considers the term 'woman writer' as derogatory as it taxes away her artistic autonomy and identity and she comes into the category of gender. She expressed her reservations on this issue, in an interview with Yashodhara Dalmia:

> "I find it impossible to whip up any interest in a mass of woman marching forward under the banner of feminism."[3]

Desai's first three novels are a study of women's depression resulting from their inability to grapple with their family situations. Some of her novels deal with the issues related to women education and their aspiration to obtain self sufficiency and a meaningful existence. She writes about women in the urban middle class who has had the privilege of receiving education and the complexities of the 'have not' section could be safely left out for considering the feminist issues in her writing considered as a whole, her novels reveal a progression in the psychic awareness of women about their position in society. From Maya in *Cry, the Peacock* to Uma in *Fasting, Feasting* there is a gap of two generations.

Maya is enclosed within her mental space and her geographical space to claim her husband's love. She has no space of her own in defiance of the heterosexual social space offered to her as a wife to a man. Gautama, Maya's husband, wanted his wife to be traditional, submissive, patient, tolerant, compromising and undemanding. Maya tried also but when she found that her physical and emotional needs were left unattended, and she was called 'neurotic', mad woman; she became a different person. Her mental state, her agony, her alienation and loneliness could not be portrayed in a better way by anyone other than the sensitive feminist like Anita Desai. The novel, *Voices in the City,* has touched upon the essential questions of being through the delineation of psychological strains of individual behaviour. However, the most significant basis of the character's psychological conflicts and dilemmas is then inability to transcend the social conditioning which compels them to view women and analyse their actions as per pre-defined chauvinistic concepts of behaviour instead of treating them as individuals. Monisha is in many ways quite like Maya. After leading a stifling life in crowded Calcutta she hoped for a freer life in Kalimpong and Darjeeling. Anita Desai probes deeper into the psyche of Monisha. Devoid of any true self-revealation and presentation, Monisha feels herself emotionally drained. And finally the perpetuation of the behavioral symbols of male dominance are ultimately responsible for Monisha's death. Another fact of traditional male psyche is critically discernible in Dharma's attitude towards his daughter and also towards Monisha's sister Amla. Whereas Monisha felt stifled in the joint family of Jiban finding the loss of privacy, of intellectual freedom, of conscience, of ethics unbearable, she expresses the plight of Bengali women in general a truly feministic concern.

> "I think of generations of Bengali women hidden behind the barred windows of half dark rooms, spending centuries in washing clothes, kneading dough and murmuring aloud verses from the *Bhagvad Gita* and the *Ramayana*, in the dim light of sooty lamps. Lives spent in waiting for nothing, waiting on men, self-centered and indifferent and hungry and demanding and critical, waiting for death and dying misunderstood, always behind bars, those terrifying black bars that shut us in, in the old houses, in the old city."[4]

Added to her misery is the fact that she cannot bear children. All she does is record her inner feelings in a diary. Her married life is devoid of love. These things lead to a sense of negation and isolation. Amla knows the value of love which helps her to shift from revolt to surrender. However, in their own ways both Monisha and Amla exhibit endurable courage. Monisha has the courage to end her unhappy life while Amla has the courage to compromise and find a way out.

A very different picture of woman is found in Nirode's mother who was more involved in her extra-marital relationship with Major Chadha rather than caring for her children. Due to lack of parental love and affection the children suffer a lot emotionally and almost become misfits in society. The idea of a woman's independence is brought in by Aunt Leila who firmly believed that women can be self-sufficient, confident and free from the clutches of men only when they are able to discover their own spirits. Aunt Leila says emphatically:

> "Women place themselves in bondage to men, whether in marriage or out of it. All their joy and ambition is channeled that way while they go parched themselves."[5]

Hence, according to Aunt Leila a woman has to set a limit for things and must find ways and means to have a little independence. A submissive suppressed life could lead to mental tension culminating in trauma as in the case of Maya.

This novel is significant as all the major and peripheral characters refuse to treat women in their own right and, compelled by the traditional mindset to treat women basically as secondary beings, pass harsh unsympathetic judgments on them. Their refusal to dissociate themselves from the social myths governing feminine behaviour leads the women to take extreme steps about their need of self-expression in diversified contexts. The idea of male superiority and stereotyped notions about female behaviour acquires the status of unshakeable truths and reflects a strong societal bias against the autonomous identity of women.

Through Sarah in *Bye-Bye Blackbird*, for the first time, Desai has taken a working woman as a character in her novels through whom she describes the problems faced by working women in a hostile society. Being a foreigner Sarah is different from the other women portrayed in the novels of Anita Desai yet her self-control, the sense of sacrifice and the attempts at compromise are appreciable. Apparently Sarah may be a pathetic creature, suffering from alienation yet her courage and stoicism in trying to adjust are qualities to be admired. Sometimes she wonders who she is, after marrying Adit — is she an English lady, or the Head's secretary in the school for English children, or just Mrs. Sen, the wife of Adit. But it is her strong will-power that often comes to her rescue. She does not allow tensions to crop up between Adit and her. Hari Mohan Prasad has pointed out:

> "In her, there is a real split, a real dilemma, a real suffering, but she triumphs over all these. She is a silent volcano, not dead, yet not bursting. She understands Dev, she knows her mother well, keeps a balanced relationship with friends and visitors and shows a feeling for Adit. Right from the beginning she has been quiet in her response. Dev's long arguments and heated discussions of other friends never disturb her calm."[6]

Malashree Lal in *The Law of the Threshold*, makes a study of the patriarchal forces which explore the Indian women's situation. She analyses three stages of Indian feminism, which moves from 'interior space' to 'doorway poise' to 'exterior adjuncts'. Anita Desai's first two novels explore the story of 'interior space'. While the 'interior space' of Indian women could be the fulfilling role of a mother, wife and daughter-in-law. The problem of women's identity in the family and society becomes more complex in the following generations. Maya's sensitive mind refuses to accept her husband's blind adherence to the detachment philosophy and Monisha tries to grapple with it till her last breath. The two women end up as two hysteries in their claustrophobic confines. In her other novel *Where Shall We Go This Summer?* Desai follows the track of Bronte sisters, who chose to study the heart and mind of women from women's point of view. This novel portrays the tragic intensity of her women characters with a feminist perspective. Sita in *Where Shall We Go This Summer?* moves beyond the 'interior space' to the 'exterior adjunct', a step ahead of Sarah, but to retreat back to the 'interior space' once again. Like the mythological Sita, Desai's modern Sita swallows her semiotic urges to determine her subjectivity through her compromise. After marriage her disintegrated personality fails to recoup and casts its shadows on her relationship with her husband and children. Bidulata Choudhary comments:

> "Between two uncompromising attitudes of Maya's madness and Monisha's suicide, Sita is the only heroine

> of Mrs. Desai to understand and succumb to the word 'only connect', the only compromising link between the prose and passion of her life. Her reaction proves that it is very difficult for a woman, however, modern she may be, to get rid of the situation she is once placed in. Inspite of her dislike to the ways of the world, to the traditional life of royalty, she resumes her return journey to adjust to the role of a wife and mother. Hence, she accepts defeat, crumbles her passion and mingles with the prose of life for the betterment of human relationship."[7]

Then comes Bimla or Bim in *Clear Light of Day* who suffered for almost twenty years. Through her character Anita Desai sends a message to all women not to be cowed down by the problems of life but to be stoic and develop the qualities of assertions and self respect. The title of the novel *Clear Light of Day* indicates the light of emancipation among women who are ardently urged to sweep away the darkness of ignorance. After this novel Desai has shifted her attention from feminism to male Psyche. *In Custody* and *Baumgartner's Bombay* both deal with male characters at the centre of the novel. But again in her more mature phase Desai has written *Journey to Ithaca* and portrays the character of Sophie and 'Mother'. In fact Desai's novels explore the issues of gender from the Indian socio-historical perspective. Desai's first three novels are a study of women's depression resulting from their inability to grapple with their family situations. Some of her novels deal with the issues related to women's education and their aspiration to obtain self-sufficiency and a meaningful existence. She writes about women in the urban middle class who have had the privilege of receiving education. *Cry, the Peacock* and *Voices in the City* depict women characters who revolt against social relationships and are forced to make a choice between life and death. Desai's women characters live a dual life—the inner and the outer. She delves deep into the inner psychic lives of her characters showing how external forces destroy their lives reducing them to mere puppets on the stage. On the other hand Desai presents Amla's mother (*Voices in the City*) as a rebel of different kind, who refuses to become a conformist. She takes an unorthodox step to get rid of the death-trap. She abandons her husband for an army officer. Her move is condemned as a manipulative act of sexuality. Society expected her to remain faithful even though the husband was a depraved man. She resented this man who was thrust on her by the law makers of society. She was even equated with Kali, the Goddess, the destroyer and the preserver.

By these novels we come to know that though Anita Desai does not proclaim herself to be a feminist writer, the fact remains that she attempts to discover life as it is. Until *Clear Light of Day*, Desai's women are sensitive and emotional misfits trying to maintain their individuality. A change in attitude comes with *Clear Light of Day* and she 'nurtures her feminine self' through acceptance and accommodation rather than withdraws and rejects. The preoccupation of Desai as a feminist writer or rather a writer of feminist psyche has been to analyse the extent of the psychic damage in women due to their respective patriarchal pressures.

Cry, the Peacock is replete with the imagery of fear and loneliness describing a feminine psyche on the verge of madness speaks of a father-daughter relationship. What continuously bewilders the reader is the absence of any recollections of mother in Maya's mind. The daughter's obsession with her father is again traced in *Where Shall We Go this Summer?* Sita's journey to the island of Manori is a psychic journey back to her childhood. Once again the mother is absent, while in *Voices in the City* Desai explores the mother-son relationship. Thus in Anita Desai, family relationships shape the feminine psyche. Desai takes the social context to analyse the gender behaviour in family and community. She finds solutions in compromise within family bondages but at the same time she makes it clear that compromise never means total submission and surrender.

Most of Desai's women characters registered protest against the circumstances which oppressed them. Yet where Maya, Monisha, Nanda, Anamika and Uma failed to tide over the crisis, Bim, Sita and Sophie succeeded in doing so. Desai's entire fiction traces the changing image of women in the face of existential dilemmas. These female protagonists assert their right to exist not as shadows of their male counterparts but as independent human beings with a will of their own. In fact this is the real aim of any feminist. Her characters realised that to live life one had to face new challenges, that hatred was of no avail, that all transcending love could overcome all obstacles, that life is indeed one single whole which is a delicate inter-connected web. It shows although Desai is not a surrealist yet her understanding of the female psyche is highly distinctive and remarkable. She views the female in relation to different kinds of organization — familial, social, national and international.

One of the primary concerns of feminism is to declare that a woman is a being. She is not an appendage a subordinate of man. Rather she is an autonomous being, capable of trial and error, finding her own way to salvation. We come across such women figures in the novels by Anita Desai, who are consciously trying to come to terms with themselves as individuals. Their voice is now gradually becoming audible and there is definitely a protest in their own voice. There is a clear tone of resentment and a pressing demand for freedom from traditional fetters which have been imposed on them and their gender. Feminism is a concept emerging as a protest against male domination and the marginalisation of women. The new woman has raised her voice against the atrocity and injustice done to her. The modern woman protests and dares to pronounce her convictions. And it is their voice of protest, their pronouncement in an overtone that has credited the difference and force us to consider and call Anita Desai as a focused feminist. Desai has presented three kinds of females. In the first group are such females who are hypersensitive and after self introspection they plunge further into dark dismal depths of neurosis, like Maya. The second group portrays women characters who silently suffer the strain of life and become idealists or commit suicide like Monisha. While the third group discloses women who discern new and important discoveries about themselves resulting in a sobering effect on them and they find a sense of fulfillment in their relation to the world. Even in a male dominated, tradition oriented society such women characters try to establish their own value system and if fail, then their inner potentiality enables them to resist unjust social pressure and they protest. For example in *Fasting, Feasting*, the disorders of Melanie and Uma might take culturally related forms — Melanie is bulimic and Uma is subject to fits — however as Arun realises, they stem from the same hungers: a desire to be understood, to be valued, for recognition of their unique being. Feminists focusing on the body as inscriptive surface argue that hysteria, a general term for the above disorders, is a form of protest — protest against society's suppression of a woman's real needs. It is probable that in future, the feminist reader could keep the expectation of texts from Indian English women writers, which will consider the repressive pressures enforced by the societies on the male as well as female consciousness to change the male attitude towards women and to reconsider gender roles for a fruitful community existence. This novel *Fasting, Feasting* deals with the issues related to women's education and their aspiration to obtain self-sufficiency and a meaningful existence. A 'semanalysis' of the structures of patriarchal oppression is brought into force through these tales of woe and social reactions. For Desai, feminism in Indian context lies in the spread of education, economic self-sufficiency, preservation of human rights and in the awareness of the desire for liberation from mythical and social values which constrain women as well as men socially, psychically and physically.

Neither Nayantara Sahgal's polemics of a clamouring feminism nor Deshpande's meticulously detailed recording of a woman's existence is there in Desai's feministic way of writing fiction. Instead, we have poignant portraits of intelligent women trapped in relationships which deny them the freedom, emotional involvement and self-respect they crave for. The women do not seek fulfillment through challenging careers but seek it within sustaining meaningful human relationships. In the process of this quest, tragically aborted in some cases, Anita Desai's women display a sensitive and subtle awareness of the forces working to repress them and question the inequalities of such systems. She has staunchly refused to be labeled a feminist but there is an incipient feminist consciousness present in the simmering anger of Maya or Sita and the studied indifference of

Monisha or Nanda. One was to consider Desai's novels in such a social context or in such a transitional stage of Indian feminism. Considered as a whole, her novels reveal a progression in the psychic awareness of women about their position in society. Her characters do not succumb to patriarchal tortures, rather they have the capacity to analyse the nature of their pain to come to a decision about their lives. Desai herself says:

> "Few Indian feminists really contemplate total change. Working towards an adjustment through the traditional role is much less drastic, much more Indian. I think Indian feminism is more practical than theoretical. It is expedient rather than ideological."[8]

References

1. Sengupta, Jayita, *Refractions of Desire: Feminist Perspectives in the Novels of Toni Morrison, Michelé Roberts and Anita Desai*, New Delhi: Atlantic Publishers and Distributors (P) Ltd., 2006, p. 52.
2. Desai, Anita, 'Secret Connivance', *Times Literary Supplement*, 14 September, 1990, p. 972.
3. Desai, Anita, Interview with Anita Desai by Yashodhara Dalmia, *The Times of India*, 29 April 1979.
4. Desai, Anita, *Voices in the City*, New Delhi: Hind Pocket Books, 1968, p. 120.
5. *Ibid.*, p. 121.
6. Hari Mohan Prasad, 'Sound and Sense: A Study of Anita Desai's *Bye-Bye Blackbird*', *The Journal of Indian Writing in English*, Vol. 9, No. 1, January 1981, p. 64.
7. Chowdhary, Bidulate, *Women and Society in the Novels of Anita Desai,* New Delhi: Creative Books, 1995, p. 77.
8. Desai, Anita, 'A Sense of Denial and a Sense of Order: Anita Desai Interviewed by Lalita Pandit' in Patrick Colm Hogan and Lalita Pandit Eds., *Literary India: Comparative Studies in Aesthetics,* London: Routledge, 1994, p. 168.

Alienation and Anita Desai

10

Alienation is a trait of contemporary life of variety and complexity. The complex ridden modern life running after more and more may be said to be at the root of this elusive term. Clearly, it is caused by a sense of deep-rooted frustration and failure, irredeemable sense of loss and loneliness. One of the cardinal characteristics of 'alienation' is anxiety (which is equivalent to German angst), about which John Macquarrie writes thus. 'It confronts the individual with his responsibility and the call to grasp his authentic being.'[1]

The feeling of alienation has become very prominent in recent times due to the growing awareness of man of the 'otherness' of himself and his surroundings. Critics have made an attempt to find out how characters get alienated from their social self and if it is possible for them to regain their normal health. The plight of modern man has been discussed by Melvin Seeman under a set of five interrelated optional conditions, viz. powerlessness, meaninglessness, normlessness, isolation and self-estrangement which he considers to be different manifestations of alienation.[2]

The Guardian said, it is an apt paradox that, at 61, the Delhi novelist who has only recently found freedom in the life of the academic should be escaping India – and rushing to embrace it. Salman Rushdie once described Desai's subject as solitude. Yet while her main characters tend to be isolaters and outsiders — whether Indian or foreigners in India — her fiction probes the tensions between their desired privacy and detachment, and the powerful family and social ties that both stifle and sustain.

Anita Desai presents her protagonist as individual who is hypersensitive and unusually tense. He or she is rendered helpless and restless when confronted with her or his responsibilities, and at the same time she or he tries hard to discover her or his true self, (authentic being). The restlessness or helplessness of Desai's protagonists like Maya, Monisha, Sita, Sarah, Nanda, Raka, Tara and Uma, may be rightly interpreted in terms of their hectic search for self-identity and self-knowledge. All of them are apparently abnormal creatures, cut off from their society and surroundings and leading a life of loneliness and frustration. In her novels, they all live in an alienated world of their own and drift constantly against the current while waging a grim fight for their existence and freedom. Hence 'alienation' is closely associated with the existential problems of man. It is pretty difficult to define 'alienation' or 'existentialism', it is quite evident that one is the offshoot of another in the modern anxious and care-ridden world. If 'existentialism' lays emphasis on 'the individual consciousness', alienation underlines the futility of human search and the modern predicament of anxiety, frustration, and loneliness. The latter is often equated with powerlessness, meaninglessness, normlessness, cultural estrangement, social isolation, and self-estrangement in an individual's life, which cumulatively tend to reinforce the idea of purposelessness and insignificance of human existence on earth.

Man oppressed with the realities of modern impersonalized life is often labelled as alienated. 'Alienation' refers to physical action not emotions, while 'estrangement' is how people feel about one another. For Marx, alienation is phenomenon of existing objective conditions. Estrangement is the word more suited to the characters of Anita Desai's subjective world. Desai's novels are replete with such characters as are estranged from self, from work, from fellow men. Her characters suffer from meaninglessness and normlessness.

The history of alienation goes beyond the modern industrial age and may be traced in the work of Plotlinus and in the theology of St. Augustine and Martin Luther. The term 'existence' and 'existentialism' were first coined by Soren Kierkegaard, a renowned Danish thinker (1813-1855), who rejected the notion of identifying man with state, society and church, etc. Kierkigaard emphatically asserts the individual's free choice and his personal relationship to God.

The most powerful Marxian sources of 'alienation', however, was Hegel, who supplied the idea to Marx. For Hegal, alienation was 'an ontological fact', rooted in the nature of man's experience in the world. There was an inherent dissociation between man as subject and man as object. This rendered man's own creations (his art, language and science, etc.) standing outside him as alien objects. The main causes of alienation for human beings are economic, technological, sociological philosophic existential and psychological. The supposed consequences are so extensive as to include psychosis, suicide, psychomatic disorder, ethnic prejudice, civil riots, and political agitations or protestations.

The problem of alienation is intimately related to the loss and quest of one's identity. Donald even rightly suggests that it is the loss of identity that results in alienation. To realise adequately the magnitude of the problems of loss of identity, it is necessary to bear in mind that it is in the centre of all problems including alienation. A sense of identity is a perennial sustaining creative force in a writer. The loss of the sense of identity may lead to rootlessness or alienation.

Alienation is so natural to Anita Desai that she uses it in almost each novel of hers. It may be noted here that in Desai the theme of alienation, though it is recurrent and pervasive, does not assume sociological or even philosophical connotations. In the opinion of Prof. D.S. Maini, the theme of husband-wife alienation — a recurring motif in Anita Desai is not developed in a slow, incremental manner such as we find in typical psychological novels.[3] By means of simile, metaphor, and symbol the two spouses are often presented before us as 'opposed archetypes':

> "Taviss speaks of two different kinds of alienation, i.e. 'social alienation' and 'self alienation'. By social alienation she means the sense of estrangement brought out by the sudden discovery that the social system is either oppressive or is complete with the individuals

> desires and ideals. 'Self-alienation', however means the loss of contact of the individual selves with any inclinations or desires that are not in agreement with the Prevailing Social Patterns, as a result of which the individuals are forced to manipulate in accordance with the social demands or feel incapable of controlling their actions."[4]

Mainly four kinds of alienation can be analysed from the novels of Anita Desai. First, there are the poor landless people, the bonded labourers, the scheduled castes, nomads, tribal and economically weak people. There is a sense of alienation and rootlessness existing among them. There is no feeling of belonging, because there is nothing to bind them. Their land, their work is snatched or being snatched away from them and they are thrown back to suffer both economically and socially. Such alienation finds expression in the novels like *The Village by the Sea* and *In Custody*. In *The Village by the Sea*, Hari represents the first kind of alienation. Hari's family land is sold to pay debts, animals are sold. He feels alone because he is the only person in the village filled with enthusiastic spirits of trying his fortune outside the village. Many factories are going to be established in Thul. But at the same time it is also a threat to the farmers, the fishermen and the shepherds. Their land will be snatched then, and they would lose their traditional jobs and houses and will be displaced emotionally as well as economically. Effluents of the fertilizers will kill fish for miles around the shore.

Hari, restless in his village, leaves it for Bombay, but feels deserted and friendless there. His position in the overcrowded city is that of a wandering lonely man. He feels alone and completely isolated. He does not find himself associated with any group or community and yet wages a heroic fight in unfavourable circumstances.

In the novel *In Custody*, the theme of alienation is reinforced herein with great ingenuity and skill. Deven, a Hindi lecturer in Mirpore, belongs to a lower middle class background. Deven is portrayed as 'marginal character who dangles' on the periphery of action. An unsuccessful teacher, Deven bores his students in the classes. The novelist brings out Deven's sense of boredom, isolation and alienation through his attitude towards his students and the locale of Mirpore. He is assigned the job of interviewing a renowned Urdu litterateur Nur Sahajehanabadi, but meets failure at every step. He feels utterly helpless. Deven's adventure in the field of poetry and art may be viewed as a search for meaningful existence. The real tragedy of alienation lies in his failure and frustration in reaching his noble goal.

Deven feels alienated. He really feels that he is not being helped by Mr. Siddiqui, Murad, Nur and his wife. He is being hunted down by these people to have their ends meet. Nobody seems to offer him any solace or assistance at this crucial juncture of his life.

This alienation of a college teacher is from his own roots and culture. The alienation is not complete but Deven feels estranged from his own job, his own family, and his own immediate environment. His vision of life and art drawn from Westernized system of education comes in conflict with the day-to-day life. Anita Desai depicts very beautifully the inner-conflict of Deven who ultimately finds the truth that life is not an ivory tower but a reality.

Deven's alienation is born out of opposite, conflicting tendencies like Western education and cultural roots urbanization and rural way of life, industrial society and placid Indian agrarian society. Deven feels estranged because he is pressurized by growing consumerism where money is all in all. Consequently he becomes utterly sad, and hopeless. The sense of isolation and self-exile often grips Deven's psyche. He feels alienated not only from his immediate environment but also within himself. The very existence becomes a burden for him.

Deven's sense of isolation and loneliness has two significant connations. He wants to break the imprisonment by taking an interview of the great Urdu poet Nur. He wants to break away from his marginality. At another level he feels ill-equipped and incapable of adapting himself to the emerging complexities of life and society. He is discontented and yearns for what is not. He feels trapped in its solidity and stubbornness. He now seeks to review his existence and its problems. Through the alienated figure of Deven, Anita Desai presents before us in the novel *In Custody* the realistic picture of the changing socio-economic Indian scene and its impact on educated Indian who feels lonely, bore, alienated, marginalized on account of materialism, consumerism and industrialism.

Second alienation is a sense of environmental alienation. Millions of men for some reason or the other leave their own roots and fail to strike roots in the alien soil and die as rootless and restless individuals. This kind of alienation is projected in the novels like *Bye-Bye Blackbird* and *Baumgartner's Bombay*; as they are richer and more ambiguous novels incorporating the experience of environmental alienation in their texture. Desai makes deeper probings into the immigrant experience and sublimates it to the universal human dimensions. In most of her novels, her protagonists are alienated from the world, from societies, from families, from parents and even from their own selves. *Bye-Bye Blackbird* mirrors alienation and lack of adjustment encountered by Indian immigrants in England. The people of England are not friendly to them and they find themselves completely isolated and cut off from the surroundings. This immensely unnerves them. Dev feels alienated in London from both Indians and English men because the former have become used to the condescending attitude of the natives, which he cannot do, and the latter consider him an outsider. Happy in the beginning, Adit, who lives in London with his wife Sarah, begins to feel alienated later on. Dev visits them and finds himself completely estranged in an alien shore. He looks for Indian things and Indianness in the High Streets of London and the English villages. While Dev is trapped in an alien land, Adit is caught up in an alien situation, the marriage with an English girl Sarah. Adit feels alienated and does not appreciate this business of always hanging together with people like ourselves, all wearing the label of Indian immigrants, never daring to try and make contact outside the circle.[5]

Like many of his fellow immigrants in England, Adit has developed a love and fascination for England right from his schooldays in India. But even then England does not accept him. He is, like others, abused, insulted, and humiliated all the time, even by school children. He lives in Laurel Lane, Clapham, in virtual isolation among people, who keep their doors and windows tightly closed taking no interest in their neighbours. All that England, the land of promised opportunities and social equality, offers him is a petty clerical job in a tiny travel agency without any prospect of further promotion. The wife of Adit Sen, Sarah feels a peculiar kind of estrangement within. She seeks her identity, which is lost after her marriage with an Indian immigrant. She is highly upset over the thought of her lost identity and desires to come out of her twin roles — one of masks and another of realities. She precisely does not know where her identity lies and hence feels lonely and dejected among the Britishers. Adit notices in Sarah, an anguish of loneliness. Sarah herself feels a loss of identity. R.S. Sharma, commenting on the theme of alienation in this novel writes:

> "The novel is about the alienation of the immigrants in a world which is alluring and appalling at the same time ... it deals with the self-awareness of the educated Indian immigrants, who keep waivering between acceptance and rejection of a world they have been educated to admire and love and which they find, on an actual contact either to be strange or to be hostile."[6]

A similar type of environmental isolation has been felt by Hugo Baumgartner with slight variations in Desai's latest novel *Baumgartner's Bombay* (1988). Unlike Adit, an Indian in foreign country (England), there is Baumgartner, a foreigner (German) in India. His fifty years stay in Bombay as an outsider, without family or country shows his isolated existence. Alone and content with the mild pleasures, he is a portrait of loneliness and alienation. Baumgartner, a German Jew, living in solitude in a shabby flat behind the Taj Hotel in Bombay, lives a solitary life with no one to look after him. Both, Baumgartner and Lotte are sailing in the same boat of isolation in an alien country, among their memories and dreams. Afterwards he comes to Calcutta. There the war breaks and he is kept a captive there for six years. The expectation of happiness in the business gets totally blurred as the lonely prison life threw him in a state of isolation. Then again he goes to Bombay and meets Lotte who often tells Baumgartner that they should have gone back to their country long back instead of living there as isolated foreigners.

One day, Baumgartner, tries to friend a young German in order to overcome his loneliness but later he is murdered by the same young German. After the death of Baumgartner, Lotte remaind an isolated figure, totally broken having lost her oldest friend.

The story of Baumgartner and Lotte gives expression to the theme of isolation and alienation. Both of the themes are solitary foreigners in India and are uprooted from their own culture. Baumgartner's story is one of inherent alienation augmented by global war, colonial war and religious war. When the familiar emotional and geographical worlds are destroyed, one gets deidentified. Cultural displacement makes Hugo and Lotte alienated and lonely inspite of their assays of adjustment.

In the present society, husband-wife alienation in their marital life creates a sense of vaccum in life values. Inspite of having everything they feel alienated, desperate, lonely; as in *Cry, the Peacock*, when alienation arises in the sense of not being able to reconcile with the existing norms and values. Existence becomes meaningless to a person while living through an experience with which one is not able to reconcile. Therefore, there is a feeling of uprootedness, estrangement from the partner, from the society itself. In fact marital alienation is the most common type of alienation in the present society. Alienation is an inevitable outcome of such societies. The breakdown of a world view, divinely ordained and supported by tradition is the primary source of alienation. Its social context is one in which man is pitted against the power of money and the cash-nexus. Alienation occurs as man is reduced to the status of a thing, as he is alienated from the earth and his fellow men.

In *Cry, the Peacock*, Maya is alienated from Gautama. By marrying a man twice her age, she probably had already minimised her chances for a good husband-wife relationship. She painfully becomes aware of her 'loneliness in this house' and whispers 'I am alone'. Their alienation is also reflected in the loneliness of the bear. The main theme deals with the total alienation of Maya from her surroundings, from her husband

and even from herself. She is made a victim of institutionalised marriage and rigid social customs. The incompatibility of their nature causes deep alienation in her mind and she becomes intensely abnormal. She finds that her feelings are not cared for, and that she is being neglected, isolated and alienated in her own home. One of the causes of Maya's loneliness and alienation lies in the romantic and delightful life that she had once led at her father's place. Gautama does not mean anything to her except a status, untouched by her presence. They live in two different isolated worlds altogether. Maya has lost even order and symmetry of her life in her deep despair. Her mental peace has deserted her completely. The accidental death of Gautama undoubtedly completes Maya's alienation and aloofness, and she becomes a strangely isolated character of Anita Desai. K.R.S. Iyengar writes in this connection:

> "The solitude and silence of the house prays upon her, and the death of the pet dog starts a chain of reminiscence and reverie and, with startling suddenness, and evrie bit of experience, long buried under the load of the years, is thrown up like lava and glares at her in all its alienness and fury."[7]

In *Voices in the City*, the theme of alienation is treated in terms of mother-children relationship, which itself is a consequence of dissonance in husband-wife relationship. All the three characters — Nirode, Monisha and Amla are alienated from society as well as from their mother who is in love with Major Chadna shirking from doing a meaningless and mechanical job. Nirode a sensitive and talented artist, drifts from one person to another and experiences an emptiness, meaninglessness and alienation in life. Nirode knew by instinct that he was a man for whom aloneness alone was the sole natural condition, aloneness alone the treasure worth treasuring.[8]

Monisha is equally alienated from her mother and husband and commits suicide. By becoming a commercial artist in which she was not really interested Amla alienates herself from her job. The alienation of Nirode, the protagonist, begins with the departure of Arun on a foreign trip. Nirode envies him for traveling in a train and going out of the dark pandemonium into the open space. Nirode returns from the station, brooding over his own helpless condition, over his wretched lonliness, contrasted to which stands Arun, a social, optimistic and intelligent person. Nirode fully alienated as he is, dislikes even marriage, family and all worldly relations hampering the healthy growth of his individuality. The female protagonist of the novel, Monisha is all the more lonely and sad. She even appreciates Nirode's sense of duty done in solitude — editing of newspaper and magazine, and helps him financially by so-called stealing from her-in-laws at the time of his serious illness. She herself wants to do her work alone, whether it be the cutting of vegetables, serving of food, or anything else. Married against her will to a 'blind moralist', a 'rotund, minute-minded and limited' official, addicted to quoting complacently and indiscriminately various authorities like Burke, Wordsworth, Gandhi and Tagore, Monisha finds her life a virtual imprisonment. She turns a sleepwalker, ghost, some unknown and dread entity (146). She is always 'eager to get away and be alone' (148). But finally Monisha's suicide is only an attempt to rebel against this meaningless existence and death-like isolation.

In *Where Shall We Go This Summer?* Anita Desai projects the theme of alienation in marital life in a more controlled and less exotic manner. The loneliness of the site is symbolic of the loneliness of a woman, a wife and a mother — a loneliness conditioned by family and society. Ironically, she is the modern version of the mythological Sita. She takes to smoking and neurotic outbursts obviously as a result of growing unbearable fever and fret of urban domesticity.

Sita does not want the fifth child nor is she prepared for an abortion. She wants to keep it, she does not want it to be born. That's why abandoning Bombay in terror leaving Raman in despair, she comes to Manori island in a mood of doubt and desperation. Her journey to this island is in fact a quest for integration of the self. She says, "I had to stay whole".

No doubt, the most recurrent themes are the problem of communication between husband and wife, between individual and the social world. Alienation in filial relation is a newly emerging idea of our modern society. Parents and children are equally alienated from each other. Desai's preoccupation with the individual, highlighting the drift between husband and wife, frustration, sense of failure and keen awareness of futility of existence radiates from most of her novels. Women are depicted as corked between their desire to assert individuality and their liability to stick to the traditional norms. Desai can be considered as the innovator of psychological study of alienated women in India.

Fourth type of alienation is alienation from society. Self-imposed isolation, which is sought by a person, when he or she tired of his or her busy life, willingly leaves the society in search of an alien place, such as in *Fire on the Mountain, Clear Light of Day* and *Fasting, Feasting*.

In *Fire on the Mountain*, both Nanda Kaul and her great-granddaughter Raka suffer from alienation – the former because, she was tired of her busy life and the latter by her instinct. Raka considers herself, shipwrecked and alone: Nanda Kaul, a vice chancellor's wife is living presently in utter solitude in her villa in the Simla hills, free from the claims and demands of the family servants and position. The individuality of her character makes her more alone and estranged. Madhusudan Prasad comments:

> "In fact this novel deals, in the main, with the loneliness and isolation as well as the resultant anger and agony in the deserted life of Nanda Kaul, who presents an unforgettable, pathetic portrait of old age."[9]

Nanda Kaul had prepared herself for a long time to enjoy the peace and beauty of this lonely place. The arrival of Raka appears as a danger to her self-imposed seclusion. Nanda wanted to be alone to have Carignano to herself in this period of her life, in stillness, but her isolation is to be intruded by one more strange character Raka. Raka places before her no demand or need, and desires only one thing — to be left alone and pursue her own secret life amongst the rocks and pines of Kasauli.[10] She is glad only when she is left alone to mount higher and climb the top of it. Raka is a complete and perfect solitary figure and solitude never disturbs her. It can be noticed that Mrs. Kaul is not an alien figure by nature or by birth. Her alienation is a thing thrust upon her by herself. She wants to live in solitude because she is fed up with the circumstances prevailing in her old house. But Raka seems to be born with it. Her isolation is natural and deliberate. Like her great grandmother, she wants herself to be left alone and pursue her own secret life amongst the rocks and pines of Kasauli.

Bim and Tara are another two truly alienated characters in the *Clear Light of Day*. The cause of their alienation lies in their nature and in the prevailing circumstances. Bim teaches in the college, to keep herself busy, having sacrificed her married life for the sake of family. She is alienated from everyone except Baba, who is himself a marble stone totally devoid of feelings and emotions. The lack of concern on the part of parents is responsible for producing ennui, restlessness and a sense of loneliness in her, Bim and Raja. Bim's growth from adolescence to adulthood brings her the experiences of anxiety, alienation, anguish and despair. She grows aware of the boredom and meaninglessness of her existence as she steps into youth. Plight of Raja and Tara is no different from hers. Bim is left alone to face the adverse circumstances into which the family has fallen, because Tara is often out to the Roshanara club or to a cinema show with the Misra sisters.

Desai's fiction continuously reveals a regular pattern in the sense that themes focus around alienation of her protagonists mostly resulting in psychosis and frustrations, though in the later novels socio-psychic analysis occurs more frequently as Andrew Kobson points out:

> "Alienation after *In Custody* and *Baumgartner's Bombay* gains a new artistic dimension. It grows into an estrangement of the adolescent in the rapidly changing spatio-temporal psychic continuum. The obsessions and fantasies of childhood no longer haunt the protagonists. They come as a fleeting impression of the past but not as a torturing obsession as in *Cry, the Peacock*. The sequestered world of the earlier novels now gives way to the socio-psychic entrapment of the

> self. The poetic outpourings of the long self are now replaced by a penetrating observation of the milieu."[11]

Anita Desai stresses the isolation and loneliness of her characters surrounded by their self-created problems. 'Their attempt to seek their refuge in their loneliness worsens their situation still more, for their solitary musings and their mobility quickens the process of their disintegration.'[12]

Her women grapple with social forces working against their individual identity. Her females are not anti-family and anti-male. They only try to overpower their solitary, marginal and oppressed situation. Their lives are full of turbulent passions, unfulfilled dreams and chaos.

The second section of the novel, *Fasting, Feasting* is narrated by Arun who is in U.S.A. for higher studies. The Patton family, with whom he stays during his summer break, is no less dysfunctional than his own. Old world had over indulgent and over interfering parents and here Mrs and Mr. Patton, Melasu and Rod have their own independent ways:

> "Everyone eats at different times and wants different means. We just don't get to eating together much now that they're grown. So I just fill the freezer and let them take down what they like, when they like."[13]

As a result the family members are alienated from each other. Though they have freedom and liberty yet this family disintegration causes emotional shocks for its members, liberty is more important here. But this excessive freedom has caused for malain bulimia, anorexia, depression, withdrawl, compulsive behaviour, hysteria, etc.

Her characters tend to be outsiders, torn between privacy and the powerful family and social bonds that both stifle and unite them. No doubt her dual heritage (half-Bengali, half-German) gives Desai an 'outsider' status. In her fictional work, characters often adopt escapist ways to cope with the banalities of everyday life. In *The Zigzag Way*, her 14th novel, Eric is a self-absorbed North American academic, bored by his studies, unable to commit to the fantasy of writing his novel. He may have reached premature domestic bliss with his girlfriend Em.

They seemed already to have reached a stage that many couples require 30 years to achieve. But Eric is beginning to stifle her with his possessiveness. Like Desai's earlier novels, *The Zigzag Way*, tackles stereotypical Western views of Indians, anti-semitism, the tensions of family life and the alienation of middle-class women. But at times, character loses out to detailed panoramic descriptions of Mexico and it is easy for readers' attention to flag. Only in the final section about Eric's grandmother, a proper, flesh-and-blood woman, does the novel stop being a poetic travelogue and really start to live. Otherwise it tells us again the story of loneliness and alienation of major characters, though with a difference. It is said, 'No other writer is so much concerned with the life of young men and woman in Indian cities as Anita Desai is.'[14]

Thus Desai's fictive world in the centrality of self is concentrated in terrifying isolation, finding it hard to reconcile with the world around 'self'. Her protagonists are constantly confronted with the stupendous task of defining their relation to themselves. Acceptable behavioural pattern is alien to them. The root is not far to find. Her central characters, by and large, have strange childhood from which they develop a negative self-image and aversion. The immediate result is their fragmented psyche to view world as a hostile place. For them the domestic life is not their world, rather, it is a trap where their individuality is endangered and thus complete lack of interest and dissonance in their relationship bring solitary confinements and show their reluctance to face reality. Desai's characters are misfit in their society largely because of either some defects in themselves or some evil in society. She is not so much interested in making philosophical, objective statements as in presenting the plight of an alienated individual and expressing compassion for him and disapproval for society.

References

1. Macquarria, John, *Existentialism,* Harmondsworth, Middlesex: Penguin Books Ltd., 1973, p. 169.
2. 'On the Meaning of Alienation', *American Sociological Review,* 24/6, December, 1959, p. 786.

3. Maini, D.S., 'The Achievement of Anita Desai', *Indo-English Literature*. Ed. K.K. Sharma, Ghaziabad: Vimal Prakashan, 1977, p. 218.
4. Taviss, I., 'Changes in the Form of Alienation', *American Sociological Review,* 34/1 February, 1969, pp. 46-47.
5. Desai, Anita, *Bye-Bye Blackbird,* Delhi: Hind Pocket Books, 1974, p. 216.
6. Sharma, R.S., *Anita Desai,* Delhi: Amold Heinmann, 1981, p. 72.
7. Iyengar, K.R.S., *Indian Writing in English,* Delhi: Sterling Publication, 1984, p. 466.
8. Desai, Anita, *Voices in the City*, Delhi: Hind Pocket Books, 1968, p. 24.
9. Prasad, Madhusudan, *Anita Desai the Novelist*, Allahabad: New Horizon, 1981, p. 78.
10. Desai, Anita, *Fire on the Mountain*, Bombay: Allied Publishers, 1977, p. 48.
11. Sinha, R.N. and Surjit Bose, 'Three Women Novelists', *Essays in Criticism,* Jaipur India: Book Enclave, 2004, pp. 85-86.
12. Raizada, Harish, *Indian English Novelist*, Delhi: K.K. Publications, 1996, p. 129.
13. Desai, Anita, *Fasting, Feasting*, London: Chatto and Windus, 1999, p. 193.
14. Kohli, Suresh, 'Indian Women Novelist in English', *Times Weekly*, 8 November 1970, p. 3.

Existentialist Vision of Anita Desai

11

The key note of existentialism is that 'existence precedes essence'. It grapples with the problems of man who is uprooted, lonely, forlorn, dismayed, anguished, fighting against destiny just to prove his identify. It is normally applied to writing that emphasizes man's responsibility for forming his own nature and that stresses the prime importance of personal decision, personal freedom and personal goals. The instinct of revolt and rebellion is at the very core of existentialism. The uncertainty of 'to be or not to be' haunts the mind of the character. Anita Desai has used this technique very beautifully to express the inner most thoughts and special characteristics of her major characters in her novels. Soren Kierkegaard stresses that uniting himself with God is necessary. Gabriel Marcel perceived that inhuman values had reduced man to a meaningless code of words. Karl Jaspers believes that morbid search for identity lies at the core of all philosophical thought while Heidegger's theory is that man is thrown in a particular situation, not chosen by him, but Sartre believes in the supremacy of man's existence in a Godless world. Albert Camus emphasizes individual experiences.

Anita Desai is mainly influenced by Jasper, Camus, Heidegger and Kafka. Her major characters are tormented by their fears and phobias as they feel circumscribed by the frightening conditions of their existence. Jaspers' existentialist concept of the border line situation figures prominently in the novels of Anita Desai. As in *Cry, the Peacock*, Maya's morbid and constant fear of death place her in a borderline situation. Monisha in *Voices in the City*, unable to bear the absurdity of her existence, commits suicide.

Anita Desai employs the stream of consciousness technique to depict Maya's moods, emotions, her existential despair, her search for identity and her dread of death. Maya is an existentialist character and world of feelings and emotions forms the core of Maya's existence. Temperamentally Maya and Gautama represent the polarities of emotion and reason which govern human existence. The clash between their irreconcilably different temperaments leads to marital disharmony in their lives. Maya grows aware of her emotional needs and of her vague sense of alienation from her husband. The undefined object that lurks in her subconscious mind is her childhood memory of an albino astrologer and his ominous prediction of her fate. As there is no emotional rapport between Maya and Gautama, she suffers in her loneliness. Left alone to herself, she reverts to her childhood memories. Through love, Maya desires to discover her identity and obtain a source of sustenance in her otherwise meaningless existence. But she fails in her attempt and finds her existence haunted by the fear of death. In her loneliness, even the serene sight of the moon does not soothe Maya's agitated mind. Instead, it makes her visualize the albino astrologer with his threatening prediction. This awareness, coupled with her superstitions belief in the words of the astrologer, becomes the source of her fears and her existential anxiety. Young and inexperienced as she is, she is unable to look at death as a fact of existence. Fear of death makes her acutely conscious of her deprivation of life and the sensuous world she loves.

Symbolically, the nightmare points out Maya's loneliness and the neurotic state of her mind. The bustling world of human activities does not engage her mind in a way so as to calm down her anguish. The thought of the train, which carries Gautama's father, makes her aware of her own misery and loneliness which haunt her incessantly. Later disillusionment with her friends, Leila and Pom, bring Maya back to her dreadful present and a painful realization that there is no one who may come to her rescue.

It is an irony of situation that the events of one evening become a source of oppression to Maya. The dinner and the cabaret after the dinner are meant to provide relief to Maya's troubled mind and diminish her loneliness, but both of them produce an effect quite the opposite of the intended one. She is overawed by the thoughts of fate and death and her sense of loneliness increases. The end of the cabaret makes her disillusioned about the false values of the human world. Her disillusionment is essentially existentialist.

Anita Desai depicts Maya's waiting for death through the Cry of the Peacock. Maya thinks of peacocks maddened by the monsoon clouds, as they dance and cry, giving calls to their mates. As she visualizes the fight in which peacocks engage themselves before they mate, Maya, realizes that life and death are the two poles of existence.

Maya is thankful to her mother-in-law and Nila who make her forget her nightmares and give a meaning to her life. But her peace comes to an end as soon as Nila and her mother announce their decision to go back to Calcutta. She becomes frightened as she thinks of her loneliness in their absence.

"What, the house empty again, and I alone with my horrors and nightmares? No ... God, to be alone with him again, my unknowing, unsuspecting and steel-hard adversary in this oneiric battle, all night, all day, for how many more nights, how many more days? God, to have to start counting them again, in utter loneliness?"[1]

Later, Maya's decision to murder Gautama is a difficult choice for her in the existentialist sense. In choosing death for Gautama she feels her responsibility towards him. The final section of Chapter VII of Part II of the novel describes the manner in which Maya leads Gautama to the roof of the house and hurls him down.

In Part III of the novel, the scene of action shifts from Delhi to Lucknow. Maya is brought to the house of her father by her mother-in-law and Nila. Both Nila and her mother await the arrival of Maya's father from Switzerland. Suddenly Maya's shrill and childish laughter changes into a desperate scream. Nila's mother rises to her feet and runs upstairs to help the frightened Maya, who jumps down the balcony and carries her mother-in-law along with her.

Her another novel *Voices in the City* is existential in character, for it explores the inward subjectivity of its main characters. As H.M. William observes:

> "It is an 'existential' novel that explore the inner climate of youth despair, epitomized by the over-acutely self-conscious Nirode, that quoter of camus, finding no meaning in his own life or in life at all. This existential 'angst' is duplicated in Monisha in whom it assumes a fatal rhythm from which Nirode was once narrowly saved but which in her reaches its inevitable end ...."[2]

The novel has been divided into four parts and each part deals mainly with the three major characters; Nirode, Monisha and Amla. Nirode is unique in his feelings and thoughts. He is disillusioned with the outward glitter of the worldly success which attracts and binds other minor characters like Jit Nair, Mr. Basu, Sunny, Bunty, Jimmy and others. Norode's belief in the negative attitude is sufficiently deep and he quotes Camus to prove the rightness of his belief:

> "I have been reading camus, you know. He says, In default of inexhaustible happiness, eternal suffering at least would give us a destiny. But we do not have even that consolation, and our worse agonies come to an end one day."[3]

He is a true existentialist. He moves from one failure to another in search of an abiding meaning in life. He is engaged in an unequal fight against the social and commercial values of life which the city of Calcutta symbolizes. Nirode recognises a lack of individuality and commitment to some higher purpose in life in all those who come and flatter him on the success of his magazine. Nirode's quest for identity and meaning in life leads him to a point where he perceives the worthlessness of all art.

Monisha craves for privacy because she is unable to share the world of her in-laws. Her in-laws are materialists to the core. The alienation between Jiban and her is rooted in their different temperaments, and Jiban's inability to understand and fulfil the emotional needs of his wife. Monisha is actually conscious of her adverse circumstances and suffers from a nervous anxiety which is certainly existentialist. She reads dismal meanings in everything she comes across. In this respect and in her alienation from her husband, she is akin to Maya (*Cry, the Peacock*).

The situation becomes unbearable to Monisha, but she does not find a way out. The dull and conventional mode of life of a Bengali woman offers her no challenge or some serious purpose of life. At the same time, she finds no escape from this meaningless existence. Monisha's anguish and despair increase in intensity with her discovery that in the absence of her present meaningless existence there is nothing she can put her faith in. There is neither love nor religious faith in her life which may support her gradually shattering self. Her lonely broodings bring her to the idea of death and her choice between death and mean existence:

> "But I have no faith, no alternative to my confused despair, there is nothing I can give myself to, and so I must stay. The family here, and their surroundings, tell me such a life cannot be lived — a life dedicated to nothing — that this husk is a protection from death. Ah yes, yes, then it is a choice between death and mean existence, and that surely, is not a difficult choice."[4]

Monisha is caught in a truly existentialist contingency when she is accused of stealing money from Jiban's wardrobe. It is true that she has taken this money but she has done so with honest intentions. She has never thought of stealing anything. She knew that Jiban had left money in the wardrobe, but by the time she remembered Nirode's hospital bill her husband had already left for his office. And Monisha cannot even dream of such a distrust, and the accusation of theft is brought against her. She is pained to think that the people, who themselves have a mean and animal existence, consider her so low as to be a thief. Apart from that Jiban utterly fails to understand her humiliation and her outraged feelings.

The third major character Amla arrives in Calcutta to find a career as a commercial artist, but her search for a career is transformed into an existentialist search for love and joy unmixed with pain and suffering. Amla becomes anxious about the unpleasant change that has come over Monisha and Nirode after their arrival in Calcutta. She begins to suffer from a sense of loneliness. Then Nirode takes her to meet his friend Dharma, who is a painter and, like Nirode, lives a life of anonymity at the outskirts of Calcutta. Dharma requests Amla to sit for a portrait, and she readily agrees to it. During the meetings she develops love for Dharma. But she is shocked to see the sketches because this dissection of her body in pictures made by Dharma suggest to her the loss of the wholeness of her being. She discovers a symbol of disintegration in it. Later Amla sees a difference in Dharma's paintings. He reveals to her that his paintings are his response to her 'charming confidences'. Meanwhile Monisha's death reveals to Amla the harsh aspect of her search for love and communion. She gives up her guest and chooses a life of compromise, even then she remains an existentialist. Her consciousness of the evil in life, her anxiety and anguish, her pursuit of absolute love, her despair at her failure in the search — all these make her a character of existentialist proportion. In fact, she commits intellectual suicide which is also a protest against the meaninglessness of existence.

Among the minor characters in the novel, Dharma is one of those who show existentialist values of life. Although the novelist does not depict his anxiety, anguish, and despair, she reveals these in his world — weariness the cause of Dharma's worldly pain and his distrust of the human world is rooted in the tragic event of the elopement of his daughter with his nephew. His existentialist subjectivity made him feel responsible towards his wife who could not bear the loss of her daughter. Feeling responsible towards her, he chose to leave Calcutta and settled at the city's outskirts. It was an effort to prevent his wife from becoming insane.

There is another aspect of it. Calcutta is not only the locale of the action of the novel, but also destroys those who come in conflict with its values. Nirode, Monisha, and Amla become aware of the challenges of existence only after their arrival in Calcutta.

Heidegger's concept of temporality manifests itself in Bim's character in *Clear Light of Day*. Nirode's desire to move from failure to failure and Sita's endeavour to retain her unborn baby is unique in itself. 'Camus' concept of the absurdity of human existence and his concept of the problem of murder and suicide are evident in the shape of Maya's murder of Gautama, Monisha's suicide and murder and rape of Ila Das, etc.

On the surface, *Bye-Bye Blackbird* treats of the problems of adjustment of Indian immigrants in England, but beneath the surface there is the existentialist theme of alienation and search for identity which the novelist presents through the different experiences and emotions of the three major characters, Adit, Sarah and Dev. The novelist reveals Adit's anguish and exasperation, which result from his sense of alienation, through his reactions to different people and situations. His sense of alienation acquires the dimensions of a morbidity that suffocates him. Adit's hatred of the London life and his sense of alienation intensify his homesickness. The war between India and Pakistan shocks Adit and he realizes that he is an Indian and decides to go back to India to achieve his real self:

> "I've got to go home and start living a real life. I don't know what real life there will mean — whatever it is it will be Indian, it will be my natural condition, my true circumstance ... Sarah, you know I've loved England more than you, I've often felt myself half-English, but it was only a pretence, Sally. Now it has to be the real thing. I must go ..."[5]

Adit's decision of returning to India is the decision of an existentialist. He makes his choice after coming to grips with the hard facts of his existence in London. His choice involves the subjectivity of an existentialist because he is aware of the pain of separation that Sarah and her parents must experience as a result of her going away with him.

In her marriage with Adit, Sarah has lost her parents, her former friends and the English world, but she has not been able to identify herself with the Indian world which she hoped her marriage would bring to her. In her anguish, she feels that she is neither English nor Indian. She is distressed to perceive the loss of her identity. She craves for a genuine identity and an authentic existence. The novelist brings out Sarah's anguish, despair, sense of alienation and the pathos of her life through her reactions to the various situations in her life. Desai reveals Sarah's existentialist potentialities through her rejection of Miss Edwina Morris's offer of a lucrative career in contrast to her voluntary choice of accompanying Adit to India. Her existentialist individuality is revealed through her reaction to his suggestion that she should be considerate to her mother who wishes that she should stay in England instead of going to India. Desai also depicts Dev's dilemma, agony and sense of isolation through the latter's instinctive responses to the London life. Dev keeps wavering between acceptance and rejection of England. He is unable to decide whether she should stay in England or go back to India where he hopes to find 'security, status and freedom'.

Dev's desperate search for employment is an organic part of the theme and structure of the novel. He comes to grips with the harsh realities of existence in his unsuccessful search for a respectable job. It is through this search that the novelist brings out Dev's frustration, anguish, despair and frightening sense of alienation. Finally Dev decides to stay in England, and does so on the strength of his inner conviction. Adit's departure from England provides him a job in the former's office, and he shifts to the flat vacated by Adit and Sarah.

In *Where Shall We Go This Summer?* Desai depicts the tumultuous state of Sita's mind through the symbols of rain and fierce monsoon wind. She swings between doubt and faith, as the rain and wind become fierce and then calm down. She feels insecure and worries about the baby she is carrying. In agony and despair, she cries out to Menaka and Karan. They appear to her as unearthly presence distressed by the evil forces of the storm. She feels that she does not belong to anyone and suffers in her loneliness. The news of Raman's arrival gives a blow to Sita's false sense of complacency.

Sita's sense of freedom enjoins on her the difficult task of choosing between the two courses of life. She can either live a life governed by her own instincts and impulses or return to a life of compromise and dull routine. She judges her situation, and chooses to live according to the values and standards laid for her by Raman. The fact that Sita consciously makes this choice is suggested by the image of the sea bird which returns to its nest at sunset. Her subjectivity to others is suggested by her thoughts of care for her yet to be born infant. As she packs her luggage and prepares for her return to the city, she feels herself like a player at the end of the performance. She visualizes her stay on the island as a dramatic episode. Sita contrasts her life in the city with her experience of uninhibited life on the island. This contrast puzzles her. She wonders whether she has not been playing roles in her city life, while her days spent on the island have given her an experience of authentic existence. She fails to understand which half of her life was real and which unreal? In her attempt to discover the fact, she achieves a solution to the mystery of existence. She perceives that illusion and reality cannot be separated from each other. She discovers that neither sea nor sky were separate or contained. She learns that existence is possible only by synthesizing the illusion and the reality of life. Her existentialist exploration of the self ends in a positive understanding of life.

In *Clear Light of Day* Bakul arrives in the Das family at a juncture when the parents have already died and Raja, suffering from tuberculosis, is confined to his room. After the sudden death of the father in a car accident, Das family comes to financial constraints. Bim is the only person to look after sick Raja, neurotic Aunt Mira and retarted Baba. Tara's marriage with Bakul releases her from her fears and anxiety about her future. It puts an end to her sense of ennui and loneliness at least for the time being. Finally, she marries Bakul and goes away to discover love and meaning in life.

A character of truly existentialist proportion, Bim is the central figure in the novel. It is through her consciousness that the novelist reveals the impact of time on human relationship. Her growth from adolescence to adulthood brings her the experiences of anxiety, alienation, anguish and despair. But her sufferings do not annihilate her personality. She lives her life in accordance with her own set of values, and ultimately evolves into a being who is capable of transcending the existential traumas of life. R.S. Sharma observes:

> "... the existential anxiety and the guest for self-hood that is pervasive in her earlier novels is transformed here in a new concept of self-hood. Bim achieves her identity and her 'self' not in isolation but in togetherness, not in rejection but in acceptance, not in withdrawal but in positive commitment."[6]

Bim grows aware of the boredom and meaninglessness of her existence as she steps into youth. Home atmosphere instills in her mind a sense of boredom and despair from which Bim fails to find a way out. She is unable to find the means by which she can give a meaning to her existence. Bim's awareness of the meaning of time in relation to eternity puts an end to her search for belonging, and completes the evolution of her self. It also brings out her existentialist subjectivity and justifies her existence in terms of her own frame of values.

Desai portrays Raja's existential sufferings of the partition of India. Like Nirode in *Voices in the City*, Raja is a rebel, but he fails to acquire the existentialist dimension of the former. It is, again, the indifference and lack of love and communication on the part of his parents that makes him sense a hollowness in his life.

Through the character of aunt Mira, the novelist reveals the meaninglessness of existence in the absence of love and relatedness. Aunt Mira's life is a spectacle of human misery and sufferings. Though her sufferings are existential, she cannot be called an existentialist for she does not have a set of her own values and lacks the will to choose a free course of life. It is Bim, the central figure in the novel, who comes out as an existentialist and transcends the absurdity of life through her sanity and wisdom.

Anita Desai was influenced by one another important existentialist Nietzsche. He declared that 'God is dead for the modern man'. He had no trust in reason because it makes man a calculating coward and withdraws him from an active participation in life. Sartre also believes in the supremacy of man's existence, in a Godless world. He declared that 'man is alone in a Godless universe'. Anita Desai's novels are apt illustrations of these aspects of the existentialist view of life. In her novels, she has ably dwelt upon such existentialist themes as maladjustment, alienation, absurdity of human existence, quest for the ultimate meaning in life. Decision, detachment, isolation and time as a fourth dimension focusing on how men and women in the contemporary urban milieu are bravely 'struggling against or helplessly submitting to the rentless forces of absurd life'. As for the themes in her novels, she has been deeply influenced by the existentialists. Desai's achievement consists in beautifully recording the emotional turbulence and chaos of her oppressed protagonist with a remarkable fidelity and seriousness. A fear of uncertainty hangs on the minds of her characters because they visualize some tragedy that threatens their existence. They encounter the harsh reality of existence single handedly. Deven Sharma, the protagonist of *In Custody* gets an insight into his authentic existence through his dread of being ruined and he finally gains the courage of his convictions.

Deven is frantically busy in pursuit of his ideal, but the fact is that he also stands in the moment and passes through the agonizing states of anxiety, dread and concern. In describing Deven's predicament in relation to time and place, Anita Desai reveals the existential significance of these two factors which govern all existence. Although she does not mention causation, the third basic factor governing existence, her emphasis on the eternal aspect of time and place clearly suggests that even the realization of existentialist awareness is possible within the limits of time and space only. Apart from the problem of choosing the appropriate time and place for the interview Deven's diffidence is another obstacle that stands in the way of the fulfillment of his ambition. Deven's repeated failures in his enterprise leads him to mood of frustration and despair. Torn by his ambition and his lack of resources, he is filled with anguish and despair, which are genuinely existentialist, but he cherishes an illusion about his free will. He is yet unaware of the sense of moral responsibility that results from the strength of one's inner convictions, and in the absence of which, use of free will reads only to illusion or absurdity.

Towards the end of the novel, the hour of daybreak symbolizes the dawn of existentialist awareness in Deven. He becomes conscious of the true nature of his predicament. As he rushes back to its home, he stops only to pull a branch of thorns from under his foot. It is through the symbol of thorns that Anita Desai crystallizes the change in Deven's attitude to the assault of existence. As Anita Desai said, "His present misfortune is no more than a prick of thorns to him and he has the courage of an existentialist to face it".[7]

Indeed, as a creative artist her central preoccupation is with the exploration and evaluation of the subjective reality of human individual. Her novels bear the testimony to this fact. Her concern with human subjectivity naturally involves her interest in the existentialist predicament of modern man. Therefore, a study of her treatment of the existentialist problems of life is central to the correct understanding and appraisal of her writings. She is often seen as a somewhat Western existential experimenter who deals with many existentialistic problems and predicaments. She does portray her characters as individuals, "facing single handed, the ferocious assault of existence".[8] The basic problem for her characters is now to exist in society, and yet maintain their individuality. It is to the credit of Anita Desai that in concentrating on the inner being of human individual, she has given a new dimension to the Indian English novel. Inevitably, her writings have a universal appeal and will surely stand the test of time.

References

1. Desai, Anita, *Cry, the Peacock*, New Delhi: Orient Paperback, 1980, pp. 162-163.
2. Williams, H.M., *Indo-Anglian Literature 1800-1970: A Survey*, New Delhi: Orient Longman, 1976, p. 91.
3. Desai, Anita, *Voices in the City*, Delhi: Hind Pocket Books, 1968, p. 40.

4. *Ibid.*, p. 122.
5. Desai, Anita, *Bye-Bye Blackbird*, New Delhi: Orient Paperbacks, 1985, p. 232.
6. Sharma, R.S., *Anita Desai*, New Delhi: Amold-Heinmann, 1981, p. 139.
7. Desai, Anita, *In Custody*, London: Heinmann, 1984.
8. Desai, Anita, Interview by Yashodhra Dalmia, *Times of India*, April 28, 1979.

Social Consciousness of Anita Desai

12

Anita Desai as a novelist is known for her non-conformist and anti-establishment views. Her characters do not conform to social values. She appears more interested in creating characters who are 'Nay Sayers'. But at the same time they are conscious about their social set-up. They know that they can fight with society but there is no escape and they will always remain a part of it. Her characters appear to be socially maladjusted. N.R. Gopal says: "Since Anita Desai specialises in creating the 'Nay Sayers' in her novels, it is but natural that her characters perforce come in conflict with society. They do not fit smugly in the socially allotted slots, they are no mere cogs in the machinery called society. Thus they are misfits as social beings."[1]

Anita Desai has not limited herself to the domestic sphere only but at times she goes beyond the limits of family exploring and portraying social prejudices and perverted social values that affect the individual. She herself said:

> "There are those who can handle situations and those who can't ... and my stories are generally about those who cannot. They find themselves trapped in situations over which they have no control."[2]

It is Anita Desai's sense of involvement in the social life of India alongwith her sensibility and keen observation that brought her international acclaim with her very first novel.

Anita Desai is a subjective writer and believes that total objectivity is impossibility. Her dependence on the instinct is so great that when she gets down to write her novel she has no plot in her mind. Her novels gradually and instinctively take their own shape. Very little happens on the physical level. Her characters reveal her vision of life. They share her perception and they set out in quest of meaning. Desai's main preoccupation is to explore the inner world. But the novelist cannot remain indifferent to the problems of the world in which he or she lives. Desai also deals with the changing contemporary situation and presents various social aspects and problems through her fiction. Her fiction fulfills the requirement as we find the details of Indian social life. All the varied experiences of people are woven together into a meaningful and effective design. Her novels are certainly reflective of social realities from a psychological perspective. She constantly highlights her character's tracts, peculiar and tender instincts as crushed by the dehumanization of society. Desai portrays women as not totally cut off from families and societies but women who remain within these orbits and protest against monotony, injustice and humiliation. Woman in her novels is not a mere goddess or a robot but a self-actualising and self-realising individual in the society. Unlike the other Indian English novelists, Anita Desai's predominant concern is not with society or social forces only, rather she is more concerned with the individual psyche and its interaction with social values.

When we interact with the gallery of women characters in Desai's world, we notice that all of them belong to the upper class of urban India. Economic independence is not an important issue for them. Only Bim works for a living. Yet, all of them directly or indirectly question the accepted codes of a patriarchal society. They refuse to unquestioningly accept the roles ordained for them by traditional social conventions. To them, even seemingly benevolent institutions like marriage or the joint family can become farcical or coercive. They go against the flow; they are driven unto some extremity of despair and turn against or make a stand against the general current of their respective societies.

Anita Desai's protagonists are unhappy with society in general and cannot communicate with the social milieu on one pretext or the other. They feel disturbed by the pretentiousness and violence in society and nurture utopian dreams. Society demands compromises, which they egotistically abhor. They are all social misfits (Maya, Sita, Nirode, Monisha, Deven, Hugo, Uma, etc.) and withdraw from society. The strained conjugal and familial relationship hampers their normal growth. Most of her characters (Adit, Hugo, Deven) are victims of strained relationship with society and with family. Desai creates characters who are non-conformist and anti-establishment and do not get attuned to the social values and relations. Her characters are mere cogs in the machinery called society. They feel observed and trapped when society imposes its norms on them and demand conformity and on refusal by them ostracizes them. Her characters play this existential drama but none of them outlines the situation.

Voices in the City is perhaps Anita's first novel of social atmosphere and locale. The novelist here ventures to juxtapose the external world with the inner one. Desai successfully captures and delineates the spirit of the surrounding place and social values. The focal point in the novel is the corrosive effects of an indifferent metropolis, Calcutta. The conflict shown here is social and Calcutta is painted as the creator of urban maladies. There is air of disillusionment, despair and perplexity around Nirode. He hates the world, which offers him nothing but endless waiting. This may be the reason why Nirode does not want to communicate with society and the world.

Desai explains various social factors connected with the climate, culture, religion, etc., in *Bye-Bye Blackbird*. Dev labels Adit as a masochist for living in rain, mildew and mud. While mocking the Englishmen's guarding their privacy, tongue and throat, Dev forgets that it is the demand of the climate. It being wet and cold, they remained in their houses and protected the throat by wearing a tie around it. In fact Dev fails to establish a link with the land and the society and therefore has to face many cultural shocks disturbing him greatly. Actually Dev represents those immigrants who cannot severe their cultural roots and yet make an effort to strike new roots in an alien society and eventually grow culturally and socially alienated. The novel, on the whole, seems as a metaphor indicating every person's difficulty of making a choice when caught in the contrary alternatives in his social life.

Anita's monumental novel, *In Custody* (1984) reveals individual nature, the relationship between people and the relationship of the individual to society. In doing so Mrs. Desai evokes the dominant attributes of contemporary Indian society through the character of Deven who acquires symbolic connotations besides his role as central figure. The aesthetic experience has a great cathartic effect on Deven and this realization indicates Deven's growth as a social human being.

The Village by the Sea depicts the miserable poverty of the village people on the one side and the impact of industrialization of the villages on the poor people on the other. In a special introductory note, Anita Desai states that the story is based on fact. That is a real village on the western coast of India. Leila and Hari have corporate family loyalty. The family motive is used in a positive and elemental manner. Supremacy of the family motive is another weighty theme in the novels. The escape from family has not made Hari cruel and selfish enough to forget his native place and family. Anita Desai's attitutde to society and human beings is humanistic and classic. Her mirror to society is not doctrinaire or existentialist, it is loving too. Anita Desai has not created a region for the setting of her novels like Hardy's *Wessex* and R.K. Narayan's *Malgudi* but she places her characters in various cities and gives a complete pen-picture of the locale, be it Calcutta, Bombay, London or Delhi. The environment has always a crucial role to play. The sordidness, the brutality and the sheer dreariness of the physical world is the force against which Anita Desai's characters revolt. They find that they are unable to fulfil social expectations or play their ordained roles. Hence, they face a sense of rootlessness, isolation and alienation. Maya needed contact, relationship, communion with society to soothe the disturbed, agitated mind but in vain presents all the problems and sorrows of an alienated being in modern society. Monisha feels totally neglected, isolated and lonely even in a bustling, joint family in crowded Calcutta. Thus from the very beginning what Desai portrays is the deeply felt and suffered rebellion against the entire system of social relationships. She looks around and refuses to accept anymore the myths created and nourished by a male ordained society. The insensibility of the people around her and the societal pressure points shrink her capacity for communality, cooperation and communication. Desai shows us how the women have repeatedly to repress their emotions, their finer impulses, due to a social code, not of their own making.

In *Journey to Ithaca* Sophie and Matteo represent the socio-religious aspect of Indian society. Matteo, Sophie's husband burns inside to possess oriental knowledge and to live his life according to the traditions of Indian society. Sophie is quite logical and modern as to believe the healing power of saints of India. She considers people's faith in such gurus, a sign of backwardness. This novel deals with the issue of traditional social pattern of Indian society and modern culture of the West.

Anita Desai's latest novel, *Fasting, Feasting* suggests that oppression of women in India today is directly related to the corrupt customs and culture. The novel throws light on certain social practices of modern India. In the first point there is elation over the birth of a boy. The status of woman is raised when she bears a son. Desai's subversion of this manifestation of patriarchal values is apparent in her tone. The deprivation of a girl child of her schooling and studies might have been normal in middle-class families. Marriage is seen as the only career for the girl and home is her confinement. The novel exposes the degrading and exploitative nature of the dowry system. The novel shows that dowry has become means of procuring money and much deception is practiced to obtain it. The treatment and humiliation meted out to a girl by her in-laws is realistically portrayed.

'Anamika had been beaten. Anamika was beaten regularly by her mother-in-law while her husband stood by and approved or at least, did not object. Anamika spent her entire time in the kitchen, cooking for a family, that was so large that meals were served in shifts — first the men, then the children, finally the women. She herself ate the remains in the pots, before scouring them.'[3]

Daughters in this society are denied autonomy. Uma and her sister Aruna are not given any privacy, as daughters are seen as possessions to be used in a manner as suits the parents. In the third attempt of marrying, Uma was married to a man who is many years her senior and who already has a wife and many children. The picture of the traditional society of India is painted here in dark colours. The novel throws light on the false dichotomy between the private and public life in this society.

Thus we have found that Desai's protagonists are, in general, unhappy with the society they live in. They are unable to communicate with social milieu around them. The novels of Anita Desai are critical essays on man's relationship to society. Her protagonists possess a defiant individuality. They discard the commonplace conformity and stick to their own vision of life. Desai wants to attract attention towards the subordination of women to men in the Indian milieu. Her novels reinforce the perception that woman's status *vis-à-vis* man is not ordained by God rather it has been determined and conditioned by society and is therefore always open to fresh determination as the social order revolves. Desai does not remain untouched from the central issue of conflict between the traditional social pattern and the modern scientific pattern. The role of inorganic forces of society brings newness in Desai's fiction. The female protagonists like Maya, Sita, Monisha, Leila, have been shown suffering because of their failure to reconcile with their social surroundings and social obligations. The social forces remain a riddle to be solved by her characters.

References

1. Anand, T.S., *Images of Women in Fiction*, New Delhi: Creative Books, 2003, p. 40.
2. Rao, Madhushree Sinha, 'Silent Spaces of Inner Vastness', *Times of India*, Delhi, 18 June 1992.
3. Desai, Anita, *Fasting, Feasting*, London: Chatto and Wndus, 1989.

13

Desai's Women Characters and Power Relation between Sexes

Anita Desai's purpose as a writer is to see her women characters as humans with their weaknesses and potentialities who are indeed caught in the web of their own compulsions. Her novels have been examined as the manifesto of female predicament and creative release of the feminine sensibility. Her feminism is not anti-male and her women need man's loving company and aspire for the bliss and thrill of life which are ever denied to them. She looks at the predicament of women and visualizes life for a woman as a series of obligations and commitments. In addition to existentialistic reality of life she evokes the sentiment and sensibility of women for their role and respect in society. She closely examines the emotional world of womankind. She sets herself to voice the voiceless miseries and helplessness of millions of married women, tormented by existentialist problems and predicaments. She focuses on how her heroines, in the contemporary urban milieu are bravely struggling against or helplessly submitting to the relentless forces of absurd life. Desai has natural preference for writing about women characters. Although she is pre-occupied with the theme of incompatible marital couples yet we come across different kinds of women characters in her novels.

Anita Desai portrays women as not totally cut off from familial and social ties but women who remain within these orbits and protest against monotony, injustice and humiliation. Her heroines are not mere goddesses or robots but they are individuals. She has presented both the extremes. If at one extreme there are sensitive women characters, on the other, we also find thick skinned women with blunt sensibility. In her very first novel *Cry, the Peacock* we find examples of two extremes. The dance of the peacock acquires a sinister significance to the heroine of the novel. Maya, the heroine is a neurotic young woman whose sanity is fast disintegrating under the pressure of marital discord and of certain vague but frightening childhood memories. Maya, a spoiled and pampered daughter of a wealthy brahman is married to Gautama, a rather insensitive advocate who fails to understand her sensitive nature. She suffers from father obsession and looks for the typical father image in her husband. Here Desai has dealt with a sterile woman, highly sensitive and emotional lady, Maya. Though Gautama loves her in his own way, yet, Maya is never satisfied and happy. She feels that Gautama never cares for her and does not have any feelings for her. Being childless she is much attached to the dog. She comes before us as a hypersensitive woman, an introvert. Maya on the one extreme is fragile, with deep cultural roots and refined sensibilities. On the other extreme is her friend Pom who absolutely does not bother and is a typical woman with love for clothes, jewellery, colour, and looks. Another woman character is Maya's friend, Leila who is married to a tubercular man. She is gloomy and ascetic wearing no jewellery. She is a contrast to Pom. *Voices in the City* articulates Monisha's plight and psychic life and intimately shows the women as female birds in the cages. Monisha dies, screaming for life, for the first experience of real feeling of pain awakens in her a desire to live. She loves to see herself as an unfettered individual and not to become at any stage a complacent, tame wife who adjusts herself to a glided cage.

Sarah in the *Bye-Bye Blackbird* is alienated from her parents. Desai treats Sarah with the sensitivity of a woman, always aware of those forces that change her destiny as a female. Even with all her acceptance Sarah remains an outsider in her own chosen world.

Sarah is laconic, reserved, self-possessed, non-syllabic, quiet and meek like gazelles. She lets her husband dominate her and take all decisions, even very important ones concerning her, without consulting her. Sarah's calm nature is also seen in the way she treats her mother's letter which is full of outrage, ill-will and warning.

'Sita' in *Where Shall We Go This Summer?* shudders at the idea of giving birth to a fifth child. She withdraws into her psyche of childhood days on the magic island. She lives in the world of fantasy thinking that going to the island and thereby to the world of childhood she could prevent the biological process of delivery. It is a strong case of neuroticism. Finally she consents to the advice of her husband and comes back to Bombay to deliver. She is irrational, childish and petulant. Through the character of Sita and Maya, Desai has portrayed the feminine psyche of neurotic women. They might be called sub-normal if not abnormal. Anita Desai's psychological probing of the women is that she includes females of different age groups. It is not that she confines herself to the young or the middle aged. She has also explored the psyche of girl Raka in *Fire on the Mountain*.

Sarla in the novel *In Custody* is usual, ordinary, compromising and a lady of normal temperament. That's why she is not like Maya or Sita or Amla, the typical heroines of Anita Desai. Sarla is a typical Indian housewife. She belongs to lower income group as her husband Deven is a temporary lecturer in a local college of Mirpore near New Delhi. Sarla's material life is not at all happy. Her responsibilities as a mother makes her frustrated as she has no money in her hands. Her predicament is the lot of every second Indian woman. Sarla may not be the heroine in the sense Desai has Maya, Monisha, Amla and others, but her alienation, boredom and loneliness makes her a typical Desai's character. Sophie in *Journey to Ithaca* is a devoted wife. Her rational mind and logical outlook on life demanded scientific answers from the Mother and others too. As a normal woman Sophie becomes jealous of Matteo's affinity to the Mother. She tries to isolate herself from Matteo's world by listening to her old tapes and stays busy with her separate world of pregnancy. Giacomo, a baby boy is her first child and after some years, staying in the ashram, she gives birth to baby girl, Isabel. Now she is worried about her kid's future as a mother and as a lady her tension builds up with the growing information of her husband for the Mother. The suspicion in the mind of a wife regarding the presence and role of other women in a man's life is authentically depicted.

In fact Desai closely examines the emotional world of her heroines. She constantly highlights their individual traits, peculiar and tender instincts as crushed by the dehumanization of the society. Desai's heroines feel exposed, vulnerable and utterly isolated. They strain and shake the bars of their cage which is their home. But they do not contemplate leaving the threshold of their cage-home even in their wildest, bitterest moods as they are family women.

Next in the line is Uma in Desai's another novel *Fasting, Feasting*. Uma is a plain, simple, uneducated, spinster daughter from a close unit orthodox Indian family. She is trapped at home, smothered by the overbearing parents and their traditions. Maya is depressed because of her loneliness, Monisha because of lack of privacy and solitude, Sarah because of her alienation from her own people but Uma's depression is thrust upon her from within. She is a loving soul for whom fate has apportioned loneliness. Uma is the elder daughter and she has to stay away from school after the birth of her brother:

> "We are not sending you back to school Uma. you are staying at home to help with Arun."[4]

The less valued child, Uma, proves to be as unlucky in the matters of wedding. The family stopped caring for this defeated girl. Mama tried hard to 'dispose off' Uma and her photograph was sent to everyone who advertised in the matrimonial columns, finally she was married to a man who seemed to be as old as Uma's own father. But her husband goes away and does not turn up and somehow the marriage is cancelled and annulled. Having cost her parents two dowries, without a marriage to show in return, Uma is considered to be ill fated by all without any fault of her own. She grows depressed and never tries to assert herself in the family. Aruna, married in a good family of Bombay, dominates everybody. Her assertiveness highlights Uma's depressed nature. Uma is reduced to the status of a maid servant in the family, a liability. Uma is kept confined to the house sans friends, enjoyment or entertainment. She is kept busy in a thankless job, not out of choice but compulsion. Her aged parents seem to be lucky to have an attendant free of cost. She has no idea of escape from the trap situation or at least she can never visualize it in the form of a career.

Another character, Anamika was simply lovely as a flower is lovely, soft, petal skinned, bumble bee-eyed, pink lipped, always on the verge of bubbling dove like laughter and with loving smiles. Daughter of a wealthy lawyer, Anamika won a scholarship to Oxford but it was used for the marriage purpose only. Her marriage to a man, so much older than herself, with higher degree, suffering from Oedipal complex, marred her life. She was beaten regularly by her mother-in-law while husband stood by and approved. She spent her entire time in the household jobs. Her own parents were not ready to protect her. She was tortured for twenty-five years before she turned into ashes at the age of forty-five.

After analyzing all the novels of Desai we find that Anita Desai is least interested in pre-marital relationship between man and woman but deals with the problem of marital relationship in all its dimensions and manifestations. Marriage, which is a means of self-fulfilment and self-knowledge, eludes most women and fails to meet their anticipations and aspirations.

Gautama and Maya in *Cry, the Peacock* have a fanatic adherence to their beliefs and ideas and neither is prepared to relent. Gautama's rationality silhouetted against Maya's fancies, speaks the inharmonious relationship between the two. One small gesture of tender understanding from her husband could make Maya fulfilld. But Gautama is 'no romantic' and having quoted forgets the couplet. This temperamental incompatibility rules out the possibility of an intimate relationship between the two. Maya wished to have an exclusive interest in the physical pleasures of life. The point of clash between Maya and Gautama is inherent in their respective mythic names. Maya wished to go to south to see Kathakali troupe of dancers, Gautama coldly tells her to wait till the group comes to Delhi for performance. She likes to go to the hills to escape the summer as she used to go in her childhood, but Gautama remains busy and is never perturbed by the scorching heat around. The gap of communication between husband and wife is felt throughout the novel. Both Maya and Gautama disagree over trifles and are tiff with each other. Maya considers her marriage to be a 'hopeless regret' and a 'broken affair'. She feels a torture, guilt, dread and imprisonment within the four walls of her private hell. Maya also complains that Gautama is unconcerned about her misery, her physical and psychological demands. When Maya desires a close contact with him to ease her anguish, he preaches the doctrine of non-attachment from 'Gita' to her. Gautama detaches himself from the sense objects so much, that he does not involve in any physical contact with his wife. On the other hand Maya involves herself in sensual life to the extreme of such attachment that her past romantic life becomes an obsession, which resulted in homicide and suicide.

Gautama's error lies in his rigidity. He desires to change Maya as he thinks she ought to be instead of understanding her as she actually is. He tries to teach her his own ways and his own philosophy but Maya's killing of Gautama symbolically suggests that Maya (illusions) overpowered and destroyed Gautama, the personification of lopsided view of detachment. Gautama symbolizes the modern, educated emancipated Indian who is extremely logical, dutiful and balanced. But somehow it became the reason of total alienation between husband and wife.

The other types of man-woman relationship is also discussed through various minor characters. Nila, Gautama's sister is not leading a happy married life. She comes to Gautama because she wants a divorce from her husband but Gautama is not in favour of this. Leila, Maya's friend marries a man suffering from tuberculosis but feels satisfied. Pom, another friend, though satisfied with her husband, does not want to live with her in-laws. In short, the dominant theme of male-female dichotomy has been dealt with successfully by Desai in this novel.

Voices in the City presents a moving picture of Monisha's married life. Her husband Jiban ranks even lower on the scale. To Monisha, her marriage is the most excruciating of all social institutions that traps and tortures her isolated sensitive psyche.

"They put me away in a steel container, a thick glass cubicle, and I have lived in it all my life, without a touch of love or hate or warmth in one."[5]

Monisha is an archetype of Indian woman and suffers quietly to death. Her relationship with her husband is characterized only by loneliness and lack of communication. Jiban is the prisoner of a conventional culture in which a woman's most important roles are child bearing, cooking, cutting vegetables, sieving food and brushing small children's hair under the authority of a stern mother-in-law. Finally Monisha's claustrophobia and exasperation ends in suicide. Monisha's childlessness is the major cause of her suffering in marriage. But she also finds it very difficult to detach herself from a worthless marriage. Jiban gives a final blow to whatever little meaning their relationship might have had when he accuses Monisha of being a thief.

The ill-assorted couple of Sita and Raman in *Where Shall We Go This Summer?* is confronted with the same problem of male-female dichotomy. Sita represents a world of emotional and feminine sensibility while Raman is a practical man with an active view of life. Sita's problem is mainly domestic but the feeling of emptiness in Sita's life gives it an existential dimension. The temperamental incompatibility of the couple further aggravates Sita's plight. Sita desires to be drenched in the rain of human emotions and love from her husband instead of running after sensual pleasures and maddening luxuries of life. She wants to attain the love of legendary figures. But her pregnancy totally shatters her. She develops differences with her husband and decides neither to give birth nor to undergo an abortive surgery but to keep it undelivered. She does not seek separation from Raman in spite of being much frustrated in love. But finally she recovers from her existential dilemma. She feels that the gap of communication between Raman and herself is after all not unbridgeable. She does not take any drastic steps as suicide but prepares to face life and find a solution. In fact Anita Desai has stressed on harmonious marital relationship in which women's individuality and identity are honoured.

Monisha in *Voices in the City* is married into a family very unlike her own. Monisha is absolutely unhappy in Jiban's house. The young, dreamy-eyed, romantic Monisha finds marriage to Jiban a very stifling experience for marriage turns her into a woman who keeps a diary.... Traceless and meaningless. Like Maya, Monisha also seeks a release from her marital-discard by an extreme step.

In *Fire on the Mountain*, Nanda Kaul's relationship with her husband is seen only through her own reminiscences and these are never pleasant. She had managed to maintain a cool exterior and keep up the appearance of being a devoted and efficient wife, inspite of being aware of her husband's liaison with Miss David. Even their house she considered to be 'his house, never hers'. She accepts her situation in life more readily than Maya, Monisha or Sita. It is only after his death that she is able to break away from the demands that her family made on her and move alone to Carignano. Marriage was certainly an unpleasant experience for her as it is for Raka's mother too.

In Custody presents Deven, an impoverished temporary lecturer, in Mirpore. He ignores the static realities of his married life as well as his household responsibilities. Sarla, his wife is a simple middle class girl. Deven follows the world of imagination even at the cost of his family life:

> "Deven had been more a poet than a professor when he married Sarla. He had only been taken as a temporary lecturer and still had confidence in his verse and for the wife of a poet she seemed too prosaic."[6]

There have been differences between them in the matters of running a household. Deven is pre-occupied in his pursuit of Urdu poetry than having interest in his family. Deven aspires for an intellectual environment while Sarla longs for a luxurious life. Sarla's dreams are shattered by her marriage to man of academic profession and moving to a small town of Mirpore outside the capital. "Deven understands the suffering of his wife but he has pinned all his thoughts on poetic consciousness. He keeps himself at a distance from his wife to avoid yoking together their joint disappointment. Deven has at least his poetry with him, Sarla has nothing and so there was an added accusation and bitterness in her looks. To live on a lecture's salary, can be an oppressive experience and though Deven and Sarla have no choice, it has given their marriage a permanent quality of despair."[7]

Deven's sense of despair on the professional front finds its ripples in his domestic life. Deven is fully aware of his personal inadequacy and incompetence in fulfilling his wife's desires and dreams on the mutual level. Obviously, the familial and social factors generate into him powerful compliant tendencies. Sarla is a plain penny pinching congenitally pessimistic wife who presents the picture of an abandoned wife. In her company 'Deven feels as if he were a stranger, an interloper'. He is pained to notice the dereliction of his marriage. Sarla's aspirations are thwarted in marriage. Deven's miserable life with unsympathetic and sarcastic wife makes him think that he looks like a caged animal in a zoo. He thinks that his marriage, his family and his job have placed him in the cage and there is no way out. Here Anita Desai accurately depicts the socio-economic problems of a middle class family causing tension between man and woman.

Psychologically most subtle and most complicated is the relationship of Nur and Imtiaz in *In Custody*. Imtiaz, an intellectual, second wife, picked from a brothel in one of the earlier poetic sessions of Nur, is both an adorer and adversary of Nur. Two opposite elements compose the character of Imtiaz. One is the fascination, the other is the jealousy for the poet. She has been successful in winning Nur's heart by her intellect, beauty and skill in singing and dancing. Imtiaz has a desire to compete with her husband. Nur, knowing the fangs of venomous malice, is yet in love with her and cannot go against her will. His another wife Safia is simple and pragmatic and love for Nur is her sole motive.

In *Journey to Ithaca*, the central issue is the search for truth, and the problem between husband and wife. There is spiritual incompatibility. Sophie, a German journalist follows her husband Matteo to India and wanders with him from one ashram to another. As a young wife she has desires to fulfil but this is not possible in the shifty and unruly environment of the ashrams.

She suffered from her husband's disgust and showed signs of nervousness and insecurity. Matteo had joined the life of an ashramite for unveiling the secrets of life while Sophie followed her husband only to share his life and nothing more attracted her as an ashramite. The dichotomy between Matteo and Sophie assumes alarming dimensions as latter's pregnancy advances and Matteo advancing on path of spirituality. According to O.P. Budholia, "Matteo represents all that comes from the heart, while Sophie represents all that comes from the mind."[8]

"Sophie, returns to Italy where she tries to fill the void created by Matteo's absence by Paolo's friendship but her life with Matteo had spoilt her for men like this Paolo, it was no longer possible."[9]

When she gets the telegram regarding Matteo's sickness and hospitalization, she reaches India to be with her husband once again.

In the latest novel of Desai, *The Zigzag Way,* though Eric and Em are not husband-wife yet through them Desai presents another man-woman relationship. This novel set in Mexico presents Eric as the central figure and not Em. Like *In Custody*, and *Baumgartner's Bombay,* this novel also has a male as the central character. Em once sets off with her colleagues to conduct field operations in Mexico, cannot pay attention to Eric, who came there in an alien land following her only. Much ink is not spelt on the character of Em.

Thus we find that women as presented in the novels of Desai present a different picture of their inner life. Desai looks at the predicament of women and visualizes life for a woman as a series of obligations and commitments. In addition to existentialists reality of life she evokes the sentiments and sensibility of women for their role and respect in society. She sets herself to voice the mute miseries and helplessness of millions of married women tormented by existentialist problems and predicaments. She focuses how her heroines, in the contemporary urban melieu are bravely struggling against or helplessly submitting to the relentless forces of absurd life. Although she is preoccupied with the theme of incompatible marital couples yet we come across different kinds of women characters in her novels.

References

1. Anand, T.S., 'Images of Woman in Fiction', Delhi: New Creative Books, 2003, p. 40.
2. Rao, Madhushree Sinha, 'Silent Spaces of Inner Vastness', *Times of India*, Delhi, 18 June, 1992.
3. Desai, Anita, *Fasting, Feasting,* London: Chatto and Windus, 1989, p. 17.
4. *Ibid.*, p. 18.
5. Desai, Anita, *Voices in the City*, New Delhi: Hind Pocket Books, 1968, p. 29.
6. Desai, Anita, *In Custody*, London: Heinmann, 1984, p. 67.
7. Kripal, Viney, 'A Perfect Bubble', *A Study of Anita Desai's, 'In Custody*', p. 127.
8. Budholia, O.P., *Anita, Desai: Vision and Technique in Her Novels*, p. 187.
9. Desai, Anita, *Journey to Ithaca*, London: Chatto and Windus, p. 143.

Desai: A Psychologist behind a Novelist

14

Anita Desai's higher education has given her a deep insight into the human psyche and a clear critical perspective to re-examine tradition. She has shed her inhibitions in a marvelous fashion in order to show surprising frankness, boldness and honesty in the fictional treatment of the workings of the human psyche. Her novels throw light on inner climate, the climate of sensibility. Her primary intention as a novelist is to depict the psyche and emotional states of her protagonists. Anita Desai has a great significance to achieve and handle the nuances of human inner psyche beautifully. In her novels we do not find political and philosophical or social idea of characters but only characters with their observations, motivations, their consciences and their tensions.

Desai is blessed with good observations, sensitiveness and penetrating analysis of the characters, the qualities necessary for a psychological novelist. It becomes natural for her to make each work of hers a haunting discovery of the inner-self. As it is incumbent for an author who wants to point out the psychological aspects of characters to employ a certain design by which the interior working of the protagonist's mind is unfolded gradually with the progress of the narration, therefore Desai's endeavour is to discover the significance of reality by plunging below the surface and plumbing the depths, illuminating those depths till they become a more lucid, brilliant and explicable reflection of the apparent world.

Anita Desai is primarily a novelist of moods, of persistent states of mind or psyche. She is interested in the psychic life of her characters and her novels reveal that her real concern is with the exploration of human psyche. Her contribution to fiction writing has been quite commendable and substantial. She comes face to face with intangible realities of life, the innermost depths of the human psyche and the chaotic underworld of human mind through her novels. Her distinctive stature as a novelist derives primarily from the fact that she has made extensive use of the stream-of-consciousness technique in her novels. Her achievement lies in the fact that she employs a relatively new technique in Indian English fiction with a remarkable consummate skill. The fiction of Anita Desai has become self-analytical and introspective and the individual's quest for a personal meaning in life has become a theme of unavoidable interest for her. Her primary emphasis is, thus on sights and sounds, on movements and patterns both physical and mental as they impinge on the consciousness of her protagonist. Her protagonists have usually sensitive sense of doom and withdraw into a sequestered world of their own.

Anita Desai has presented in her novels the predicament of sensitive women characters, who find it very difficult to adjust in the present mechanical and urbanised set-up. She sincerely broods over the fate and future of modern woman. She has explored different aspects of feminine psyche like man-woman dichotomy, their very personal relations, presentation of neurotic characters, etc. In fact most of her novels are a study of feminine psyche, which comprises women of all ages. Images and symbols are employed freely to reveal the inner psyche of the characters and illuminated their obsession changing and contrasting moods, and psychic deviation besides emphasizing the obscure and weird atmosphere of her tale.

Desai portrays her female characters on the verge of psychological breakdown with a view to capture the prismatic quality of life in her fiction. She uses the stream of consciousness technique, flashbacks and interior monologues. Her female characters are educated, well to do and hypersensitive ladies burdened by chaotic milieu. Desai reflects the inner struggle of such characters, their desire to break the shackles and come out of their shells and assert themselves as human beings. Desai can be considered as the innovator of psychological study of alienated women in India. She deals with the problems of meaninglessness in life and lack of communication not from the philosophical or sociological but entirely from psychological point of view.

As a psychological novelist she tries to delve deep into the emotional built-up and crevices of her characters. She employs very beautifully all techniques of psychological novel like zigsaw puzzle, diary entries, self analysis along with stream of consciousness and flashback.

She makes each work of hers an accelerating exploration of the psychic self. The psychological turmoil creates psychic imbalances, which in turn, handicap them in establishing harmonious and gratifying inter-personal relationships. There is a complete compatibility between her theme and technique. With the help of colour and symbols she reveals the hypersensitive nature of her heroines. Her language has three major characteristics — love of words, sensuous richness and sensitivity, which suit her expression of personal vision. She is much interested in life with its hopes, frustrations, negations, rejections and chaotic flow of events as she is concerned with the art of giving shape, purpose and wholeness to life.

The novelist's language and theme also reveal the meaningful correlations between the psychic conditions of the characters. Her deft handling of language, imagery and syntax in order to convey an acquainted expression of the interior psyche of her characters is superb and unique. She presents with a keen view that how moral values of women are conveniently altered to suit the demands of men who treat them as their objects of possession to be ruled and controlled by psychological insecurity nurtured in them through myths, customs and social discourse.

Desai's use of various linguistic devices in order to present the submerged psychic truth is unique in itself. Clusters of images, symbols, myths, fresh collocations, parallelisms, alliteration, consonance, rhyme, different levels of semantic interpretation are some of the devices used by her.

From the very beginning, her first novel *Cry, the Peacock* shows her interest in the psychology of her characters. Maya's psychic disintegration is presented and to do this Desai moulds images in such a way that the objects get increasingly blurred and confused. In the beginning only the edges of the images are mixed e.g. the tail of the rat gets merged with father and father's voice becomes the voice of the peacock, yet they are recognizable. Later they all get mixed up leading to an imagistic disorder which sets forth effectively the chaos of Maya's psyche. Desai uses the stream of consciousness technique to explain the causes and growth of her despair. The second section of the novel reveals the gradual stages by which Maya moves from sanity to insanity. The final section which acts as the epilogue provides a powerful picture of the effect of the calamity on the important characters. Maya's heart craves for love and understanding, solace and support from her husband. Gautama is a normal gentleman interested in his profession of an advocate, perhaps too practical and materialistic to allot time for expressing his love. Maya does not tell him about the albino's prophecy for fear of hurting him. At the same time she is unable to bear the oppressive burden of the secret.

Because of Gautama's age and cold attitude to sex, Maya remains a much disappointed woman. The image of fighting and mating peacocks, apart from being the central motif of the novel, underlines Maya's sexual frustration too. Psychologists suggest that a healthy emotional and sexual life would have given Maya a sense of security and stopped her psyche from decaying. Fraud attributes neurosis of women to sexual dissatisfaction resulting from the rigours of civilized sexual morality. Various incidents representing her longing for outdoor life in which she bears frustration mainly by Gautama also affect her psyche. The neurotic defence mechanisms such as sleep rituals, hallucinatory visions and nightmares, experience of split personality, adverse somatic symptoms and religious avoidance of violence woefully fail to blunt the edge of her unconscious wish. At most places she appears to reel under the pressure and break to pieces as a result of the struggle within. And it resulted in psychosis which progressively moves towards a psychotic solution to Maya's neurotic struggle.

Monisha in *Voices in the City* seeks loneliness and privacy in order to be her ownself. She is oppressed by a sense of claustrophobia and longs to be free. Even her most private self is not spared by the members of the joint family. Love has no place in her relationship with her husband, Jiban. What she means by love is only a condition of conscience. She feels desperate and finds her life a conundrum that she shall brood for ever with passion and pain, never to arrive at a solution. She desires to be complete and fulfilled. Confronted by unconducive atmosphere, she turns inward and realizes that alone she can feel better. The gulf between expectations and reality throttles Monisha with the result that her bruised self withdraws into her private world where darkness is the natural element. She feels like a caged bird. Meenakshi Mukherjee rightly observes, 'Monisha's claustrophobia and exasperation culminate in suicide and appropriately enough the style and imagery in the pages from Monisha's diary come closest to the language of the heroine of *Cry, the Peacock*, another desperate woman.'[1]

Sleep cannot comfort her. The loneliness and the rejection of the uncongenial external world are the characteristic features of Monisha's life. In a sudden frenzy to experience desire and to experience feeling, she rushes to her room with a tin of kerosene, pours it over herself and sets fire. It is true, 'Monisha's suicide is as much the result of her morbid nature and emotional insufficiency as the result of her uncongenial surroundings'.[2] Thus, through this novel Desai portrays the agony, a sensitive soul experiences, in its quest for meaning and fulfillment in a hostile world.

In *Where Shall We Go This Summer?* the problem of Sita is again more a psychological problem than being external, that resulted from unfulfilled wishes. The husband-wife relationship is dragged into difficulties as they are opposite to each other. Raman is an extrovert and Sita is an introvert personality. She hates Raman for being cold. Her reactions like she starts smoking, abusing her children for trifles and her becoming extremely angry when the servants talk in the kitchen shows her hypersensitivity. Desai views her as a psychologist. Sita suffers from nervous disorders, a void in her life, emptiness, even in her married life resulting in her loss of identity. Her alienation from her surroundings, from the world around her forces her to live in a dream like world of fantasy which is the outcome of a serious psychological confusion. At a deeper psychological level Sita's quest for her identity is an outcome of the husband-wife conflict. Raman's insensitive nature causes serious libidinous problems to the mental life of Sita.

Desai achieves the cohesive design of content and form in her psychological novels and bridges a thought-provoking harmony over different streams of feelings and sensibility, found in different settings of human society. On many places, she delves deeper and deeper in the inner world of her characters and brings out many realistic truths of psychological interest. For Desai, the inner climate, the climate of sensibility that lovers or dears or rumbles like thunder on suddenly blages forth like lightning, is more compelling than the outer weather, the physical geography or the visible action.

We find that the structural pattern of this novel *Where Shall We Go This Summer?* is strikingly similar to that of Virginia Woolf's *To The Lighthouse*. Similar to Woolf's novel, it has three parts. Part one 'Monsoon' 67; Part two 'Winter' 47; Part three 'Monsoon' 67. Each section of this novel is concerned with a particular season, time and space. The psychological cosmos of Sita's life moves around the island and her father's fantasy. In the core of her heart, she believes that the magic of the island will wipe out the evil spell and her unborn child will remain within her womb for ever. Sita appears a bit abnormal and introvert. She wants to escape from the brutal realities and harsh facts of human life. She also thinks that no one cares for her. She becomes defiant in her words and deeds in the fit of depression. Sita has travelled a long distance from Maya and Monisha though she is yet to achieve perfection. She identifies herself with the jelly fish stranded on the shore. She becomes aware of the need to be related in order to gain protection. Her escape to Manori island symbolizes her need to acquire a 'place' for her 'self' both in the real and metaphorical sense of the term in order to maintain her mental equilibrium. Her urgent desire to leave the 'madness' of domesticity and the degree of triviality the outside world attaches to it sums up the traditional concept of the place destined for married women. In this novel Anita Desai follows the track of Bronte sisters, who chose to study the heart and mind of women from women's point of view.

The next novel *Fire on the Mountain* explores the inner emotional world of Nanda Kaul and Raka. Desai draws a picture of the tragedy of Nanda leading a segregated life like a recluse in lonely hill hut. In *Clear Light of Day*, again heroine prefers to lead a solitary life in a decaying house. We find that Desai penetrates into the hidden depth of mind of her characters, who are obsessed by nostalgic reminiscences of their past life and events. In this way Desai heralded a new era of psychological exploration of inner mind in her novels. We find that most of Desai's protagonist pass through a psychological crisis which damages their value system. Some of them are lost, whereas some get out of their alienation. The psychological turmoil creates psychic imbalances, which in turn, handicap them in establishing harmonious and gratifying inter-personal relationships.

But it is wrong to say that Desai deals only with the female psyche. Her successfully probing into the male psyche establishes her as a psychological novelist whose interest is in human psychology. In her novel *In Custody* the main focus is shifted towards the male psychology. The major protagonist, Deven is the representation of male psyche. Deven comes from a lower middle class family and his consciousness is directed towards a wide world beyond himself and his family. At thirty-five Deven feels already having spent all the empty years waiting for a break, waiting to do something worthwhile, something great. Deven is presented as a romantic and an escapist, a weak person incapable of facing crisis. A chanced visit by Murad brings a dramatic change into the monotonous and purposeless existence of Deven. Murad's offer to take an interview of Nur appears the very summon, Deven has been waiting all these years.

> "Deven felt another warm, moist tide of jubilation rise and increase inside him at being recognized, named and invited into the presence of a man so clearly a threshold into the house."[4]

To be successful has always been an anxiety with Deven. Nur in this sense is Deven's alter ego. In this novel there is a different category of psyche in the sense that here Desai attempts to study the helpless nature of male protagonists due to poverty, helplessness and lack of initiative. The diverse trends that affect the contemporary middle class Indian are unified into the sensibility of the protagonist, Deven. He undergoes experiences of various shades and complexities and eventually emerges as a wise man with a more mature and complete knowledge of being in this world. During the period of undergoing shades of various experiences, he suffers from the problem of marital dissonance. He is also disappointed with the atmosphere of the institution, Deven's psyche is probed. He is aware of his personal incompetency to fulfill his wife's desires and dreams. He lives with a sense of defeat and failure. The sense of defeat and failure bring disappointment in the lives of Sarla and Deven but it had not brought them any closer. The motif of despair, failure and mediocrity that underlines the lives of each of these people is repeated in several situations in the novel in the kind of homes, D-II types, that Deven a low paid employee in the same grade live in the phenomenon of 'brain drain' and migration to more prosperous countries for lucrative jobs. The prime characteristics of Deven that attract our attention are his helplessness, humility, suffering and nobility. Socio-economic factors colour his personality and mould his psyche. Desai uses some colour, bird, and animal images, relating to the character's despair, death and suffering. Except in the end, when Deven feels his epiphany that instills in him a new courage and clarity of vision. The novel by and large offers only negative images of characters and situations.

As a psychological novelist Desai has symbolically used the town of Mirpore. It symbolizes the basic nature of the entire class of society, to which the hero Deven belongs. Deven regards Mirpore as a prison where he is sentenced forever to live a gloomy and empty life.

In Custody is important as a psychological novel as it is recreation of the problems and the agonies of the wounded self. It is primarily about the functioning of human psyche. It is different from other novels as here we find neither a sensitive and highly strong woman protagonist nor any violent neurotic woman. It explores the psyche of male character whose problems are social. Similar kind of portrayal we find in *Baumgartner's Bombay*. Anita Desai, an expert in delineating the lacerated psyche portrays the ontological insecurity, alienation and anguish of uprooted individuals, in this novel too. It narrates the story of Hugo from his affluent childhood days in Germany to the horror of his murder in India by another German. This series of calamities losing his home, business and finally his mother makes him mute and accepting. When his frantic attempts to get connected to his mother fails, he withdraws into his own world, disinterested in the way of the world, in his own physical appearance, in anything except the company of his feline friends. Peer group experience is essential for the proper growth of child psyche. His complete schooling denied Hugo this opportunity, cultural uprooting, geographical displacement and failure to connect, torment his psyche. Frustrated with the world, with himself, having no where to go, not getting recognition for his simplicity and honesty the 'pagal firanghi' is saved out of his unpleasant past and unknown future by the German youth who murders him. He lived in doubt and distractions in his quest for identity, but he died in faith. The novelist peeps deeper into Baumgartner's mind and brings the inner fibers out of it. To force a way into the inside of human psyche is indeed an arduous work, but it fits into the narrative skill of Anita Desai. Desai's inside revelation of the character invites a wonderful parallel with George Eliot who also displays the inner threads of human psyche. Hugo's urge to escape into a world of dream and memory from his childhood becomes a source of pleasure for his tense nervous system, but his leaning upon past memories creates an urge in him to escape the dreadful reality of his social existence. Like the characters of Virginia Woolf, Hugo too sometimes in a fit of his fear psychosis shifts from his present to his childhood memories. The use of nostalgia regulates the protagonist's language which conveys his inner experience and the true meaning of life. This way the sequestered world of the earlier novels now gives way to the socio-psychic entrapment of the self.

Thus Desai's fiction is symbolic, sensitive and psychological. Her fictional word reflects her concerns with psyche of her characters. Brati Biswas says in *Perspectives on Anita Desai*:

> "By writing novels and stories that are psychological and purely subjective, She (Anita Desai) was free to employ, simply the language of the interior. She further states 'even when two characters meet, they use this particular type of language — the language of their thoughts, of their interior selves — which has nothing to do with geography."[5]

Anita Desai prefers simple words to polysyllabic words. A discreet mixture of Saxon and Latin words give her English a native touch. While writing about human psyche she uses more concrete nouns than abstract. This is to eliminate the 'disjunction of self and world'. As a result of this, her writing gains in authenticity, since man's two halves, the subjective and the objective make a whole. For vividness and visibility she includes adjectives, referring to physical and psychological tracts. The narrative voice is mirrored in evaluative epithets. A large number of adverbs of time, place, direction and degree give her writing a palpable quality and the adverbs of manner throw light on the personalities and the psychology of the characters. A balanced use of transitive and intransitive verbs adds speed to the progression of images, which are created in order to dramatize an inner conflict and symbolize it objectively through a situation or object. A well-known feature of her style is her use of figures of speech, metaphors and similes, personification, pathetic fallacies, alliteration and assonance are very common, but the towering figure employed by Desai is that of irony. Desai, in the garb of beautiful words and phrases, has tried to probe deep into human psyche. Few Indian English novelists have surpassed Anita Desai in psychological delineation of protagonists.

A characteristic use of symbols and images also helps the novelist like Desai to reveal her protagonists' psyche. Every colour, sound, odour, emotion and every visual image has its correspondence in tracts of human self. Whether it is the cry of peacock, or the city of death—Calcutta, or the locale of Manori island or sleepy Mirpore, Desai has used them symbolically. Her novels also abound in recurrent motifs. Her use of colour symbols convey the awareness of a confusing duality of existence. The two dominant colours in *Cry the Peacock* are black and white. Red is probably symbolic of Maya's craving for a colourful life. In *Voices in the City*, however, scenes and characters have been presented in terms of black or dark. Black has been accentuated occasionally with streaks of white. 'Everything is dark', clamours Sita, in *Where Shall We Go This Summer*'? She finds her Manori house 'pitch dark', with its 'crowded darkness inside'.

We come to the conclusion after a close survey of her novels, that her novels are psychological dramas, surfacing an inner conflict through aesthetic objectivity. She has adopted a controlled method of stream of consciousness. Internal narration, a point of view within a character's consciousness, manifesting character's feelings about and evaluations of the events and characters of the story. In the novels of her first twenty years of writing, Desai has used a uniform structural pattern with marked features of a modern psychological novel. Meena Belliappa rightly says, "What is new in Anita Desai is the effort to delineate a sensitivity to locale, as it operates within the consciousness of her characters. ... The nature of the central character is crucial to a fictional technique which places the centre of the novel within a single consciousness. The perceiver whose thoughts and feelings constitute the story, is also the instrument for registering the values of the objective world."[6]

'Free Indirect Thought' and 'Narrative Report of Thought Acts', dominate the writings of Anita Desai. The psychological nature of her novels makes it a natural choice. From the Spatio temporal point of view, the novels of Anita Desai give the impression of slow motion pictures with sharpness and perspicacity. The movement is in full control by the recurring monologues and implicit dialogue very frequent in her novels. Desai's writing gains in depth and intensity mainly due to her psychological perspective. The various kinds of discourses at different levels is a result of the combination of internal and external perspectives. The technique of 'Free Indirect Discourse', which has been freely used in these novels is a distinctive feature of her psychological novels. Madhusudan Prasad gives voices to our feelings when he says:

"She has added to Indian English fiction an existentialist dimension, a lyrical splendour and a technical richness that were hitherto lacking."[7]

References

1. Mukherjee, Meenakshi, *The Twice Born Fiction*, New Delhi: Arnold Heinemann, 1974, p. 190.
2. Bulliappa, Meena, *Anita Desai: A Study of Her Fiction,* Calcutta: Writers Workshop, 1971, p. 51.
3. Iyengar, K.R. Srinivasa, *Indian Writing in English*, New Delhi: Sterling Publishers, 1994, p. 464.
4. Desai, Anita, *In Custody*, London: Heinemann, 1984.
5. Srivastava, K., *Perspectives on Anita Desai*, Ghaziabad: Vimal Prakashan, 1984, p. 147.
6. Bulliappa, Meena, p. 27.
7. Prasad, Madhusudan, *Anita Desai the Novelist,* Allahabad: New Horizons, 1981, p. 144.

Desai: A High Priest of Nature

15

The fiction of Anita Desai from *Cry, the Peacock* (1963) to her latest mind blowing novel, *The Zigzag Way* (2004) have natural environment in which she embroiders dreams of despair, defeats and illusions of individual characters. It is amazing that critics and scholars have overlooked this aspect of her fiction. In fact the nature and the natural environment are the material on which she weaves her tragic tales. Nature is a familiar presence in Desai's novels. Natural landscape fuses with the character's inner milieu and provides a new dimension to her view of nature. Her love for and obsession with nature is not superficial. It is deep seated in her mental make-up and is part of a large vision which guides her novels in the stark barren and lifeless lives of the protagonists. Nature acts both as a metaphor of hope and life and as an ironical presence that sharpens the awareness of a grim existence in the hollow metropolis. Desai's perception of the city is deeply interfused with a subtle awareness of nature in all its diversity, the flower and the grass, the seasons and the hills, the animals and the birds. While Desai's perception of nature is in itself quite delightful, nature also provides a symbolic dimension to the total meaning of her fiction and thus becomes a sharpening element of her form and style.

In fact nature in Desai's novels appears basically in two forms (a) as horrid and enclosed, perceived through the metaphor of the garden and (b) as open and benign, perceived through sights and sounds. Nature in her fiction plays an important role in sharpening the spirit of the protagonists. Through its different moods and elements nature casts a deep shadow over the spirits of the characters who are but helpless victims of a cruel, indifferent and malignant nature. She presents an unbreakable relationship between society and nature. Nature also associates the conscious mental forces. *Cry, the Peacock* (1963) begins with the description of seasons. The spring season comes with the long insistent call of the brain fever bird. The spring is combined with the qualities of the autumn as the trees shed their leaves and new leaves are about to appear in them. The silk cotton trees are first to flower. Her garden has an element of fantasy attached to it. The garden of Maya's childhood and the garden at present intermingle as the flow of thoughts cascade down from past to present. Garden strikes her as a symbol of symmetry, pattern and order that are absent in her own life. She also gages at the gardens of others and searches for a pattern and a design that has 'deserted her own life.'

But the fragrance and the flowers have no meaning for Gautama. The loneliness and insanity in Maya are suggested through several images taken from nature — the wind, the dust storm, the snake, and the desert. The vision of desert makes Maya conscious of her loneliness alongwith the rats, the lizards and the snake. As storm approaches Maya turns restless. The description of the cloud is lively and metaphorical. While the storm reveals the violent and malignant aspect of nature and its impact on the spirit of the protagonist corresponding to a similar storm inside her shattering the balance of her mind, the cry of the peacocks has an element of pathos in it which sharpens Maya's sense of separation, alienation and death.

Monisha in *Voices in the City* feels that the garden of Kalimpong is her abode of peace. She is delighted by the solitude of the jungles; the aqueous shadows of the bamboo groves and the earth led with great fallen leaves (116). In her letter, Monisha's mother refers to the profusion of spring in the garden of Kalimpong. Monisha's dull existence in the house and the lack of any communication with others drive her towards an inner garden, a garden of her own creation. Dharma's paintings seem to be the 'studies of the finer secrets of nature'. Looking at the still pond where the white geese swim silently, Dharma says to Nirode: "So it has, Nirode, like you. I find myself inexorably drawn away from my island back to the main land again."[1]

In the *Bye-Bye Blackbird* nature acts as the agent of change in the taste and attitude of Dev. His strong resentment turns to appreciation as he wanders through London enjoying its natural scenery. The beautiful daffodils in the parks the patches of bright sunshine, the grass under the green canopies of the new garden have a great impact on him. He is intoxicated by the beauty of the countryside. The field of tall, ripe hay and wheat and barley swaying in the gentle breeze look luxuriantly green and golden.

The major novel dealing with this aspect is *Where Shall We Go This Summer?* (1975). Structurally this novel has been divided into three parts:

'Monsoon 67', 'Winter 47' and again 'Monsoon 67'. Even the title *Where Shall We Go This Summer?* and the repetition of the term 'Monsoon' indicates clearly towards the lively presence of nature in the novel. Desai discusses social intricacies, the sensibleness of city, the environmental pollution, the influence of nature on man and the correlation between man and nature apart from working on the ancient Indian myth of the *Ramayana* through the characters of Sita and Rama(n). In her delimma, there was, however, a relief to her that she enjoyed the company of nature at the island of Manori village. In her forties, her fifth pregnancy shatters her severely and she takes an odd decision-neither to give birth to the child nor to undergo the process of abortion. Like Bimla, Maya or Leila, Sita too had the strained human, the symbolic experience either of nature or anything related to it. At the instance of other heroines, Sita also thinks of coming to the island of miracles. Desai shows some resemblance between the foetus inside and the natural image of the 'soft flushed fish in a bowl of warm sea water.'[2] Amidst the company of nature of Manori village, Sita tries to seek constantly the real meaning of life. The foetus thus becomes a sense of constant worries, and she wishes to relieve herself from the burden of these worries in the company of nature on this island:

> "The island had been buried beneath her consciousness deliberately, for years. Its black, its subtle glamour had grown too huge, had engulfed her at time when she was still very young and quite alone."[2]

This shows Sita's association with nature. She develops the universal cognition in the company of natural objects on the island at Manori village. Admitting the importance of nature in her fiction she says in an interview that natural objects are of primary importance to her. The visual images and sounds, smells and textures of the places she knew are her material. Sita, as a very young girl perceives the free and frank environment of nature in such a way as it becomes a glamour to her. The fresh air of the island, the animals of the sea and the differences and dissention between her mother and father are writ large as permanent forces of the unconscious mind for seeing life beyond the island. With the rich store of her natural memories that she collected on the island, she comes to the mainland in a flat at Bombay with her husband, Raman. Again the cleanliness and the natural environment of the island is compared with the most awful sensation through the noisy and dusty atmosphere of Bombay. She then decides to leave it and come to the natural environment of the island again. Her arrival at Manori village in the company of nature hardly minimizes her fear psychosis. Desai has decorated the inner thoughts of Sita with wonderful images from nature. The inner tumult of Sita resembles the external monsoon, the processes of inner and external natures. Desai remarks:

> "I wanted the book to follow the pattern of monsoon together darkly and threateningly to pour down widely and passionately, then withdraw quietly and calmly."[3]

Sita, the protagonist, swings between two natures — the inner and the outer forms and the being and the process of becoming in the association of nature. When the water touches the sand, the heat created so in the sand subsides and removes Sita's all illusory passions. Her constant companionship with nature on the island shows the metamorphosis in Sita and she begins to think of her home. Sita's understanding of human relationship is revealed through the dialectics of nature.

Another novel *Fire on the Mountain* (1977) includes two natural epithets, the fire, and the mountain. This novel goes a step ahead in voicing forth the effects and shaping power of nature on human beings. The novelist shows that nature works out its two forms as malevolence and benevolence for human beings. If man obeys the subtle and suggestive pattern of nature, it brings well-being for man and if he disobeys it brings the curse and destruction. Nanda Kaul lives as a widow of a vice chancellor on a mountain at Carignano in an old house. Her great granddaughter Raka comes there. She compares the mode of two worlds only in the company of nature; the rotten world of city and the inspiring force of nature. Insufficient parental affection and parental callousness also shapes the psyche of Raka in *Fire on the Mountain*. She in insecure and lonely and yet she wishes to be left to herself to enjoy the nature around her. The topography of Kasauli attracts her because of its 'ravaged, destroyed and barren places' (91). She raised herself on to the tips of her toes — tall, tall as pine (146). At Carignano, in the company of nature, there are neither sickly sweet smells of illness, sadness, drink, medication nor any kind of tension. Every object of nature draws and inspires her:

> "It was the ravaged, destroyed and barren spaces in Kasauli that drew her: the ravine where yellow snakes slept under grey rocks and agaves growing out of the dust and rattle, the wind, the wind-leveled hill-tops and the reared remains of the safe, cosy, civilized world in which Raka had no part."[4]

Raka shows some extraordinary traits as a lover of nature, for she desires to know the secrets of nature 'amongst the rocks and pines of Kasauli' (48). She tries to seek the meaning of life in the company of nature. With an eagle's eye, she explores her existence beyond the surfacial meanings of life. Like a discoverer she scrutinizes each and every object of nature with a keen intensity of a scientist. Anita Desai uses such images from nature as to analyse the inner threads of Raka's mind. She links Raka's presence with the images of 'cricket' and 'mosquito'. She also sees 'a scraggy-necked ken' in Raka. Even the language of the novel is regulated through working out the poetic images from nature. Desai handles these images from nature in such a way as to create a specific semantic purpose of her narrative power.

In the novel *In Custody* nature is symbolized by the neem tree growing outside the wall of the courtyard of Deven's house. It does not provide any peaceful shade to Deven, but only obstructs the free flow of fresh air. Desai shows that even nature is not able to help a person escape from this trap and get full freedom. Again, a cricket chirping incessantly stands for Deven's unconscious mind. It suggests that his unconscious self is greatly agitated under strong pressure from all sides. On his way to Delhi, Deven sees all around him nature without any sign of joy. Thus, the novelist suggestively projects his impending disappointment through nature imagery effectively and artistically, 'Bushes and grasses all appeared to have died, the land was shown or shrouded.'

The thirsts of summer, the parched and barren atmosphere of summer, correspond to the dry and parched existence of the protagonist Deven. When Deven returns to Delhi he stands near the doorway and sees the sparrows nesting in the skylight twitter and quarrel, scattering twigs as they rustle about their nests. The coming of the devastating summer announced by 'Surahi' however outside is already a felt experience for Deven. But the summer with its dryness, its heat and thirst is not going to continue forever. When the heat becomes unbearable for Deven, he hears thunders in the distance, perhaps, announcing that the monsoon is drawing close.

Nature takes a different colour with the change of outlook of the main protagonist. Deven could never see any beauty or comfort even in the landscape. The sky is gradually filled with a grey light, slowly dissolves the dense blackness of the night. Consequent upon the resolution of the protagonist's inner drama, nature is seen to cover itself with beauty and splendour. The sunlight dissolving the darkness of the night before, is symbolic of the emergence of the new courageous 'self' of Deven; dispersing his previous timid self. There is delightful fusion of colour, light and sound reflecting the regenerated spirit of Deven.

In her another novel *Baumgartner's Bombay*, the different aspects of nature are so influenced by the life in the city that they lose their inherent charm and turn insipid, blank and colourless like the lives of the characters. As Lotte observes out of her window: 'Right at the top, a layer of sky, a blank sky, as always with neither colour, nor form. Empty, afternoon light, daylight, perpetual light and blankness' (4).

In a city like Bombay people very seldom find time to look at nature during day time. It is also due to the hot sun and the busy life of the day that they come to the seashore in the evening to spend some time away from the hurly burly of city life. Desai narrates:

> "Baumgartner did not turn towards the sea. That was for the evening, when the breeze came up with the tide and the sun fell headlong into the waves, livid and melodramatic in its orange and purple flames and people strolled, for pleasure buying themselves peanuts to eat or coconut to drink from, and one was not conspicuous if one loitered too.[5]
>
> But for the Baumgartner, nature loses all charm when he finds her mother playing a duet with the young Friedmann. Nature also becomes a metaphor of indifference. Garden as nature for Hugo appears as a disturbing presence and not a benign shaping spirit.
>
> *Journey to Ithaca* presents nature in a slightly different form. Matteo joins the life of an ashram in India for unveiling the secrets of life while Sophie has only followed him. Matteo shifts his place and comes to the terrains of Himalayas. This ashram is run by a woman known as Mother."

Fasting, Feasting describes the natural atmosphere of the ashram. Further the scene is described. The temple at one end of the courtyard was brightly painted pink and blue and green but seemed deserted. Mira masi went straight up a gravel path neatly edged with shrubs to the long low building with "its deep veranda and flat roof shaded by an immense banyan tree in which parakeets were contented by picking at berries and scattering them down in the dust."

Desai compares Uma with the natural objects. She narrates:

> "So that everyone had to come to her attracted to her as bees to a lotus. A lotus, with her deep, creamy, still beauty that was what she was. Or a pearl, smooth and luminous."[6]

At another occasion when Uma is alone and her Mama Papa have gone to the club to play bridge, her loneliness is reflected through the images from nature and natural objects:

> "At least the air is clearer here and has something free about it. Still as it is. Over the top of the dusty trees, there is a new moon to be seen, very pale and far away. The jasmine bush at the foot of the stairs is in full bloom, releasing its perfume in white clouds in the dark."[7]

While sitting in the garden she remembers a tune from a film 'sweet, sweet moonlight' from her past and now she sings 'pale pale moonlight' to the flower in the cup of her hand. At another moment when she goes to wake Mali down the steps, Desai gives a detail description of the natural scene through Uma's eyes. "It is not so dark that she cannot make out the familiar path beside the hedge of night flowering jasmine, or the dusty bush from which pink oleanders hang in bunches, or the trunk of the ancient tamarind tree."[8]

In her latest novel *The Zigzag Way*, Eric is drifting in his chosen career path, writing a book on immigration with the help of a grant, an extension of his thesis, daily losing focus caught up in an aimless cyle of wasted days. Eric grabs the opportunity to travel to Mexico with Emily. He was certain that a change of scene will invigorate his sagging self-discipline and commitment to his project. When they arrive in Mexico, Eric is stunned by the colour and beauty of the area, the unflinching brightness of the days appear as a sharp contrast to Boston.

Not only has novels but her short stories too taken images from a large variety of services depending on the aptness of the situation. In her short stories, her most important source is nature and she has a whole range of images drawn from vegetable and plant life, birds, animals and other natural phenomena.

Desai also presented the starkness and barenness in nature corresponding to the pattern of life led by the protagonists. Trees, birds, seasons, hills, and gardens symbolize hope, regeneration and freshness as well as the grim reality of existence. Nature also shapes the spirits of the protagonists. Violence, murder, madness also occur in the world of nature. Through its different moods and elements nature casts a deep shadow over the spirits of these characters who are but helpless victims of a cruel, indifferent and malignant nature. The element of violence in nature are presented through different sights and sounds. The destructive aspect of nature is suggested by images of violence and destruction. Usually through the image of prey and predator Desai depicts the violence in nature. The images are not static rather they change according to the change within the characters. Sometimes nature also becomes a metaphor of indifference.

Thus, we had seen that the human world always interacts with the world of nature in novels of Anita Desai. Nature in the novels acts both as a consoling agent and also as a disturbing presence. There is a constant interaction between the inner world of the protagonist and the outer world of nature and in the process of this interaction, an intense vision of the life is projected. In the novels of Anita Desai nature thus appears as an ironic presence that pervades the life of the main characters of the novel. It fulfills Desai's two main objectives. She reveals the lulling and soothing effects on violently disturbed psyche of her protagonists, and that she extends the original range of her fiction through the use of appropriate symbols, metaphors and images from nature. This also includes her cinema technique. As Desai approaches the Mexican landscape like a master cinematographer in the novel *The Zigzag Way* and *In Custody*, it suggests that novels of these types can easily and popularly may be transferred into films.

References

1. Desai, Anita, *Voices in the City*, New Delhi: Hind Pocket Books, 1968, p. 224.
2. Desai, Anita, *Where Shall We Go This Summer?* New Delhi: Orient Paperbacks, 1982, pp. 57-58.
3. Desai, Anita, quoted in Kung Bala Goel, *Language and Theme in Anita Desai's Fiction,* Jaipur: Classic Publishing House, 1998, p. 37.
4. Desai, Anita, *Fire on the Mountain*, New Delhi: Orient Paperbacks, 1985, p. 91.
5. *Baumgartner's Bombay*, New Delhi: Harmonds Work: Penguin, 1988, p. 8.
6. *Fasting, Feasting*, London: Chatto and Windus, 1989, p. 68.
7. *Ibid.*, p. 99.
8. *Ibid.*, p. 148.

Desai's Concept of 'Marriage' as a Social Institution

16

'Marriage is the destiny traditionally offered to women by society', says the feminist Simone De Beauvoir. Desai in her portrayal of man-woman relationship mostly concentrates on the predicament of modern woman in this male-dominated society and her destruction at the alter of marriage. According to Desai most marriages prove to be unions of incompatibility. Her women long for love and communion of the spirit which they perceive as the panacea of the ills of the world. In an interview dated 16th November 1979 in Jaipur, Jasbir Jain asked Anita Desai, "Do you feel the man-woman relationship doesn't have the capacity to be a satisfying one, is it inadequate in every respect?" Anita Desai replies, "I think all human relationships are inadequate. Basically everyone is solitary. I think involvement in human relationships in this world invariably leads to disaster."

Almost all female protagonists of Anita Desai are the victims of marital disharmony. All the marriages in her novels are more or less business transactions. A marriageable daughter is handed over to the male partner without considering the delicacy of her mind and feelings. She has to fulfil either the parent's obligation or the relative's demands with different intentions.

Desai has presented marital disharmonies as they exist in Indian male dominated traditional families. A marriage is a union of souls. Some adjustment must be there from both sides. But very often, a marriage in Indian society becomes successful because of the woman's grace, love, wisdom, sense of understanding, tolerance and sacrifice. Desai focuses on the inadequacies between the couples who attempt it.

Within the private hell of maladjusted marriages, Desai presents the repressive forces of patriarchal attitudes. In her novels there is a sustained presentation of failed marriages, posing unstated questions regarding the functioning of marriages within the patriarchal structures of the Indian family. In the sophisticated upper middle class ethos generally depicted by Desai, severe economic deprivation or physical brutalization (except Anamika) is largely absent, what is foregrounded is the psychological repression created through a male supremacist ideology which consumes any possibility of mutual love and concern, corroding the woman's self-esteem and devouring her sense of identity and selfhood. In these fictional representations of reality, marriage becomes an institutionalized form of domination of women by men within the most personal of relationships.

Desai's forte is her handling of maladjusted marriages — Maya, Monisha, Sita, Tara, Uma, Sophie are all woman of deep emotions and fine sensitivities who are entrapped in marriages with men who are never outrightly cruel, who carry out their husbandly obligations assiduously but are impervious to their wives pleas for understanding, communication and respect for their individuality. Such emotionally incomplete relationship have a fatal effect on the finely tuned female psyche and Desai's women find themselves tortured by a painful sense of alienation. P. Bhatnagar discovers in Desai's novels the view that 'most marriages prove to be unions of incompatibility.'[1] Infact Desai makes use of the subtlest understated means to question the institution of marriage through the consciousness of her protagonist narrator. Her attitude to the hypocrisy, the shallowness of marriage as an institution is clear. Desai also portrays her emancipated woman as single, but by this she does not necessarily negate the institution of marriage because some of her women characters, like Tara (in *Clear Light of Day*) do achieve fulfilment in their marriages. Instead, through Bim or Bimla, Desai points to a kind of feminist emancipation that lies in not limiting women to their traditional roles but in expanding and awakening them to several other possibilities. This kind of life, apart from being invigorating also frees them from dependence on men. Bimla through her individual freedom, exemplifies Simone de Beauvoir's description of an independent woman in her individual freedom.

Desai also tries her pen to discuss the various reasons of disintegration of marriages. Incompatibility in marital relationships, spell insecurity in children as is the case of Raka in *Fire on the Mountain* and Raja in *Clear Light of Day*.

Desai's very first novel, *Cry, the Peacock* is about Maya, who is unable to relate her emotions to her husband Gautama. Unlike the Western tradition, in the Indian middle class-families, the couples generally go through arranged marriages and do not choose each other. Though times have changed, the tradition of negotiations in the name of marriage is still very much in vogue. Maya and Gautama's marriage is one such case where they both are ill-matched as a couple. There is absolutely no understanding on the intellectual as well as sensual plane. Maya being the more sensitive of the two is unable to bear the strain of the relationship and is driven to insanity by the end of the novel. She craves for 'contact, companionship and communion', which Gautama with his rigid understanding of the Hindu Philosophy is unable to fathom.

Maya's marriage with Gautama in *Cry, the Peacock* is more or less a marriage of convenience. Gautama's friendship with Maya's father resulted into the marriage of Gautama and Maya. This marriage could not gratify Maya's basic need for love and belongingness. The death of a beloved pet and her husband's genuine inability to understand its impact on her stirs Maya from the complacency of a 'happy' marriage. Gautama's casual indifference to her desperate need for sustenance brings her to a sharp awareness of the incomplete nature of the relationship. In Maya, Anita Desai creates an epitome of the many women who have passively accepted their dependent, inferior status within marriage; unable to find sustenance either from within themselves or from any broader interests, they cling desperately to their husbands, pathetically grateful for occasional moments of intimacy or companionship. The hire of security which marriage offers, the confinement within a self-enclosed world have reduced them to the status of emotional beggars. The resentment is strong, yet unexpressed. Maya's psychic problem lies not in the 'loss' but in an 'absence'. Maya emphatically lacks the emotional security and longs for the understanding and the sacred communion with her husband which she never had. Turning away from her insensitive husband, she attempts to find an outlet for her pent up emotions and passions through her experience of nature but the final answer, she gets in the murder of Gautama and her suicide.

Monisha in *Voices in the City* is totally dissatisfied with her life after marriage. Like Maya she is also a miserable misfit among her in-laws. So she weaves a web of her own and remains imprisoned in its privacy. She feels lonely even in the company of Jiban, her husband. She feels alienated from him and ponders over the problems of attachment and detachment. Monisha and Jiban's marriage is the most pathetic illustration of maladjustment in marriage. In the marriage market, the Sita, Savitri — Pativrata tradition is deeply engrossed in the Indian feminine psyche as well as the masculine psyche. The joint family household hinders their relationship and they fail to reach out to each other. Their marriage is rendered meaningless as it is merely based on role playing to cater to the codes of the larger family they belong to. Her relationship with her husband, Jiban, does not offer her any happiness and contentment. Her infertility and lack of intimacy with her husband, lack of primary and charge of theft by her in-laws prove too much for her and she is driven to commit suicide. In a fit of uncontrollable emotional turmoil, she decides to put an end to her nightmarish, unhappy, loveless marriage. She pours kerosene over her clothes, sets herself ablaze and dies before any help could reach her. Thus she tries to give meaning to her death since her married life has had none.

Nanda Kaul in *Fire on the Mountain*, is a great grandmother, completely disillusioned with all matrimonial bonds. Her husband was the Vice Chancellor of Punjab University. But he treated her simply as some useful object in the house. He carried on an affair with the Maths teacher Miss David. Nanda just played the role of wife in his life. She is deceived and betrayed in her marriage. Raka remembers the unsatisfactory married life of her parents. She thinks of her father beating her mother with fists and her mother crying helplessly. Then again the news of her mother's serious illness reminds Raka of her father's cruelty to her. Both these important female characters negate the institution of marriage. Nanda's bond with her husband did not involve her 'self'. She could not over come the trauma of her married life. The infidelity of her husband caused such a deep anguish in her heart that she has lost her faith in the sanctity of human relationships, she distrusts all attachments.

In reality Nanda Kaul's apparently tranquil story of retirement in the mountains allows for a whole set of secondary plot to be hinted at. Subplots concerning ill-treated wives, children who die without medical assistance, child-marriages as a tradition which goes against the laws of modern India, but still persists in rural India and as well as Nanda's own unhappy marriage, Tara's unhappy marriage, etc., are there. Thus, again Desai concentrates on the negative side of marriage.

After Maya, Monisha and Nanda Kaul there comes a change in the concept of marriage for Desai's heroines. Sarah, Sita, Bim, Sarla, Leila, Lotte, Aruna and Uma represent the positive side of life. They face their problems boldly. They too go through the emotional predicament, mental and spiritual conflict, domination of the male community, suffering at the hands of their in-laws, marital disharmony, etc. Still they fight and try to compromise in their married life and survive. They believe that inspite of disillusionment, disharmony and unfavourable circumstances, life is worth to be lived.

Bye-Bye Blackbird presents Adit and Sarah. Sarah gets herself alienated from her society through her marriage. Her inter cultural marriage does not offer her anything grand and fabulous. By marriage, 'She had become a nameless, she had shed her name as she had shed her ancestry and identity.'[2] Sarah tries to build up a harmonious matrimonial relationship by keeping the past and present to two watertight compartments. Hence, her life becomes mechanical keeping an emotional distance from anyone and anything. Sarah has sacrificed her past to gain a new life after marriage. She decides to go to India as atleast in India, she hopes, she will have only one face — Adit's wife. Her reluctance to discuss her Indian husband before her colleagues shows her identity crisis and bewilderment. We find that the two female protagonists in the first two novels of Desai fail in thus reconciliation with marital lives. But the scene is a bit changed in the novels of second phase. Sita in *Where Shall We Go This Summer?* attempts to come to terms with it. She chooses her own exile from her husband and her frequented domestic world. Anita Desai magnifies the tyranny of monotonous existence in the role of a housewife to hyperbolic proportions in Sita's rebellion. However, the rebellion is abortive as Sita through a process of self-analysis gives in to a reconciliation with her husband. This also indicates that the Indian wife hardly has any choice apart from her learning to accept her situation. The sex is something that 'happens' to them by the fact of marriage. The main theme of the novel is marital discord emanating from the conflict between two irreconcilable temperaments and two diametrically opposed viewpoints. As B. Ramchandra Rao suggests:

> "Sita and Raman represent the external opposition between the passion and the prose of life. Raman, the husband, says the 'great yes' and follows the path of honour and social success. Sita says 'No', and although she is not destroyed by life, she is compelled to arrive at some kind of a compromise with life."[3]

Sita realises that genuine happiness is not possible in her marital context, that hope rises only to be crushed in an insensitive and cruel setting, that her husband and children are alien to her nature and her needs.

Clear Light of Day tries to probe the subconscious where love and frustration create enormous shadows. Marriage to Bakul affords Tara a means of escape. For Raja, marriage is a means to become rich and fat by marrying the one time landlord's only daughter. The central character Bim is left alone after her parents' death and Tara's marriage. She is the only one to attend to the aged, alcoholic aunt and look after her mentally retarded brother Baba. It is these burdens and responsibilities that shatter her marital bliss and destroy her conjugal identity. Tara seems to have lost her identity in marriage. But she gains in terms of family and motherhood. She assumes a new identity with her marriage, the identity of a mother. Raja too relinquishes his Byronic longings in marriage, but experiences a new kind of freedom and a new kind of awareness linked with his marital and conjugal life. Bim seems to have lost love, marriage and domesticity. She plays the foster mother to her brothers and sisters. In fact Bim reflects Desai's vision of the identity of the new Indian woman, who is not dependent on the institution of marriage, for her survival. Unlike most Indian girls, she opts out of marriage for the life of a spinster. She is reluctant to play the conventional role of a sex-object and a yoked wife. In fact she is the symbol of the emancipated woman. And marriage, which in Desai's earlier novels, was a destructive institution, breeding alienation assumes a positive significance.

In Custody analyses the problem of Deven Sharma an impoverished college lecturer. After his marriage with a sullen and dull wife, Deven sees a way to escape from the meanness and hopelessness of daily life. His extreme devotion to art leads him to indifference to his wife rather he has cultivated an aversion to and dislike for his wife. Like Zola he lets his wife feel widowed. Here Desai deals with a purely marital problem of this materialistic world of glittering civilization in a city like Delhi, where the relationship between husband and wife is always under strain because of the undue indulgence of husband in extra activities and his attachment with other women. The relationship between Sarla and Deven is not satisfactory because they have never attempted to build up their marital relationship on the basis of love, companionship and equality. Both of them are frustrated in their own ways but they are unable to do anything for each other. Deven feels as if he was in a prison. Marriage, his family, his job had placed him in a sort of trap. Deven lives in a dreamy world and plans a utopian scheme. Sarla is puzzled by these dreams of Deven as how can she become satisfied with a husband who thinks of others, love others, have ties with them but maintains a distance from his wife and son. Problems of post-marital life are dealt in this novel. In such circumstance Deven often feels as if his marriage has stood behind his imagination like a heavy weight. He also believes that marriage has clogged his progress in life. Had he shown his love and affection to his own family life, his wife and son, he would have led a happy and contended life, full of satisfaction and peace. Deven could never understand that as a wife Sarla needs love and affection more than money. In their married life what is missing is the real feelings of love and affection. Here Desai presents a kind of humour and pathos of married relations that he wants to be more familiar and closer with others, not with his wife and child. He could not understand that marriage is a means to combine two souls and two bodies into spiritual harmony.

Deven thinks that Sarla does not care for him and his feelings while Sarla thinks that he neglects her all the time and is engaged with some other girl. Both feel insulted and humiliated living in one room. As Desai narrates beautifully in simplest words, "Deven had been more a poet than a professor when he married Sarla — he had only taken on as a temporary lecturer and still had confidence in his verse and for the wife of a poet she seemed too prosaic."[4] In the common problems of post-marital life, he came to understand her predicament also. But there is another aspect of this loveless marital relationship. Deven wants money but that too for Sarla, to buy gold jewellery for her.

Another aspect of marriage is shown by Nur and his two wives, while his elder wife stands for duty, the second one for love. Nur and Imtiaz Begum do care for each other to a certain extent. There is enormous attachment of husband and wife. But wife is the controlling agent in this case, unlike Deven and Sarla. Nur's own life is miserable on account of it. We have no details as to how Nur married Imtiaz Begum, but it has been clearly shown how inspite of his infatuation for her, he is not able to derive any happiness or satisfaction from her.

Journey to Ithaca presents Matteo and Sophie as husband and wife who are not Indians by birth but Matteo is fascinated by Indian spiritualism. Sophie, unknowingly, following the ideals of Indian wifehood comes to India after her husband Matteo. She suffers and remains in Mother's ashram just for the sake of her husband, where her identity crumbles and her children suffer. She returns to her country. Even then, love for her husband remains dominant in her heart. And she rushes to India as she gets the news of Matteo's illness and hospitalization. She feels as if she was waiting for this time only. For her, her marriage is of primary importance. To a secular reader it is a novel about marital problems, adjustment and life thereafter. That's why the novel revolves around Sophie, the wife. In *Fasting, Feasting*, for Anamika's parents marriage is the only path for women. The offer of a scholarship to study in Oxford made to Anamika, Uma's cousin, is ignored by her parents. Instead, the letter making the offer is used to procure a husband for her. The novel throws light on the misery that can follow a marriage too hastily arranged and the lot of women in a typical joint family, in which the new bride is a virtual prisoner and a slave to the mother-in-law. The beautiful and talented Anamika is regularly beaten by in-laws and finally she was slaughtered at the alter of marriage. Before that when she had a miscarriage after being beaten, people consider her as 'damaged goods' and for them it is a great shame for a woman once 'given' in marriage to return to her parents' home. Anamika's mothers' explanation that her daughter's marital family loved her so much that they couldn't bear to let her out of their sight for a single day, is startling and shocking.

On the other hand Uma's parents make several attempts to get her married off at any cost to any one. With each successive attempt they lower their expectations. The third attempt sees Uma married to a man who is many years her senior and who already has a wife and several children. Through distress in married life Uma presents the common problem of an Indian girl for whom marriage becomes her destiny.

The discussion points out to another side of the coin too. In her fictional world female protagonists are so acutely and assertively observed with their own individuality that they do not care for the individuality and emotional needs of the persons with whom they try to establish their relationship, especially their husbands. This failure of understanding on the part of both lead to marital disharmony and lack of interpersonal fusion. Most of these protagonists are so vehemently inclined to keep their individuality intact that they ignore the basic fact that marital love demands surrender, a fusion not on the sexual level alone but deeper than that, an emotional interaction which is unifying and mutually gratifying. In this connection Jasbir Jain has made a very apt and revealing observation:

"The world of Anita Desai's novels is an ambivalent one, it is a world where the central harmony is aspired to but not arrived at, and the desire to love and live clashes — at times violently — with the desire to withdraw and achieve harmony ... surrender of the self, appears to her protagonists, to be a subtraction from their personal freedom and wholeness. In each successive novel the problem of involvement versus detachment, of surrender versus freedom is viewed from various angles and psychological perspectives."[5]

References

1. Bhatnagar, P., 'The Theme of Man Women Relationship in the Novels of Anita Desai', *Indian Women Novelist*, Set I, Vol. 2, New Delhi: Creative Books, 2003, 143.
2. Desai, Anita, *Bye-Bye Blackbird*, New Delhi: Orient Paperback, 1985, p. 31.
3. Ramachandra Rao, B., *Technique in the Novels of Anita Desai: Perspectives on Anita Desai, op. cit.*, p. 87.
4. Desai, Anita, *In Custody*, London: Heinman, 1984, p. 28.
5. Jain, Jasbir, *Stairs to the Attic: The Novels of Anita Desai,* Jaipur: Printwell Publishers, 1987, p. 16.

Socio-Religious Aspect in the Novels of Anita Desai

17

Social change is not possible without changing ourselves, and the discipline which helps us to change ourselves is religion. Indian society and religion are entwined, unlike Western society. As a matter of fact society and religion are complementarily serving different needs of mankind. Religion, if it is to survive must become a social force. It must permeate every aspect of our personality and extend into all the vocations of our daily life. The study of socio-religious aspects of the Indian society together is necessary because social values and religious thoughts are so much admixed with each other that they cannot be set apart in watertight compartments.

Religion is part of the cultural systems. As such, religious beliefs provide guidelines for human action and standards against which man's conduct can be evaluated. Many of the norms of the social system are integrated by religious beliefs. As a part of the cultural systems, religious beliefs give meaning to life, they answer man's questions about himself and the world he lives in. Changes in the forces of production are mirrored by changes in religious beliefs and practices. The internal aspect of religion is the body of ideas, convictions and emotions concerning man's relations to God, while its external aspect is the system of prayers, ceremonies and rules through which the religious feeling is manifested. Religion satisfies the social interest as the bond that unites men to God, and tends also to strengthen the bonds of unity existing between man and man. This is the basis of brotherhood of man under the fatherhood of God. Religion through religious places establishes a centre of human fellowship in which persons unite to pray and worship, to collect funds and work for the poor and needy. These pursuits are not always of a religious nature, but directly or indirectly they may be termed as socio-religious.

Religion is not to be confused with magic, witchcraft, quackery, outdated dogmas, incredible superstitions, which are hindrances and barriers which spoil the simplicity of spiritual life. Infact religion is a way of achieving union with that ultimate 'Reality' called God. The plurality of religions in India seem to be a matter of utter confusion or conflict, but all religions in their true spirit seem to be varied manifestations of the essentials of true religion. Hinduism, which is a religion of the majority in India is not confined to temples or other places of worship, it is a way of life which seems to be the reason for nearly everything and influences life at every juncture.

Including Hinduism, in all religions there are religious teachings or doctrines, which have been revealed to many a holy man, not only in India, but in different countries of the world as well. The aim of it is to enable man to guard himself against evil and to do his righteous duty. In Hinduism, *Bhagavad Gita* is the book which contains religious teachings through its eighteen discourses in seven hundred shlokas delivered by Lord Krishna to Arjun during the battle of Kurukshetra. The *Gita* is said to be the essence of the *Vedas* and the *Upanishads*. It is a landmark in the tradition of religious and philosophical texts of India. Warren Hastings was probably the first European to have drawn our attention to the literary merits of the *Gita*. During the course of his brief letter, Hastings also compared the best translated verses of the *Gita* with those of *Iliad* and *Odyssey*. Apart from him, William Blake, Carlyle, R.W. Emerson, Henry David Thoreau, Walt Whitman, Arnold, W.B. Yeats, E.M. Forster, Aldous Huxley, T.S. Eliot are some of the names, whose literature is influenced by the philosophy of *Bhagavad Gita*.

In this series to a certain extent, names of Ruth Prawar Jhabvala, Nayantara Sahgal and Anita Desai can also be added. Desai too, relates religion with life. In her novels the pursuit of religion means largely, if not exclusively, the pursuit of peace of mind. Hence, she emphasizes on detachment, other worldliness, prayer, meditation and sanyasa. It is often claimed that this peace of mind produces clearer thinking and creative activity. In her very first novel *Cry, the Peacock* (1963) religion is admixed with the inner psyche, in other words with the philosophy and thinking of the social creatures. Gautama, Maya's husband believing in the philosophy of detachment from the *Bhagvad Gita*, unfolds the traps of attachment to his childlike wife and preaches:

> "Thinking of sense objects, man becomes attached thereto. From attachment arises longing and from longing anger is born. From anger arises delusion, from delusion loss of memory is caused. From loss of memory the discrimination faculty is ruined and from the ruin of discrimination, he perishes."[1]

Gautama's philosophy of non-involvement implies denial of mundane matters of love. Maya, being so much in love with life feels bored by Gautama's act of pouring out wisdom from the *Bhagvad Gita* which to her, appears dry and inhuman. Gautama wants to be her friend, philosopher and guide, while she wants him to be her lover. Though she herself was quite familiar with the shooting effect of religion, particularly of *Bhagvad Gita*, she remembered some phrases from *Bhagvad Gita* that calmed her with their cool, steadfast wisdom. She says:

> "Phrases came to me from *The Gita*, so long unread, that calmed me with their cool, steadfast wisdom. He is fit to attain immortality who is serene and not affected by these sensations, but is the same in pleasure and pain ....
>
> 'He whose mind is not agitated in calamities and who has no longing for pleasure, free from attachment fear and anger, he indeed, is said to be of steady wisdom ....'
>
> 'He who is free from all attachment and neither rejoices on receiving good nor is vexed on receiving evil, his wisdom is well established ....'
>
> 'When he completely withdraws his senses from sense objects as the tortoise withdraws its limbs then wisdom becomes well established."[2]

Through these solid, simple, deeply consoling words that had remained, somehow, surprisingly fresh and crystalline in her untidy mind, she felt herself relieved from the recurring tension of death, though for a very short time. When Maya was in the neurotic state of mind Gautama said:

> "A question that has employed thinking minds for centuries. The answer of course is there in the *Gita* — once again, the *Gita*. He whose joy is within, and whose light is within, that yogi, being well-established in Brahman, attains to absolute freedom. The freedom of the lotus from water, of the lamp from winds, of the tortoise from all contact. Detachment, in a word, detachment."[3]

The most significant factor that remains as far as religion and ritual are concerned is that the woman, despite religious descrimination is more religious, God-fearing and accepts unquestioningly the role of preserver of tradition and guardian of culture that has been imposed upon her.

In *The Village by the Sea*, which is based on facts, Anita Desai has pointed out the religious practices of villagers. The inhabitants of this village, fishermen and farmers are hardworking, poor though self-centered and religious. But it is especially the woman who does religious practices:

> "Women would come and offer flowers at the sacred rock. Some would say a little prayer for the safety of the fishermen at sea because they were all the wives and daughters of fishermen. Some would simply bow, like Leila and say a greeting to God. It seemed a good way to start the morning."[4]

In her recent novel *Journey to Ithaca*, Ithaca is but an evocative mythical place name. In fact it is the home for a long-wandering, long-suffering, searching soul. Desai presents here an unequivocal rejection of the western religious ethos of sin-evil-guilt-penance. Matteo, the only child of well-to-do Italian parents, exhibits signs of worldly failure from the beginning. His wife Sophie is a confident journalist. Thanks to his confused ideas about India; Matteo was distracted and deceived by a series of 'face yogis' (65) and other 'ridiculous delusions' (66-70). After running from pillar to post in search of a guru (master), Matteo reaches an ashram on the mountains in the north and coming here at last Matteo finds peace, joy, deep contentment. Matteo seems to get closer and closer to his goal under the blessings and guidance of the Mother, the head of the ashram. Matteo, the seeker of truth seems to have found his guru at last. Sophie had come to India with no intention to find Truth or God or guru. And finally exasperated by Matteo's obsession with Truth and spiritual India, Sophie leaves him within months of their arrival in desperate rage to join the drugtribe on the beach of Goa. She leaves India and returns to Europe, her spiritual journey to the essential 'India' begins. While the Mother was the guru for Matteo, Sophie had taken her to be a hypnotist, a magician. She was sick of 'damned ashrams' and 'mad gurus' and, therefore, approached her subject as a sceptic, a perfectly rational intellectual, set on the task of dethroning the Mother's image from the high pedestal the devotees had put her on. But the very route of chilly bleak bitterness, of renunciation and unfaith, ironically brings her, in a roundabout way, closer to faith and devotion. She returns to India, and after the Mother's death goes ahead on her journey as a lonely pilgrim.

As Sophie tries to dig out and reconstruct the Mother's past, the reader gets a glimpse of another remarkable, journey through the interstices of an interwoven fabric of skepticism and admiration. Leila had yearned with her entire body and soul since childhood for some vision of supreme joy and beauty. So she could not confirm to the conventional religion of her society or the common ways/norms of life as upheld by her relatives and acquaintances. An undefined urge for some sublime life and experience stirred within her. Unfortunately, however, she first heard the call of India through of 'false master' who mesmerized her into believing that he was Krishna, Leila, in her innocent eagerness and devotion to her spiritual goal had mistaken the guise for the man. Her avowal at this turn — 'Krishna is my country and my religion' (227) shows the extent and degree of her honest infatuation.

Though her spiritual journey still continued, it was now swathed in peace, joy, harmony. Incidentally, 'master' (guru) has a special connotation in the Indian context, here it means not just teacher or expert, but one's spiritual leader who guides the disciple towards truth and God, and before whom one surrenders with complete devotion-trust-faith.

Thus in this novel, though Desai has unsparingly pointed out the orthodox, superstitions, inhuman, vulgar practices of Hindu society and rites, she also goes beyond this to capture the essence of Vedantic Hinduism - the message of joy - light - truth.

The same theme continues in her next novel *Fasting, Feasting*. Thematically it appears to be a partial sequel to *Journey to Ithaca*. The religio-spiritual awareness purports to be a momentous aspect of the novel because the title of the novel derives its root from a popular Hindu mythological metaphor. The title of the novel is explicitly symbolical. Fasting alludes to the life of self-discipline, renunciation and inner purification connoting in spiritual gnosis. Alessandro Monti interpreted on the basis of the myth of Shiva. To quote him:

> "By introducing the God Shiva into the thematic texture of the novel, Anita Desai constitutes the mythical backdrop for the two cognate aspects out of which the Hindus shape their way of life as a continuous balance between asceticism and eroticism. He quotes W.H.O's Flaherty who says, Shiva quarrels with Parvati in his ascetic aspect and reunites with her in his erotic aspect; the myth begins with fasting and ends with feasting."[5]

Shiva is the Hindu god that threatens the well-disposed order that culminates socially in the trimmed figure of the householder. As a roaming and semi-naked ascetic the god combines the accumulated strength of the yogi with the excessive lust and virility of the unrestrained seducer. He deregulates both mundanity and retirement, making a 'fasting' of 'feasting' and vice versa. Uma's implied metamorphosis into an erotic yogin introduces the passional mode of 'Sringara' into the ashram, so as to move the devotional emphasis from the lugubrious figure of the divine extreme God Shiva.

Again the character of Mira masi and her life as a widowed devotee brings another view of Indian socio-religious life. Desai narrates:

'Even since her widowhood, she had taken up religion as a vocation. Her day was ruled by ritual, from the moment she woke to make her salutations to the sun, through her ritual bath and morning prayers, to the preparation of her widow's single and vegetarian meal of the day, and through the evening ceremonies at the temples she visited'(39).

It affected Uma deeply and casteism was introduced by means of religious ritual.

> "It was her passion to attempt this miracle that made her follow Mira masi through the cycle of the day's rituals."(40)

In fact Uma was fascinated by Mira masi since her childhood. She used to listen attentively to the ancient myths of Hinduism being narrated in a realistic and lively manner. Stories about Lord Krishna, Mira — the poet saint, and Raja Harishchandra specially appealed to Uma. She abounded in ecstasy when Mira masi allowed her to participate in some of the rituals including the otherwise forbidden dip in the river. Such scattered religious experiences converted Uma into a day-dreamer and in moments of loneliness she would think of Mira masi feeling her soothing hand descend upon her shoulders and also imagine the tender whisper in her ears: "You are the Lord's child — I see His mark on you."

> "After many purgatorial rituals, like taking holy dip and pronouncing Har har Mahadeva!, She returned to the Shiva temple in the Himalayas devoting herself to intense meditation and worship. Masi's religiosity touches Uma to the core of her heart who craved to accompany Mira masi to various places of pilgrimage. Succeeding in strengthening Uma's faith in God, Mira masi's religious favour reveals the creativity of maintaining a balance between the societal and the spiritual melieu."[6]

When Uma suffers dejection in life later, she turns to religion, cultivates spiritual awareness craving to visit an ashram as a means of escape from the problems of life.

In the second part of the novel the life of Arun in America represents this fact in a different way. Desai presents ironically that inspite of the idea of unifying religious ritual, the family of Patton is the most disjointed one because they lack the sense of spiritual unity. There, religious issues like Arun's refusal to eat the non-vegetarian food because of being a pious Hindu adds a special element to the novel. Mr. Patton's failure to draw the family members together for his specially prepared meal symbolizes the growing menace of the new religious, values in the American society where materialism was suffocated by the spiritual consciousness and hence religion has failed to attract the masses leading to negation of the spiritual power. Anita Desai concludes that be it east or the west, family and society need spiritual and religious anchorage to sustain human beings. As is evident by a comparative study of Uma and Mira masi on one hand and Mrs. Patton and her daughter on the other, Uma and Mira masi could survive due to the compromise between their social and the spiritual spectrums. Desai, through these characters, leads up to a new realm where socio-spiritual or religious awareness results in lasting ecstasy.

References

1. Desai, Anita, *Cry, the Peacock,* New Delhi: Orient Paperbacks, 1980, p. 112.
2. *Ibid.*, pp. 108-199.
3. *Ibid.*, p. 119.
4. Desai, Anita, *The Village by the Sea*, New Delhi: Allied Publishers Pvt. Ltd., 1982, p. 8.
5. Alexandro, Monti, 'Failed Households Renouncement and Distributive Strategies in *Fasting, Feasting*'; *The Atlantic Literary Review*, Vol. 2, No. 1, January-March, 2001, New Delhi, p. 68.
6. Alexandro, Monti, 'Failed Household: Renouncement and Distributive Strategies in *Fasting, Feasting*', *Post-Independence Indian English Fiction,* New Delhi: Atlantic Publishers and Distributors (P) Ltd., p. 55.

18

Four Decades of Her Prose: Her Comments

Anita Desai seems to have had a simple middle class upbringing with German angle to it. Her mother, Toni Nime was of German origin. Perhaps that is why Desai has confluence of sorts in her writings. As a woman writer, Desai has given her literary work an unmistakable edge. She can no longer be claimed as the exclusive property of India; her work and her narrative art belong to the world. Desai's novels and short-stories evoke characters, events and moods with recourse to a rich use of visual imagery and details, which has led to comparisons with the modernist sensibilities of T.S. Eliot, William Faulkner, and Virginia Woolf.

> "Professor Anita Desai, an award-winning fiction writer who, after nine years of teaching in MIT's Program in Writing and Humanistic Studies, is retiring this summer to devote herself to writing novels on a full-time basis."
>
> —*Carly Kite*

Anita Desai, an Indian novelist, the John E. Burchard Professor of Humanities, Emeritus at the Massachusetts Institute of Technology, started her literary career in 1963 with the publication of her first novel *Cry, the Peacock*. From 1963-2004, she has covered a span of four decades and every decade is different as far as her writing is concerned.

Awards

The Booker Prize - Best Novel Nominee (1980)
- *Clear Light of Day*.

The Booker Prize - Best Novel Nominee (1984)
- *In Custody*

The Booker Prize	-	Best Novel Nominee (1999)
	-	*Fasting, Feasting*
Orange Prize for Fiction	-	Best Novel Nominee (2005)
	-	*The Zigzag Way*

In an interview Desai admitted that her work changed over time. She said; "My literary style has changed over the years. Now my writing is bare compared to my earlier work. My schooling as a child in India had an impact on my writing, I grew up, reading the major English writers. As I grow older I feel less a need to prove my skills. I realize I don't always have to write in their style. I think *Fasting, Feasting* is an example where my style has changed since *Clear Light of Day.*"[1]

Anita Desai never tried, or never got her work published in India because no publisher in India would be interested in a fiction writer from India. She states, "I can't really write on it with the same intensity and familiarity that I once had. She is glad she left later rather than sooner because she believes she has been drifting away from the culture ever since. At the age of 21, she married a businessman named Ashvin Desai and they raised four children together. She believes she was noticed in England because of her Western style of writing and their interest in India. She believes her feministic style of writing came from the changing times when she was growing up. "The feminist movement in India is very new and a younger generation of readers in India tends to be rather impatient of my books and to think of them as books about completely helpless women, hopeless women." (Desai)

S	We enjoyed reading and analyzing your novel *Clear Light of Day* and your story 'Rooftop Dwellers' knowing that we will be meeting you. We wonder what you think about when you are writing?
Anita Desai	When I am writing, I focus 100 per cent on my writing. Then, by the time I'm half way through the book, I'm already thinking about the ending. People think that because I write about India, I must be trying to portray India in a way I am to

tell the truth about any subject, not a romance or fantasy, not avoid the truth.

S What sort of process do you use to write?

AD My style of writing is to allow the story to unfold on its own. I try not to structure my work too rigidly. I don't make outlines for my novels. Instead, I jot down notes, then formulate characters. I try to trace the connection between the characters and that way a story or plot emerges.

S How do you feel after you have finished something?

AD Usually a feeling of disappointment follows the book, because what I hoped to write is not what I actually accomplished. However, it becomes a motivation to write the next book.

S When did you know you were a writer?

AD Ever since I could first write I have been doing so. When I was taught how to write and read at school, I made up my mind that this was what I love to do best and this was the world I was going to occupy. So I started writing little stories at that time. When I was very young, I used to share much of what I wrote with my family, but as I got older and more self-conscious, it became a much more private process.

S Our class read and discussed *Clear Light of Day*, and we have many questions to ask you.

AD Wait.

S Can you say something about the book?

AD It is the one closest to my heart. When I wrote it I was in love with literature and under the influence of great English writers, so it was a very literary novel.

S We noticed the time period of Partition in 1949 and then twenty years later and also that two of the characters are girls — these might match your background. Is it somewhat autobiographical?

AD The setting is autobiographical, but (being partly set in 1949) it is also about India becoming independent and de-colonized. It is set in my home city of Old Delhi, in a period of my childhood, during a time when I was becoming a woman. It was the coming together of two momentous events in my life, growing up and india transforming from a colony to independence. Even such a quiet, protected, enclosed place as the family's home could be affected by the great events of history. But Bimla in this novel and also Moyna, in the story 'Rooftop Dwellers' stay alone to represent the growing independence of women in India and having the choice of not getting married.

S Our class noticed that the parents were very remote, but we couldn't find a reason in the novel for it.

AD The main reason for the parental absence is to protect my parents' private lives. I felt that I might inadvertently give some of my parents' private aspects when I was writing so in order to prevent that, I decided to make the parents conveniently absent and aloof. The reason were subconscious too. In part the novel was autobiography, but I was shying away from writing about my own parents. I sidestepped the issue. But decades later, in my recent *Fasting, Feasting*, I faced up to this relationship.

S The novel is divided into four parts. What was your purpose in this design?

AD The book begins and ends with the visits to give the impression of a tunnel into their ancestors and family history. I believe in going backwards into the past. I felt I was digging a tunnel back to the past. Originally I had planned to go even further back, to infancy and ancestors, but I stopped I ran out of energy.

S The character of Baku, the husband of the visiting sister, is an ambassador. Why is he so pompous?

AD Many characters in the novel are representative of types that exists in India. He represents the caste system in India with an air of superiority, the caste system in India and the people thinking that Western things are better.

S But the brother Raja is interested in Urdu poetry and is friendly with a Muslim family though they are a Hindu family.

AD I grew up in Delhi in the north of India. There it is very Islamic, with the history of the Mughal dynasty and everywhere Urdu spoken, and Islamic architecture and food and dress. Islam was as much a pent of our lives as Hindu things. Many of us regarded the Partition as a tragedy. Raja represented an India that had an Islamic tradition. This is another unfinished business that is taken up later in my book *In Custody*, where a character sacrifices his life.

S At the end of the novel an elderly guru sings a song by Iqbal, what is the significance of this song?

AD The song of this famous Urdu poet shows that poetry art is significant in the history of India. India is a curious place that still preserves the past religions and its history. No matter how modern India becomes, it is still very much an old country.

S Do you have a favourite piece among your writings?

AD I have the same feelings for almost all of my writings. Every book has unfinished business, but may be *Fire on the Mountain* is one book I have never been disappointed with.

S Do you have any advice to give to young writers?

AD Someone who wants to write should make an effort to write a little something everyday. Writing in this sense is the same as athletes who practice a sport everyday to keep their skills honed. When you are writing, you must be 100% focused on the writing. Also, when I write I often stop and check by asking myself, 'Does this make sense to anyone besides me?'

S Are any of your own children writers?

AD One of my daughters, Kiran Desai, is a professional writer. She wrote the novel, *Hullabaloo in Guava Orchard.*

S What do you think is the future of literature in the Indian languages, now that Indian literature in English has become so strong?

AD It has become strong in the last ten or twenty years. When I started to write, it certainly wasn't. There were just a few of us, we had a lot of problems finding publishers, there were very few readers, and no one seemed very interested. I think things changed very dramatically.

S Does it bother you when people don't get what you wrote?

AD No, people do see my works differently, but that is how it should be. I believe that once a writer creates a novel, it takes on a life of its own. I feel dissociated from a book in the bookstore — it belongs to the reader.

S Thank you very much.

INTERVIEW WITH MAGDA COSTA

Magda Costa interviewed Anita Desai in Barcelona, 30 January 2001. Desai was in Spain to launch the Spanish and Catalan translations of *Fasting, Feasting*.

Q How was it to grow up in a family like yours, with a German mother and a Bengali father, in India?

AD When you are a child you take for granted what your family is; you don't question it. The fact is that my mother adopted so completely to the Indian way of life that nobody thought of her as a foreigner anymore. It's sure that we spoke German at home, which is unusual in India, but I think it was only as I grew up that I realised our home was a bit unusual. We spoke German, we listened to Western music, read Western literature to a greater extent than our friends and neighbours, but in every other way we were exactly as any other Indian family in that neighbourhood.

Q You say your mother adapted completely to the Indian way of life. Did she also convert to Hinduism?

AD No. She didn't change her religion, but she didn't bring us upto be Christian either.

Q However, you went to a Christian School, St. Mary's.

AD It was a missionary school. My parents simply sent me there because it was nearby. In India children are often sent to a convent school because the education there is supposed to be of high standards. They are sent there for the sake of their education, but very few Indians ever convert. There's a very small Christian community. When it comes to religion, when it comes to food, music, or cinema, Indians like their own ways, they don't change very much. Indians manage to slip back and forth between the modern world and the ancient world, the Indian world and the Western world, with a great ease, without feeling any strain. If there's one characteristic of India, it is very inclusive, it's not exclusive.

Q Later on you went to University in Delhi. Was it very unusual to be a woman in an Indian university at that time?

AD No, it was a women's college that I went to. Both my sisters had university education too. One became a civil servant, and my other sister became a doctor, a pediatrician. It was not unusual at all. I heard one story, which is quite astonishing, about an Indian woman from Bombay who went to England, to the University of Cambridge, and got a degree in medicine. But in those days women weren't given degrees. They could attend classes and study, but they wouldn't get a degree. She went back to India and got her degree, in Practice Medicine.

Q How did you become a writer? When did you decide that was what you wanted to do?

AD When I was a very little girl. We had a house that was full of books. All of us were great readers. We were always going to the library and the bookshop. When I was taught how to write and read at school, I remember I made up my mind that this was what I'd love to do best and this was the world I was going to occupy. So I started writing little stories in that time. I never really wanted to do anything else. I think it was simply a love of books, and the pleasure I found in imagining images within words.

Q Did you really publish your first story when you were nine?

AD Yes I did, in a children's magazine, so my family also thought of me as the writer of the family. That was the label I got.

Q Why did you wait so much for your first book *Cry, the Peacock* (1963) then?

AD Well, I was in my twenties and I had got married, I had two children, so ...

Q Was it very difficult to deal with writing and taking care of a family at the same time?

AD It wasn't at all difficult, because I had four children as a very young woman. I stayed at home, I didn't go out, so when the children went downstairs to play or they went to school I would immediately go to my desk and start writing. Then I would put it away as soon as they came back. I learnt to work according to the school time table, and now that I teach I find myself still following it.

Q As a teacher of creative writing, do you think that writing can be taught?

AD No, I don't think so. I can't teach the students how to write. They can learn from reading. I try to show them what books to read, how to learn from other writers. Basically what one does in the writing class is simply give the students time, space, in which to write. Otherwise their schedule is very full of their studies and exams and no one takes writing very seriously. Here's a class which does take it seriously, and does give them time and framework in which to work. They seem to find that helpful. All on their own they might hesitate to start or not at all, but at least this gives them the opportunity to try their hand at it. They may give up, they may pursue it, then.

Q Do you follow any specific method?

AD I set them little exercises to begin with, like practice pieces. I always tell them it's like practicing music; you have to play the scales before you can play a symphony. And from little practice pieces go on to learn how to develop stories.

Q Where do you start from when you think of a novel to write?

AD Usually quite a small detail, may be just a single image. That image stays in your mind, so that you keep returning to it, and you keep adding other images to it, which are fit, which are suitable and appropriate. Sometimes an image doesn't grow, it remains where it is and never becomes a story, but sometimes it outs the branches, leaves, fruit, and then becomes a book.

Q What is the first thing you tell your students?

AD On the first day I make them take out a piece of paper and write down on four ideas they have for stories, just the seed I tell them: now you start thinking about these ideas and how to write them. If you get stuck and you can't think I'll give this paper back to you to look at once again and recover that part.

Q What are your aims as a writer?

AD I don't have an agenda as a writer. People think that because I write about India I must be trying to portray India in a way. But, really, when you write you don't think about your readers at all; you don't imagine what your readers will look for or what they expect from a book. You are alone with that page and with your pen. You are really only playing a game by yourself; of imagining thoughts and images with the best words suitable. It's an exploration of language, how much can language do, how far can it pretend human experience and feelings.

Q Are there any subjects you prefer writing about?

AD Specially in my earlier work I found myself addressing the same things over and over again. Very much about the life of women, specially those women who are confined to home and family, also the solitude from which a person can suffer even if living within a big family or surrounding by crowds. But after several years and several books I began to feel suffocated myself by the confinement of these subjects. I felt I was limiting the territory to such an extent that it created a kind of suffocation even for me. So, I very deliberately opened the doors, to widen the canvas, and started writing more about male characters and their lives, because I felt they had a wider experience of the world and I could address a greater variety of experiences.

Q In *Fasting, Feasting*, though, the two main characters, Uma and Arun, being a girl and a boy, have similar experiences.

AD They are brought up by the same parents; they share the same childhood and background. As Arun grows he finds himself as incapable of grasping the opportunities he's given and developing individually a personality of his own, any more than Uma can, because she is confined by her parents and the household. But Arun is also confined, he is in a way crippled by his childhood, and goes no further than Uma.

Q In your book *Diamond Dust and Other Stories*, there's one story — 'The Rooftop Dwellers' —

which looks like a continuation of *Fasting, Feasting*. Is it so?

AD Yes. Originally I thought of writing a third part of that story, which is about the neighbour's daughter, who goes to Delhi, takes up a job, has a career, learns how to live independently. It meant to be the third part of the book, but its tone was so different. It was very lighthearted. I put all the humour, and the fun, and the laughter into that section. It just didn't fit in *Fasting, Feasting*. After writing it I saw it didn't really belongs. So I separated it and put it in a collection. Arun does appear in that story too. He returns from America with a degree and becomes this suitable husband possibly for the neighbour's daughter. There are links between the novel and this short story.

Q In *Fasting, Feasting* two families are compared; One Indian and the other American. Was it a way of replying writers such as Chitra Banerjee Divakaruni or Bharati Mukherjee, who seem to say that America is the promise land at least for women?

AD It was partly a response to all the literature that has been written by British authors about India. I felt it's about time that Indians, who now live in large numbers in the Western world, start writing about them too. It was about a foreigner's experience, not really an emigrant's experience like Bharati Mukherjee's characters. It was more about the fact that, no matter where you travel, you come across the same emotional hungers and needs. What is different is our ways of satisfying them? In India one imagines religion should satisfy him. If you have nothing else in the world, at least you have religion. In America people might think that a trip to the shopping mall is best.

Q Do you think Americans are like that? They look quite caricatures.

AD It was a bit of a caricature. I do feel as a foreigner in the US. There is a lot I miss. I don't understand I could never write about American characters, except from this perspective: a foreigner's. Of course they see themselves differently, and if they were to write about the same thing they would do it differently.

Q Do you feel your work has become more occidentalised with time?

AD I don't think so, because the first thing I wrote was *Fasting, Feasting*. The Indian section is very much the way I would have written it, had I been in India. The material is entirely Indian and it is written from an Indian perspective. But it was already when I was in India that I started writing about Indians from a foreign perspective too. Some of my books have foreigners as the central characters and I write about their experience of India. *Baumgartner's Bombay* was the first book in which I did that, and then *Journey to Ithaca*.

Q *Baumgartner's Bombay* even has full paragraphs in German—

AD Yes. I wrote that book to begin with, as a starting point. It was a matter of language again, really. I wanted to use the German language in an Indian context the way I had always used it, and it took me so many years to find a subject that would allow me to do it.

Q Does it have to do with your mother's experience?

AD Not really. It has to do with a German's experience of Germany in the thirties and the rise of nazism. It has to do also with being a German in India, so in that sense it has something to do with my mother, but it's about a German, Jew, a man not someone who marries and has a family like my mother did. It's a totally different experience.

Q This character in *Journey to Ithaca*, 'Mother', is based on a real person, isn't it?

AD Yes. She was a French woman who set up this ashram in Pondicherry with a very famous Indian sage, Aurobindo. She outlived him by many years and died in her nineties. She was very much revered in India. What intrigued me was that, being a foreigner, she became this Indian mystic.

Q Do you think any Indian writer has influenced your work?

AD It's difficult to say, because there are Indian writers in so many different languages. I can't say any of them has been an influence on my writings simply because I didn't read as many of them as I did of Western literature. But of Indian writers there are certainly many I admire very much.

Q In your novel *In Custody* you wrote, as a matter of fact, about the decay of Urdu literature.

AD I was trying to portray the world of Urdu poets. While living in Delhi I was always surrounded by the sound of Urdu poetry, the fact that most Muslims left India to go to Pakistan meant that most schools and universities of Urdu were closed. So it's language I don't think is going to survive in India. To some extent it is still written there. There are many Muslims and they do write in Urdu; but it has a wind of very artificial existence. People are not going to study Urdu in schools and colleges anymore. So why are we going to be their readers? Where is the audience? I was writing about this very regrettable decay.

I also wanted to write about the male world. I wanted to try my hand at writing about how life is like for men, how different it is from the life of women.

Q And that was from the point of view of men, moreover. Is that why the female characters in the book are so awful?

AD They are awful. I didn't mean to add any women characters, because the world of Urdu poetry is very homo-sexual; there are not many women in it, it's mostly a male's world. I thought I would try to write without any female characters, but it proved impossible. I could hear them always screaming in the background, banging on the doors, being very hysterical. I asked myself why have I made all these women so awful? and I thought well, if that was the house they were made to live they would probably be awful.

Q The poet's wife, in the novel, intends to be a poet herself. Were you trying to refer to the recent eruption of women writers in Urdu literature?

AD There are quite a few women writing in Urdu, yes; it tends to be extremely strong and feminist poetry. But really I was writing about a perfectly individual drama, I wasn't making it typical or representative of a bigger world, these were individual characters. And I wanted to show how much easier it is for a man to live this life, how much harder it is for a woman's words to be taken seriously, or even have the time, the space and the privacy .... Imagine they would write without any of that. The ones we are writing we don't have that, but we still write.

Q *In Custody* was made a film in 1993. How did you feel when you saw it?

AD Very shocked, because in my imagination it was all very grey, very dark and dirty and I just couldn't believe my eyes when I saw it in gorgeous technical colour, and everyone beautifully dressed looking very handsome. That's the world of Ismail Merchant, he makes everything look so beautiful, gorgeous. I had to distance myself from it, I had to detach myself and accept the fact that it's his vision of the book. He is very happy with it, it is not my vision I would have preferred it in black and white, more in the school of New Realism. They were things that I did enjoy very much in the film, like the music, and actually hearing the Urdu poetry.

Q In the book you took poems from several Urdu writers, while in the film they belong to one only, Faiz Ahmed Faiz, whose idea was that?

AD That was Ismail Merchant's choice. He does know a lot about Urdu poetry, so he was able to choose very fine poems. But it had an unfortunate effect, which I was afraid of that people would think that the poet in the film was in some way connected with the actual poet. Some people took it to be biographical, when it isn't at all.

Q What do you think is the future of literature in Indian language, now that Indian literature in English has become so strong?

AD It's become strong in the last ten or twenty years. When I started to write it certainly wasn't. There was just a few of us who were writing in English, we had a lot of problems in finding publishers, there were very few readers, and no one seemed very interested at all in our work. I think things changed very dramatically and I can put a date to it, it was 1980 - when Salman Rushdie published *Midnight's Children*, and it had such a huge success in the West. I think in India also readers and publishers took notice of it. After that there was a whole new wave of new writers. I think it was the success of his book that gave them such confidence, encouraged them to write. I think we all need models, and he was a model for that whole generation in the 80s. Also it is a growing confidence in the English language. When I started to write there was a lot of questioning. Can you really express the Indian experience, and Indian ways of thinking and speaking in the English language — a foreign language? But I think by the 80s everyone accepted the fact that English had become an Indian language, it was not going to disappear, it had taken roots and had started growing not in any artificial manner but in a very natural manner. Indians have taken it to our world and turned it into an Indian language. So now they are writing with a kind of confidence I think it is not questioned anymore. I was always questioned about using English and I no longer am. I don't think my daughter has ever been, questioned about it. There was a certain amount of resentment by writers in the Indian languages, because of all the attention it has received in the West .... But recently I read an article in a publishing journal comparing sales figures of writers who write in English and writers who write in say Bengali, or Malayalam and were more less comparable. Well-known writers in Bengal were selling as many books as well-known writers in English.

Q Another hit in the tradition of Indian writing in English was Arundhati's Roy's *The God of Small Things*. Do you think it changed anything?

AD You know, I don't believe so. I know its had a defect. People have started looking at Indian writing in a quite different way after reading her book. I don't myself see it as an innovation. I think innovations were made by other writers, such as G.V. Desani, much earlier, Salman Rushdie, certainty, I think Kiran's voice is extremely original. She brings something totally fresh and new to the writing scene. For me Roy's book was very much in the tradition of the British novels in the 30s or 40s.

Q It has been said that your work expresses nostalgia.

AD Its' something I wish to avoid, because I think nostalgia is a falsification. If you are nostalgic you tend to sentimentalise, or to fantasise, and you are no longer facing reality. So it's something I try very hard to avoid, in books like, *In Custody* or in *Fasting, Feasting* to gloss over Indian life out of sentimentality, not out of fear of losing that I would prefer to think that the books face the truth and don't create illusions.

Q Could that be the reason why sometimes you give such negative images of places like Bombay, or Goa?

AD Well, in *Journey to Ithaca* it was only about the foreign community. It wasn't about India from an Indian point of view. I wrote about the part foreign tourism mostly experience the beaches, the drugs. They don't take any part in Goan life.

Q According to the *Encyclopedia Britannica,* your novels shout a tragic view of life. Would you agree with that?

AD No. A lot of people tell my books are extremely pessimistic, and extremely dark, but I would prefer to think of them as facing the truth, not having illusions. But I do make an attempt also to show the fact that India is full of laughter, even in a family like Uma's, there is room for humour.

— Thank you Ma'm

Source: http://www.baruch.cuny,edu/wsas/Harman/desai-interview.html

Bibliography

Acharya, Shanta, "Problems of the Self in the Novels of Anita Desai". R.K. Dhawan, Ed. *Exploration in Modern Indo-English Fiction,* New Delhi: Bahari Publications, 1982.

Asnanai, Shyam Mohan, "Anita Desai's Fiction: A New Dimension". *Indian Literature,* Vol. XXIV, March-April, 1981.

Asnanai, Shyam Mohan, "Contribution of Women in Indo-English Novel". *Treveni.* July-Sept., 1975.

Bala, Suman and Pabby, D.K., Eds. *The Fiction of Anita Desai.* Vol. I & II. New Delhi: Khosla Publishing House, 2002.

Bande, Usha, *The Novels of Anita Desai.* New Delhi: Prestige Books, 1988.

Beauvoir, Simon De and Friedian, Betty, "Sex, Society and the Female Dilemma: A Dialogue". *London Saturday Review.*

Belliappa, Meena and Anita Desai: *A Study of Her Fiction* Calcutta: Writers Wrokshop, 1971.

Bhatnagar, Paravati, "The Theme of Man-Woman Relationship in the Novels of Anita Desai", *The Fiction of Anita Desai,* Vol. I, New Delhi: Khosla Publishing House, 2002.

Budholia, O.P., *Anita Desai: Vision and Techniques in Her Novels.* Delhi: B.R. Publications, 2001.

Chaddah, R.P., "Symbols and Cities of Anita Desai". *The Tribune,* June 13, 1992.

Chaudhary, Indranath, "Indianness in Indian Literature". *Comparative Indian Literature.* New Delhi: Sterling Publishers, 1992.

Chttopadhyaya, Kamla, *The Awakening of Indian Women*, 1939.

Dalmiya, Yasodhara, "An Interview with Anita Desai". *The Times of India*. Sunday Edition, April 29, 1979.

Desai, Anita, "The Indian Writers Problems". *Exploration in Modern Indo-English Fiction*. New Delhi: Bahari Publication Pvt. Ltd., 1982.

Desai, Anita, *In Custody*. New Delhi: Penguin Books India (P) Ltd., 1984.

Desai, Anita, "Contemporary English Literature in India". *Literary Criterion*, January, 1982.

Desai, Anita, "Replies to the Questionaire". *Kakatiya Journal in English Studies*, Vol. 3, No. 1, 1978.

Dwevedi, A.N., Papers on Indian Writings in English, Vol. II. Delhi: Amar Prakashan, 1991.

Dwevedi, A.N., *Studies in Contemporary Indian Fiction*. Allahabad: Kitab Mahal, 1987.

Gupta, Santosh, "Bridging the Polarities of Imagination and Reason in *Clear Light of Day*". R.K. Dhawan, Ed. *The Fiction of Anita Desai.*

Jain, Jasbir, "Anita Desai Interviewed". Rajasthan University, *Studies in English*, Vol. XII, 1979.

Jain, Jasbir, "Anita Desai". Madhusudan Prasad Ed., *Indo-English Novelist*. New Delhi: Prestige Books, 1989.

Jain, Jasbir, "The Use of Fantasy in the Novels of Anita Desai". R.K. Dhawan, Ed., *Exploration in Modern Indo-English Fiction*. New Delhi: Bahari Publishers, 1982.

Kripal, Viney, "The Perfect Bubble: A Study of Anita Desai's *In Custody*". *The Indian Novel in English, 1960-1985.*

Krishna, Swamy Shanta, "Anita Desai: The Sexist Nature of Sanity". *The Woman in Indian Fiction in English*. New Delhi: Ashish Publishing House, 1984.

Lal, Malashri, "Literary Feminism in India: In Search of Theory". The Tribune News Services, *The Tribune*, June 16, 2001.

Lawrence, D.H., "Morality and the Novel". David Lodge, Ed., *20th Century Literary Criticism*. London: Longman, 1972.

Maini, Darshan Singh, "The Achievement of Desai". K.K. Sharma, Ed., *Indo-English Literature*. Ghaziabad: Vimal Prakashan, 1970.

Pathak, R.S. Ed., *Indian Fiction in English: Problems and Promises*. New Delhi: Northern Books Centre, 1990.

Pathak, R.S., "Alienated Self in the Novel of the Anita Desai". R.K. Dhawan, Ed., *The Fiction of Anita Desai*. New Delhi: Bahari, 1989.

Prasad, Madhusudan, *Anita Desai: The Novelist,* Allahabad: New Horizon, 1981.

Raizada, Harish, *Indian English Novelists: Some Points of View*. Delhi: K.K. Publishers, 1996.

Ram, Atma, "An Interview with Anita Desai". *World Literature Written in English*, November, 1977.

Rao, B. Ramachandra, *The Novels of Anita Desai: A Study*. New Delhi: Kalyani Publishers, 1972.

Sharma, K.K. Ed., *Indo English Literature: A Collection of Critical Essays*. Ghaziabad: Vimal Prakashan.

Sharred, Paul, "Tradition and Tragedy: Anita Desai and R.K. Narayan". *Australian and Indian Literature: Studies in Mutual Response.*

Srivastava, Romesh, K. Ed., *Perspectives on Anita Desai*. Ghaziabad: Vimal Prakashan, 1984.

Tripathi, J.P., *The Mind and Art of Anita Desai*. Bareilly: Prakash Book Dept., 1987.